Toward a
Speech Act Theory
of
Literary Discourse

TOWARD A
SPEECH ACT THEORY
OF
LITERARY DISCOURSE

Mary Louise Pratt

INDIANA UNIVERSITY PRESS
BLOOMINGTON · LONDON

Manufactured in the United States of America
Library of Congress Cataloging in Publication Data
Pratt, Mary Louise, 1948–
    Toward a speech act theory of literary discourse.
    Bibliography
    Includes index.
    1. Discourse analysis.   2. Style, Literary.
I. Title.
P302.P74   808   76-26424
ISBN 0-253-37006-X   2 3 4 5 81 80

Contents

Preface

For some years now in this country, the Modern Language Association and the Linguistic Society of America have held their annual meetings at the same time and in the same city, but in different hotels. This custom provides a handy and not entirely frivolous measure of how relations stand between the two disciplines represented by these organizations. Both clearly feel they belong in each other's vicinity, but they don't exchange programs or street guides; so to get from one to the other you have to find your own way. It is with good reason, then, that the title of this book begins with the word "toward."

The chief aim of this study is to suggest, to the people in both hotels, that it is both possible and necessary to develop a unified theory of discourse which allows us to talk about literature in the same terms we use to talk about all the other things people do with language. Methodologically, the study suggests that much can be gained if we abandon the traditional assumption that literature exists by opposition to other uses of language and if we adopt instead an approach which looks at literature in terms of what it has in common with other varieties of discourse. Ultimately, I believe such an approach can enable the literary critic to make fuller and more legitimate use of linguistics than has been possible in the past and can provide him with a linguistic description of literature much richer in explanatory power than those presently available to him. On the other hand, it is an approach which obliges the critic to forego the comfortable assumption that his subject matter is autonomous and self-defined. For the linguist, integrating literature into the general schema of discourse theory means taking into his purview a body of data he has often been more than content to ignore. But that body of data is also one that can provide him with important insights into areas and aspects of nonliterary discourse that have been problematic or invisible to him in the past.

The issues under consideration here are not new ones; rather, they emerge from much larger discussions taking place today in both linguistics and literary studies. In the latter field, this discussion has caused a movement from intrinsic to reader-based criticism; in the former, a movement from syntax-based, meaning-independent linguistics to semantics-based context-dependent linguistics. Both movements suggest and support a view of literature as a linguistic activity which cannot be understood apart from the context in which it occurs and the people who participate in it. Both form the background for the present study and, it is hoped, will provide it with an audience.

Needless to say, this book does not claim to present anything approaching a full-fledged theory of literary discourse. No such thing is possible at present, nor even in the near future. Here, I have undertaken only to carry out some preliminary groundwork in the hope of providing some basis for future discussions. Three limits in particular have been imposed on my subject here: the discussion of twentieth-century poetics deals only with the Russian Formalists, the Prague School, and certain of their contemporary descendants; the treatment of literary texts is limited to a single genre, prose fiction; the discussion of the theory of language use is based on a single linguistic model, speech act theory. It is hoped that these essentially pragmatic limits will not conceal the larger implications of the argument.

Certain measures which have been taken to make this book accessible to readers in both linguistics and literary studies, deserve comment. I have avoided formal linguistic notation and have tried to provide explanatory background for the linguistic theoretical constructs I introduce. Literary examples have for the most part been chosen from well-known works originally written in English or readily available in English translation. All quotations and titles are given in English, and wherever possible standard English translations have been used. In a few cases where English translations were unavailable or failed to reflect the original, the translations are my own and are as literal as possible. The reference conventions adopted are those normally used in linguistic scholarship; that is, all references are given briefly in the text with full reference information in the list of works cited. Since the histories of both linguistics and literature are of some importance to the argument presented, all texts are referred to by their original dates of publication. Where necessary, the specific edition or translation in question is given in the list of works cited. Literary scholars will doubtless be startled to see *Pride and Prejudice* referred to as (Austen, 1813), but they will be spared many footnotes in return.

In writing this book, I have relied on the help of many people. I wish to express my gratitude to Prof. Herbert Lindenberger for the guidance and encouragement he so willingly extended to me during my graduate student years, and for his unfailing assistance and support on this project. I would like also to thank Prof. Elizabeth Traugott for her generous help throughout my graduate studies and especially for her many thoughtful comments and suggestions during the writing of this book. I am grateful to Profs. Richard Ohmann, Paul Smith, Charles Bird, Edward J. Brown, and Stanley Fish for their careful criticism and commentary on the manuscript and to my friends Toni Guttman, Sandra Drake, Elisabeth Boisaubin, and Constance McCorkle for many hours of discussion. Any errors of fact or judgment which remain were made by me, and in spite of everyone else.

- Labov — as template no formal narrative
- S-a-theory - context
  illocution
  perlocution — contribute to meaning

Grice - implicature — appropriateness conditions
  notion
  for whole language —
  (maxim).
  one — tellability — display texts
  - intended deviances (implicatures)
  - :

Introduction

Over the past decade there has developed a growing consensus among Anglo-American critics that the traditional structuralist opposition between poetic and nonpoetic language is an inadequate foundation on which to construct a linguistic theory of literature. Theoretically, there is no reason to expect that the body of utterances we call "literature" should be systematically distinguishable from other utterances on the basis of intrinsic grammatical or textual properties. Nevertheless, the belief that such a distinction could be made and could give rise to an interesting and adequate definition of literature underlies nearly all of the language-based intrinsic or formalist criticism of this century, from Russian Formalism through Prague School poetics and Anglo-American structuralism to present-day French literary semiotics. The contributions of these schools to our understanding of specific literary texts have been enormous and valuable, but their point of departure, the poetic/nonpoetic opposition in its various guises, has indeed been, as Roger Fowler says, "one of the greatest sources of confusion and error in poetic aesthetics" (Fowler, 1971:ix). My aim in this study is first to make a few suggestions about where the "confusion and error" in the "poetic language" approach lie and second to show how more recent developments in linguistics can be used to correct that approach.

The origins of the poetic/nonpoetic language opposition in its modern form go back at least to Romanticism and probably to the rise of scientific language in the seventeenth century. Ultimately, of course, the distinction comes down to us from Aristotle's *Poetics*. The point of departure of the present study, however, is the point at which modern linguistics entered the "poetic language" scene in the first decades of this century, the point at which the concepts of "poetic" and "nonpoetic" (or "ordinary," or "everyday," or "practical") language were incorporated by the Russian Formalists and the Prague School into the framework of structural linguistics, as formal linguistic categories.

This attempt to build the poetic/ordinary language opposition into linguistic theory has given rise to a number of widely held misconceptions about the relation between literature and the rest of our verbal activities. The most serious of these is the belief that literature is linguistically autonomous, that is, possessed of intrinsic linguistic properties which distinguish it from all other kinds of discourse. In objecting to this view, my main concern is not with what formalist and structuralist poeticians have said about literary texts but with the drastic misrepresentation of nonliterary discourse which their approach fosters. It is this misrepresentation which, I believe, has vitiated nearly all our attempts to develop a satisfying theory of literature.

What makes the poetic language doctrine most suspect is the fact that although its disciples claim empirical support for the poetic/nonpoetic opposition, they in fact have never tested their assumptions about nonliterary discourse against real, "ordinary language" data, and indeed have felt no need to do so. As I try to show in the opening chapters of this study, when such a test is performed those assumptions collapse altogether and with them collapse the two central notions on which structuralist poetics is based: the belief that literature is formally and functionally distinct from other kinds of utterances and the concomitant belief that literature is linguistically autonomous. It then becomes necessary to consider literary discourse in terms of its similarities to our other verbal activities rather than in terms of its differences from them.

The greater part of this study is devoted to this latter enterprise, that is, the development of an approach which allows us to describe literary utterances in the same terms used to describe other types of utterances. Departing from the claim that literary discourse must be viewed as a *use* rather than a *kind* of language, I have advanced the hypothesis that a descriptive apparatus which can adequately account for the uses of language outside literature will be able to give a satisfactory account of literary discourse as well. Needless to say, no such apparatus exists at present. However, the hypothesis itself finds ample support in some fairly recent developments in sociolinguistics and speech act theory, the two areas of linguistic inquiry most deeply concerned with language use. I have tried to demonstrate how some of the general principles of language use worked out by sociolinguists such as William Labov and Emmanuel Schegloff and speech act theoreticians such as John Searle and H. Paul Grice can be used to describe what writers and readers are doing with the language when they are participating in works of literature. Of equal importance is the observation that when these principles fail to account adequately for literary discourse, they fail to account for certain areas of nonliterary discourse as well, and for the same reasons. The theory of language use is still in its infancy, and its application to literature is younger yet. For the most part, then, the present study confronts only the most obvious preliminary issues.

To avoid misunderstanding, I wish to comment briefly on a few questions which relate to my subject, but which I have not undertaken to explore here. First, my discussion of the Russian Formalists and the Prague School in the opening chapter is by no means intended as a complete analysis or appraisal of their work. I have used only texts available in English and French and have concentrated only on the poetic/ordinary language issue. In addition, I have not attempted to discuss the exceedingly complex and intimate ties between these movements and the contemporaneous political and cultural circumstances in Russia and Czechoslovakia. As the Prague

School's Theses of 1929 attest, Czech linguistics was from the beginning bound up with questions of national language development; a fact which is not surprising since Czechoslovakia itself had only recently come into being. In his 1965 study of the Russian Formalists, Victor Erlich is particularly careful to stress the importance of viewing early Formalist writings in their polemical context:

> The shrill exaggerations of the early stage could be attributed, in large degree, to the natural belligerence of a young school of criticism bent on dissociating itself at any cost from its predecessors. One would be equally justified in relating the half-deliberate overstatements of the early Šklovskij and Jakobson to the Futurist tradition of shocking the Philistines.
> This, however, does not tell the whole story. The strident tone of the *Opojaz* studies was not merely an echo of the Futurist brawls. It reflected, not unlike the latter, the temper, or, more exactly, the timbre of a generation. One had to talk loudly indeed to make oneself heard in the market-place of contending ideas during the years 1916–1921, the turbulent and eventful years of War and Revolution. (Erlich, 1965:78)

In a sense, however, Erlich's warning has not been heeded. To a great extent, Formalist and structuralist poetics have come to France, England, and America without their immediate Slavic cultural context, and it is this fact which justifies my own elliptical treatment of them. The aspects of Formalist and Prague School doctrine to which I am objecting are precisely those which have had the greatest impact on literary studies outside Eastern Europe, as my references to the work of Todorov, Barthes, Jakobson, Stankiewicz, Wellek, Levin, and others attest.

Furthermore, the poetic language doctrine which I am trying to refute constitutes the main area of overlap between structuralist poetics and Anglo-American "New" or "Practical" criticism. Regardless of their differences, there is no question that both structuralist poetics and New Criticism foster essentially the same exclusivist attitude toward the relation between literary discourse and our other verbal activities. This affinity no doubt accounts for the ease and enthusiasm with which structuralist poetics was received on this side of the Atlantic in the 1950s and 1960s. To the extent that New Criticism encourages a poetic/ordinary language split and the concept of a linguistically autonomous literature, it too may be considered susceptible to the arguments I have proposed to refute these dogma.

The second issue I wish to clarify concerns the relevance of linguistics to the study of literature. Throughout this study, I have intentionally avoided claiming that linguistics can offer the literary critic new insights into works of literature. I do not believe such a claim can be made, certainly not at this point, when linguists are still struggling with utterances of a single sentence. Nor do I believe, however, that such a claim need be made in order to justify the "application" of linguistic analysis to literary texts. Since they are utterances, literary works by definition form part of the data for which linguistic theory must account. Both linguists and critics have been at fault in regarding the linguistic analysis of literature as some kind of special case of applied linguistics. As Michael Halliday (1964) has suggested, any theory of language use will ultimately have to describe literary utterances to the same extent it can describe any other utterance. Given this fact, the present study can be taken as a contribution to linguistics, though it is primarily intended as a corrective to literary theory.

In refuting the poetic language doctrine, I have taken its advocates at their words and have treated the concepts of "poetic" and "ordinary" language as the value-free linguistic constructs the poeticians claim them to be. Obviously, it is their attempt to claim empirical support for the doctrine, to "detach" the study of poetic language "from the concept of values," as Edward Stankiewicz puts it (1961:11), that leaves the poeticians open to the criticisms I have leveled. In fact, of course, the poetic/ordinary language opposition is anything but value-free and, in its origins, anything but a data-based linguistic construct. The Prague School's claim in its Theses of 1929 that "poetic language must be studied in and of itself" amounts to a restatement of the art for art's sake credo of the avant-garde. For the past century at least, the belief that literature is intrinsically distinct from and opposed to all the other things we do with language has had at its heart the belief that literature is somehow intrinsically superior to them, a belief which is still accepted without question in many critical quarters today. And this belief generally comes accompanied by a number of others. For Valéry and Mallarmé, for example, the opposition between poetic and practical language held also between poetic and practical experience, a poetic and a practical universe, and ultimately, the poet and the practical man. For Valéry, "everyday language" is "a medium essentially practical, perpetually changing, soiled, a maid of all work" (Valéry, 1938:81); for Mallarmé, "speech is no more than a commercial approach to reality" (Mallarmé, 1886:41).

Despite their linguistic terminology, Formalist and Prague School statements on poetic language have more in common with the pronouncements of the avant-garde poet-critics than with the rest of structural linguistics. Jakobson's statement in 1960 that:

> In poetry the internal form of a name, that is, the semantic load of its constituents, regains its pertinence. . . . In other words, poeticalness is not a supplementation of discourse with rhetorical adornment but *a total re-evaluation of the discourse and all its components whatsoever.* (Jakobson, 1960:376–77, emphasis mine)

finds an antecedent in Rilke (1922):

> The poet's task is increased by the strange obligation to set apart his word from the words of everyday life thoroughly and fundamentally. No word in the poem (I mean here every "and" or "the") is identical with the same-sounding word in common use

and conversation; the purer conformity with the law, . . . the
constellation it occupies in verse or artistic prose, *changes it to
the core of its nature*, renders it useless, unserviceable for mere
everyday use, untouchable and permanent. (Rilke, 1922:326,
emphasis mine)

The Prague School's impassive claim in 1929:

> In its social role, language [*le langage*] must be specified accord-
> ing to its relation to extralinguistic reality. It has either a com-
> municative function, that is, it is directed toward the signified,
> or a poetic function, that is, it is directed toward the sign itself.
> (Cercle Linguistique de Prague, 1929:14, translation mine)

is based on the same values and assumptions as Valéry's less "scientific" statement in 1938:

> It is the same with utilitarian language: the language I use to
> express my design, my desire, my command, my opinion; this
> language, when it has served its purpose, evaporates almost as it
> is heard. I have given it forth to perish . . . and I shall know that
> I was understood by the remarkable fact that my speech no
> longer exists. . . . The poem, on the other hand, does not die for
> having lived: it is expressly designed to be born again from its
> ashes and to become endlessly what it has just been. (Valéry,
> 1938:71–72)

Similarly, the Prague School thesis of 1929 which states:

> Poetic phonology includes: *the degree to which the phonological
> repertoire is utilized in comparison with communicative language*,
> principles of phoneme grouping (especially in sandhi), repeti-
> tion of phoneme groups, rhythm and melody. (Prague Linguis-
> tic Circle, 1929:19, emphasis mine, translation mine)

is not as far removed as it sounds from Mallarmé's (1886) description:

> Language, in the hands of the mob, leads to the same facility and directness as does money; but in the Poet's hands, it is turned above all, to dream and song; and, by the constituent virtue and necessity of an art which lives on fiction, it *achieves its full efficacy*. (Mallarmé, 1886–95:43, emphasis mine)

In similar fashion, Šklovskij's (1917) "law of obscurity" very easily boils down to Mallarmé's "art is a mystery accessible only to the very few."

Such statements as these lead one to suspect Stankiewicz's (1961) assertion that the "significance of internal analysis . . . lies in its claim to objectivity, in its conviction that poetic language can be defined in terms of its internal, inter-personal and empirical features" (Stankiewciz, 1961:11–12). It is one thing for the poet, or even the poet-critic, to claim that his art exists in a universe of its own and bears no relation to the society in which he and his readers live. It is quite another for the literary analyst to unquestioningly accept such a view as the basis for a theory of literature. The poet's declaration that he no longer wishes his work to be associated with "society" or "reality" or "commerce" or "the masses" is hardly grounds for the critic to decide that the associations have in fact ceased to exist or ceased to pertain to the critical enterprise. To study a religion, one does not have to be a believer, and if one is, one is at any rate obliged to make an attempt to distinguish between facts and one's beliefs. In the case of poetics and of intrinsic criticism in general, the claim that this dissociation of literature from all other realms of human activity had empirical justification and could thus serve as the basis of a "scientific" theory of literature in effect serves to build a whole range of ideological assumptions into literary studies in such a way that they never have to be made explicit. It is a claim that frees the critic from any obligation to refer to the poet's values, the society's values, or his own values. He may prescribe under the guise of describing.

Yet the very concept of literature has values built into it. Not all books get published, not all societies agree on what constitutes literature, and not all varieties of verbal art are recognized as literature. Marxist and sociological critics, of course, have been objecting for at least fifty years both to the concealed ideology behind intrinsic and formalist criticism and to the tendency of such criticism to conceal ideology. The few steps I have taken here toward supplying the literary speech act with its context and toward reintegrating it into the broader schema of our verbal and social activities will, I hope, suggest that a socially based, use-oriented linguistics is a prerequisite toward sealing the breach between formal and sociological approaches to literature.

Toward a
Speech Act Theory
of
Literary Discourse

Chapter One

The "Poetic Language" Fallacy

> It is of the utmost importance
> to overcome naive antinomies of
> sacred and secular. They prevail
> not only in historiography
> but also in personal and even
> national psychoses. Anthropology
> has helped to overcome them
> by showing that the sacred is
> not a class of special things but
> rather a special class of things.
>
> GEOFFREY HARTMAN,
> "Structuralism: The Anglo-
> American Adventure"

In his 1926 article, "The Theory of the Formal Method," Boris Éjxenbaum explains the role played in Russian Formalist literary theory by the opposition between poetic and nonpoetic language:

> Their [the Formalists'] basic point was, and still is, that the object of literary science, as literary science, ought to be the investigation of the specific properties of literary material, of the properties that distinguish such material from material of any other kind. . . . To establish this principle of specificity without resorting to speculative aesthetics required the juxtaposing of the literary order of facts with another such order. For this purpose one order had to be selected from among existent orders which,

3

while contiguous with the literary order, would contrast with it
in terms of function. It was just such a methodological procedure
that produced the opposition between "poetic" language and
"practical" language. . . . Thus, instead of an orientation toward
a history of culture or of social life, toward psychology, or aesthetics and so on, as had been customary for literary scholars, the
Formalists came up with their own characteristic orientation
toward linguistics. (Èjxenbaum, 1926:9)

According to Èjxenbaum, then, the opposition between poetic and
practical language was supposed to provide "literary scientists" with
a method of empirical verification, a kind of external evaluative criterion against which their observations about literature could be
tested. By establishing a systematic relation between literary and
nonliterary data on which to base their work, poeticians would be
able to claim for their observations the same empirical validity
granted to the statements of general linguistics. Notice, however,
that Ejxenbaum makes a number of assumptions about the nature of
that relation that are not obvious. Among other things, he assumes
that (1) language functions in literature differently than it does
elsewhere, (2) the relation between the literary and nonliterary
functions of language is one of opposition, and (3) this opposition
is fully manifested in the observable properties of literary and nonliterary data; thus, literature has properties that other utterances do
not possess and is defined by those properties. Literature, in other
words, is linguistically autonomous. And literature and nonliterature
can be taken as self-consistent, homogeneous bodies of data, at least
in their relation to each other.

In his 1919 article, "Potebnja," Viktor Šklovskij makes the same
set of assumptions and in addition claims that "massive evidence"
exists to support them:

If a scientific poetics is to be brought about, it must start with
the factual assertion, founded on massive evidence, that there

are such things as "poetic" and "prosaic" languages, each with
their different laws. (quoted in Èjxenbaum, 1926:14)

("Prosaic" in Šklovskij's terminology is synonymous with "everyday." See, for example, his article in Todorov, 1965:81.) There is no
question in Šklovskij's mind that the poetic/nonpoetic distinction,
the different laws, and the massive evidence exist. Throughout the
seventy-five-year history of modern poetics their existence has hardly
ever been questioned. They have existed as presuppositions without,
to my knowledge, ever having been tested as hypotheses. The verification procedure which Èjxenbaum claims motivated the comparison of literature with nonliterature in the first place was never actually applied.

I mean simply this: throughout the exhaustive literature this century has produced on metrics, rhythm, syllabification, metaphor,
rhyme, and parallelism of every kind, the role these devices do play
in real utterances outside literature was never seriously examined or
recognized. Likewise, throughout the brilliant body of Formalist
scholarship on prose fiction, nary a scholar seriously poses the question of whether or to what extent devices like palpableness of form,
estrangement, foregrounding, and laying bare of devices do exist outside literature. Not a single reference can be found to the myriad
types of narrative utterances which make up a formidable part of
everyone's day-to-day verbal behavior. Examples from literature are
virtually never accompanied by data from extraliterary discourse.
Instead, devices observed in literature were assumed to be "literary,"
to constitute "literariness" (the term is Jakobson's) because nonliterature was assumed a priori not to possess the properties of literature. Hence even terminologically, the right-hand term of the
poetic/nonpoetic dichotomy scarcely mattered at all. "Nonpoetic"
could be specified variously as "practical," "utilitarian," "spoken,"
"prosaic," "scientific," "everyday," "communicative," "referential,"
or any combination of these without in the least disturbing the

notion of what "poetic" was. That the poeticians themselves have never been able to agree on a term for designating nonliterature should have led them to doubt the existence of any such monolith. That they have so far felt no need to resolve the question of how nonliterature should be baptized is, as I shall show shortly, an important symptom of the vacuous role this concept plays in their theory.

Had the Formalists and their descendants used their verification procedure, had they actually asked whether their so-called literary properties really did "distinguish literary material from material of any other kind," they would have found Šklovskij's "massive evidence" seriously lacking. One simple negative proof of this is the fact that texts cannot always be identified as literature on sight. In addition, even the most cursory glance at the day-to-day behavior of a speech community can tell us that neither the formal nor the functional distinctiveness that the Formalists attributed to literature has any factual basis. Before I develop and illustrate this claim, however, I should like to show in a little more detail what the real motivation for the poetic/nonpoetic duality was and what happens to the Formalist argument when that duality begins to break down.

We could begin by posing two questions. First, since the Formalists were only interested in the structural properties of literary utterances, why bring nonliterary discourse into the picture at all? Secondly, since their claims about nonliterary discourse are almost never supported by real data in their writings and since linguistic theory at the time of the Formalists had specifically excluded the question of language use from its scope of inquiry, where did the Formalist assumptions about the nonliterary uses of language come from, and on what basis was the category of "practical" language defined in the first place?

Èjxenbaum, in the passage quoted earlier, provides us with his answer to the first question: "practical language" was introduced to "establish a principle of specificity without resorting to speculative aesthetics." Èjxenbaum here appears to be proposing the comparison of two types of data, but his statement (quoted in full on p. 3) makes sense only if one assumes the existence of a pre-established "order of facts" called "practical language" whose identity has been defined without the devious intervention of "speculative aesthetics."

And so we face question two: where did this "order of facts" come from? Èjxenbaum and his colleagues evidently believed it came from linguistics. Linguistics provided the facts about nonliterary language; the job of poetics was to juxtapose those facts and the facts about literary language. In other words, coupling "poetic" and "ordinary" language was a way of coupling poetics and linguistics, and thus of laying claim to a respectable empirical basis for observations which had previously only been "speculative." Notice, however, that this "methodological procedure" entails a rather drastic redefinition of what linguistics is. For, as I have already suggested, the linguistics of the Saussurian structural tradition does not claim to describe real utterances of any kind but rather the abstract set of rules which underlies real utterances. While a structuralist grammar can make statements about the grammatical relations which obtain among elements in a given real utterance, it emphatically does not claim to make statements about that utterance's function or use and remains effectively blind to those aspects of an utterance's organization which may have been determined by its intended function in its speech situation. By means of the *langue/parole* distinction, Saussurian linguistics intentionally "brackets" all structures other than basic, rule-governed grammatical and phonological ones. Prague School structural linguistics, though it made a point of calling itself "functional," was, like Saussure, almost uniquely concerned with the function of elements within the linguistic system rather than with the functions the language serves within the speech community. In the pre-World War II days of the Prague School, the poeticians themselves were virtually the only members interested in this latter question,[1] with the result that in the all-important Prague School Theses of 1929, the poetic/nonpoetic opposition is built right into the pronouncement on the social function of language:

> In its social role, language [*le langage*] must be specified [*distinguer*] according to its relation to extralinguistic reality. It has either a communicative function, that is, it is directed toward the signified, or a poetic function, that is, it is directed toward the sign itself. (Prague Linguistic Circle, 1929:14)[2]

Given the limited scope of structural linguistics, then, the Formalist and structuralist belief that statements arising from general linguistics were available as evidence in support of a theory of linguistic aesthetics rested on a number of questionable assumptions. Schematically, we could say that the Formalists established their "principle of specificity" by:

1. defining literature as a linguistic category
2. postulating an opposing linguistic category containing all and only nonliterature
3. redefining grammar in such a way that its domain is all and only nonliterature
4. ascribing to nonliterature all and only those properties described by structuralist grammar.

----

1. One important exception here is Vilém Mathesius, whose interest in language as a social phenomenon crystallized even before the Russian Formalists were in existence (see, for example, his 1911 paper in Vachek, 1964). However, Mathesius himself showed little interest in the poetic language question, and I have found almost no reference to his work among the poeticians. In addition, Professor E. J. Brown has called to my attention a still untranslated essay by L. P. Jakubinsky titled "On dialogic discourse" (*Russkaya rech'*, 1923) in which Jakubinsky criticizes the inadequaciy of the poetic/practical language opposition and tries to produce a more detailed inventory of the uses of language.

2. Here and throughout, references to the Prague Circle's Theses refer to the French original in the *Travaux du Cercle Linguistique de Prague*, vol. I (1929). Since the Theses are not available in English, translations are my own and are as literal as possible.

Obviously, I am not suggesting that these four points represent the stages of a conscious attempt to mislead the public. Rather, they represent a set of assumptions, in some cases only attitudes, which gave rise to the poetic/nonpoetic opposition in the first place and which underlie its various manifestations today. It is worth examining more closely how this relation between poetics and linguistics came to be. Consider the following statement by Jakobson and Bogatyrev concerning the relation of a work of folk literature to its tradition:

> A folklore work is extraindividual and exists only potentially; ... it is a skeleton of actual traditions which the implementers embellish with the tracery of individual creation, in much the same way as the producers of a verbal message (*la parole* in the Saussurian sense) act with respect to the verbal code (*la langue*). (Jakobson and Bogatyrev, 1929:91)

Here, the Saussurian *langue/parole* distinction is used as an analogy. The folklore work is to its tradition as the individual utterance is to its grammar. In an earlier article, Tynjanov and Jakobson apply the analogy to all literature. Referring to *langue* and *parole*, they write:

> The principles involved in relating these two categories (i.e., the existing norm and individual utterances) as applied to literature must now be elaborated. In this latter case, the individual utterance cannot be considered without reference to the existing complex of norms. (Tynjanov and Jakobson, 1928:80)

René Wellek elaborates the same argument in his 1936 article, "The Theory of Literary History." Discussing the problem of a work's relation to the individual, he says:

> Roman Jakobson has supplied the necessary corrective meeting the objections here voiced. He prefers to speak of "collective ideology," a system of norms which is implied in every work of

art though not every individual may be able to materialize these norms. The parallel between language (*langue*) and speech (*parole*) in the sense defined by de Saussure is instructive. A system of actual norms (*langue*) is materialized only in the individual pronouncements (*parole*), but only the existence of this system of norms makes the individual pronouncements possible and comprehensible. So every work of art materializes (becomes effective) only in the minds of individuals, but no individual ever realizes it as a whole, just as he will never "materialize" the whole of his language. (Wellek, 1936:180)

Wellek, you will notice, posits not one analogy here but two. The *langue/parole* distinction is used to represent both the relation of a given work to the literary canon of its time and the relation of an individual reading of a work to the work itself.

The fact that, analogies aside, there is a real *langue* shared by literary and non-literary utterances alike is quite overlooked and seems almost irrelevant to the line of argument these quotations indicate. But the analogy is flawed in a more serious way, for it implies that this metaphorical *langue/parole* relationship is unique to literature, that only literary utterances are subject to norms other than the rules of grammar. But this is clearly false. In addition to the rules of grammar (or *langue*), any utterance is subject to rules governing the use of language in the context in question. All utterances take place against the background of a whole range of contemporary norms governing what styles, what subject matter, what degrees of formality, politeness, and so on are appropriate in different contexts. The *langue/parole* analogy used in these quotations obscures the fact that such norms exist for extraliterary discourse and are of the same type as those making up the so-called *langue* of literature. Indeed, the two overlap to a significant extent.

In a 1935 lecture, Jakobson developed the analogy even further by attributing to this hypothetical poetic *langue* its own peculiar set of minimal units: "Each concrete poetic canon, every set of temporal poetic norms, however, comprises indispensable distinctive elements without which the work cannot be identified as poetic" (Jakobson, 1935:85). Here the analogy becomes more concrete. The literary norms that are compared to *langue* in the first three quotations are here depicted as configurations of discrete minimal units ("distinctive elements"), in the same way that morphemes are configurations of phonemes. The *langue* of poetry, it seems, has its own universal categories and units of analysis, just like the *langue* . . . the language of what? "Of practical language," is Èjxenbaum's answer; "of everyday language," is Šklovskij's answer; "of communicative language," is the Prague Circle's answer. It is exactly at this point that the analogy becomes a distortion, for it is taken here as a fact. Postulating a separate grammar of poetry which is related analogically to the grammar of language very easily obscures the real relation that holds between poetic utterances and the grammar of the language in which they are written, namely that of *parole* to *langue*, the relation that all utterances in a given language hold with respect to the grammar. It was a simple step indeed for the poeticians to lose sight of this fact and to establish their relation to linguistics on the basis of their analogy instead. It is the analogy that leads to the belief that there *is* a poetic language with its own laws, which poeticians discover and specify, and a nonpoetic language with its laws, which linguists discover and specify (cf. Šklovskij, quoted above, p. 4). According to the analogy, grammaticality is to linguistics what poeticality is to poetics, and the difference between the linguist's grammar and the poetician's grammar is the difference between literature and nonliterature.

Notice that at this point the methodological parallel ceases to be an analogy at all. The definition of poetic language offered by the Prague Circle in its Theses of 1929 bears no traces of its metaphorical underpinnings:

> It is necessary to develop principles for the synchronic description of poetic language [*langue*] without making the common mistake

of identifying the language [*langue*] of poetry with that of communication. Poetic discourse [*langage*] has, from a synchronic point of view, the form of speech [*parole*], that is, the form of an individual creative act, which is realized on the one hand against the background of existing poetic tradition (poetic language [*langue*]), and on the other hand against the background of contemporary communicative language. . . . All levels of the linguistic system, which have only a subordinate role [*rôle de service*] in communicative discourse, take on in poetic discourse some degree of autonomous value. (p. 19, translation mine)

The poetic *langue* here is regarded not as a metaphor but as an autonomous phenomenon of the same order as, but also contrasting with, the *langue* of nonpoetry, here labeled "communicative language." The following statement made by Tomaševskij in 1928 illustrates what happens when the results of the linguist's and the poetician's procedures are compared as facts of the same order:

The chief trait of poetry is that it no longer presents an expression merely as a means or the action of an automatic mechanism, but as an element which has gained an original aesthetic value and has become an end in itself of the discourse. (Tomaševskij, 1928:230, translation mine)

The implication, obviously, is that nonpoetry does present an expression "merely as a means or the action of an automatic mechanism." But of course it is structural linguistics that presents language in this way (Saussure's chapter on syntax is titled *Mécanisme de la langue*). What Tomaševskij takes to be characteristics of nonpoetic utterances are actually characteristics of a structuralist grammar.

Similarly, Osip Brik describes the interaction of rhythm and syntax in the following terms:

Syntax is the system of word combination in ordinary speech. Inasmuch as verse language is still subject to the basic laws of prose syntax, the laws of word combination are laws of rhythm. And these rhythmic laws complicate the syntactic nature of verse. ... Verse is regulated not simply by the laws of syntax, but by the laws of rhythmic syntax, that is, a syntax in which the usual syntactic laws are complicated by rhythmic requirements. ... The very fact that a certain number of words coexist with the two sets of laws constitutes the peculiarity of poetry. (Brik, 1927:121–122)

Assuming that syntax, as it is specified in a grammar, constitutes a description of how words are combined in spoken discourse is for Brik a way of assuming that rhythmic organization is alien to non-literary discourse and can thus be taken as a distinctive feature of the poetic language. Hence, according to Brik, one can "translate" an utterance from poetic to nonpoetic language by wiping out its rhythmic organization: "By rearranging words we can deprive any line of poetry of its poetic shape and turn it into a phrase from the sphere of ordinary speech" (p. 124).

But of course the syntacticians who formulated the "laws of word combination" had never *posed the question* of rhythmic organization and in fact located such questions squarely outside their concerns, along with everything else that concerned the use of language. Brik's comparison is thus illegitimate.

Nearly forty years later, Samuel Levin makes the same mistake in his influential monograph, *Linguistic Structures in Poetry.* "In poetry," writes Levin, "structures are not merely dummies to be filled in by just any form as long as it is grammatical and communication is effected" (1962:34). Once again, note the implication: outside poetry, constructions *are* "merely dummies to be filled in by just any form. ..." Within the context of the linguistics which invented it, the dummy construction (whereby a sentence is conceived as a series of slots, each to be filled in by a given part of speech) is no more a characteristic of nonliterary discourse than it is of literary. It is a descriptive device used in specifying grammatical relations. Besides being an inadequate representation of the way syntax works, as Chomsky has shown, the dummy construction was never intended to represent the aesthetic structure of any real utterance and was obviously not conceived with aesthetics in mind at all. In fact, it was above all a device linguists could use in field research to elicit responses from informants (by asking them to "fill in the blank" in the sentence). It was designed, in short, by and for linguists whose concern was to derive the phonological, syntactic, and morphological systems of (often unwritten) languages up to the level of word order within the sentence, linguists who were very far indeed from *posing the question* of aesthetic organization either within literature or outside it.

Levin, Tomaševskij, and Brik all make the same far-reaching mistake. They derive their view of what extraliterary utterances are like from structural linguistics' idea of what a grammar is like. In the process of defining poetics by analogy to linguistics, they in effect redefine linguistics in the way I outlined earlier: the domain of grammar is taken to be all and only extraliterary discourse; extraliterary discourse is assumed to possess all and only the properties attributed to it by the grammar.

In point of fact, let me repeat, the structural linguist's grammar is not a description of any set of utterances at all, and it is even more emphatically not a description of how language is used in a given utterance and context. A structuralist grammar—an inventory of phonemes, morphemes, and rules for combining them—bears no substantive resemblance at all to the inventory of devices, conventions, and norms which makes up the *langue* the poeticians were postulating for literature. Nor are there grounds for equating the two. The so-called grammar of communicative language can exist apart from the so-called grammar of poetry, but the reverse is not so; the latter exists only by contrast to the former. The often voiced claim that "poetic language must be studied in and of itself" is thus meaningless. The "poetic morphology, phonology and syntax" which the Prague Circle outlined in their Theses (1929:18ff.) can only consist of the search for points of contrast. Attempts to define the terms positively seem unintelligible: "Poetic phonology deals with the degree to which the phonological repertoire is utilized in comparison with [*par rapport au*] communicative discourse [*langage*]" (p. 19).

In short, it is clearly illegitimate to infer that a linguistic theory asking the question "Is this utterance grammatical?" should have answered, in the realm of nonliterary discourse, the question "Is this utterance poetic?" And although this inference does not always emerge as blatantly as in the examples I have cited, it lies at the center of the structural poetic conception of "ordinary language." The faulty analogy I have been discussing underlies the overwhelming tendency to view style as an exclusively or predominantly literary phenomenon and to equate style outside literature with mere grammaticality and conventional appropriateness. "Ordinary language" looks utilitarian, prosaic, mechanical, practical, and automatized to poeticians not because it is, but because structural linguistics is utilitarian, prosaic, and mechanical in the sense that it only undertakes to describe those aspects of language that can be accounted for in terms of dummy constructions, grammaticality, *rôles de service* and the "action of a mechanism." Small wonder that poetic language should seem to "impose on the discourse some structure in addition to that which derives from ordinary language" (Levin, 1962:18) or that rhythmic structure should appear to be a second set of syntactic laws. These are not structures in addition to those nonliterary utterances possess. They are structures in addition to those which structural grammar describes.

We are now in a position to return to the first question posed earlier: why bring extraliterary discourse into the picture at all? Attempting to distinguish literature from nonliterature at the level of *langue* has the effect of locating the concerns of poetics outside those of general linguistics, while retaining an analogy between the two disciplines allows the disparity of their aims to remain hidden behind a uniformity of terminology and method. It is this separation of powers that, I believe, "ordinary language" as a linguistic construct was invented to support. Extraliterary discourse was brought into the argument so that linguistics could be brought into the argument, but only in such a way that it would provide seemingly empirical support for an idea that is very dear indeed to the defenders of avant-garde aesthetics, the idea that poets speak a language different in essence from that of "the tribe." The category labeled "ordinary language" (or just about anything else) furnishes not an experimental control or verification procedure as Èjxenbaum would have, but insulation, a way of building the linguistic autonomy of literature into the theory without referring to actual evidence from nonliterary discourse. "Ordinary language" fills in a blank in a faulty paradigm. It would be foolish to suggest that we critics have been consciously misled over the years by a tacit conspiracy of poeticians. I mean to say only that since linguistics had no theory of language use to offer, poetics simply invented its own in accord with its aesthetic ideology. But it isn't a very good theory. It has trouble explaining the fact that literary and nonliterary utterances are alike at all. Ultimately, it renders poetics and linguistics mutually exclusive, and in so doing it misrepresents the status of literary discourse in the grammar as completely as it misrepresents the role of aesthetic considerations in our speech behavior outside literature.

Once this peculiar "separate and equal" relation is established between poetics and linguistics, such misrepresentations become very difficult to correct from within poetics, first because they seldom become apparent and second because the poetician is left with no theoretical obligations to linguistics. He is set free to raid the linguist's toolbox at will and to use what he finds in whatever way he likes. Richard Bailey (1972) has voiced this same objection:

> Only seldom, however, has the relationship between linguistics and criticism been a happy one, for the literary parasite too often violates the integrity of his linguistic host. Examples of the misapplication of the models and methods of one discipline to the

tasks of another are easy to find, particularly in the analysis of literary style. (Bailey, 1972:98)

Linguists have not been eager to call poeticians to account for their theoretical frivolity, however. Indeed, it is more than safe to say that the division between linguistics and poetics fostered by the poetic/ordinary language split has not inconvenienced linguistics in the least. In fact, this division of labor has been reinforced from within linguistics in a number of ways. Saussure, noting the extent to which his philologist predecessors had been led astray by their reliance on written documents, was extremely suspicious of all written forms of language. In the *Cours* he stresses the derived nature of writing and its tendency not to change with the spoken language, and he generally excludes written texts as a source of data except in the case of dead languages.

Furthermore, Saussure makes a point of excluding what he calls "la langue littéraire" from the scope of linguistics, although his reasons for doing so have nothing to do with the Formalist ideas of poeticality or "literariness." Saussure sets literary language apart from the study of *langue* for the same reasons he excludes dialect phenomena on the one hand and "langues spéciales" like juridical language on the other. In Saussure's view, all such language-internal subdivisions are conditioned by geographical circumstances, cultural and political developments, or other extralinguistic contingencies and thus belong to "la linguistique externe" rather than to the study of *langue* proper. Saussure's definition of a literary language, stated in terms of its cultural and social function rather than its intrinsic properties, bears no resemblance to the "poetic language" of the Formalists:

> By literary language I mean not only the language of literature but also, in a more general sense, any kind of cultivated language, official or otherwise, that serves the whole community. (Saussure, 1915:267)

> At every point the literary language oversteps the boundaries that
> literature apparently marks off; we need only consider the influ-
> ence of *salons*, the court, and national academies. (p. 21)

Yet Saussure does seem to share some of the Formalists' interest in
contrasting literary language with the spoken norm:

> The linguist must also examine the reciprocal relations of book
> language and the vernacular; for every literary language, being
> the product of the culture, finally breaks away from its natural
> sphere, the spoken language. (p. 21)

In spite of the enormous difference between Saussure's view of
literary language and that of the Formalists, it is easy to see how
Saussure reinforces the poetics/linguistics split. By separating spoken
language from both written and literary language and by insisting
on spoken language as the norm for linguistic description, Saussure
undoubtedly set the stage for the erroneous view that a Saussurian
description of *langue* constituted a description of nonliterary language that was equatable to poetics' description of literary language. The poetics/linguistics split was reinforced even more
strongly by Saussure's *langue/parole* distinction itself. As long as
the subject matter of linguistics was understood to be *langue* in the
Saussurian sense, poeticians and linguists were virtually guaranteed
to be doing different things. The term "literature" refers either to a
particular use of language or to a particular body of real utterances.
Either way, in Saussurian terms, it belongs to *parole*. Linguistics in
the Saussurian tradition has no theory of *parole*, not even a rudimentary way of stating how real utterances differ from one another
or how they are related to their speakers, hearers, and context.

As I mentioned earlier, the Prague School did consider questions
of language use to be part of linguistics. The theory outlined in the
1929 Theses aims to describe language as "a system of means

adapted [*appropriés*] to an end" (p. 7). In practice, however, the *langue/parole* split, and with it the linguistics/poetics split, reasserted itself almost immediately. The seven volumes of the Prague Circle's *Travaux* which appeared after 1929 concentrate overwhelmingly on internal morphological, phonological, and syntactic systems and concomitantly contain almost no articles on poetics. Nearly thirty years after the 1929 Theses, in another set of theses presented at the Fourth International Congress of Slavicists in 1958, B. Havránek and others agree that:

> In structural linguistics more progress has been made in the study of *langue* than in the study of *parole*. In the area of *parole*, attention has been given chiefly to artistic texts. (Havránek et al., 1958:42, translation mine)

As Karl Uitti (1969) has shown, the breach between poetics and linguistics asserted itself even more emphatically in the United States, where linguistics developed without even the vestiges of a literary arm, while the study of "poetic language" became the province of the New Critics, few of whom were interested in the linguistics of nonpoetry at all. Since the late 1950's, when interest in structural poetics did begin to gel in the U.S., attempts to bridge this institutional gap have burgeoned within the literary establishment, beginning with the 1958 Indiana Style Conference (see Sebeok, 1960, for the proceedings). The proceedings of the 1960 conference on poetics in Warsaw (Davie et al., 1961) contain an impressive number of American contributions. It is not surprising that the American partisans of poeticality should have thus sought out their European fellows, for in America poetics has caused scarcely a ripple among linguists. The two disciplines have remained apart here for the same reason they did in Europe: poeticians and linguists have been doing different things, and oftentimes the linguists know it while the poeticians do not. Uitti has discussed the achievements of structural poetics in America fully enough, and I need not repeat here the observations which led him to conclude that "so far, by and large, no general linguistic theory in America has been implemented in such a way as to deal systematically with the language of literature. 'Poeticalness' remains a concept analogous to 'grammaticalness' " (1969:200).

Uitti perceptively attributes the tendency for poetics and linguistics to repel rather than attract each other to a more general and deep-seated characteristic of linguistic investigation: the fact that in linguistics, "the point(s) of view will always shape the material to be studied" (Uitti, 1969:109). Uitti refers to Saussure's formulation of this problem, which I think is worth quoting:

> Other sciences work with objects that are given in advance and that can then be considered from different viewpoints; but not linguistics. Someone pronounces the French word *nu* 'bare': a superficial observer would be tempted to call the word a concrete linguistic object; but a more careful examination would reveal successively three or four quite different things, depending on whether the word is considered as a sound, as the expression of an idea, as the equivalent of Latin *nūdum*, etc. Far from it being the object that antedates the viewpoint, it would seem that it is the viewpoint that creates the object; besides, nothing tells us in advance that one way of considering the fact in question takes precedence over the others or is in any way superior to them. (Saussure, 1915:8)

Perhaps even Saussure might have been able to point out to poeticians that the difference between their discipline and linguistics was not the difference between two kinds of language or even between two uses of language but between two *views* of language.

To the extent that it has concentrated on the internal phonological, morphological, and syntactic systems of language, then, linguistics has given tacit support to the distortive poetic/ordinary language dualism. With some exceptions, the dominant trends in linguistics, both in Europe and America, have not been concerned with the question of language use. This state of affairs has two main consequences for the linguistic theory of literature. On the one hand it means that the analytic equipment with which structural poeticians approached the question of how language is used in literature was ill-adapted to their undertaking. In this sense they can hardly be censured for relegating linguistics to the domain of ordinary language. On the other hand, it means that only a linguistics which has a theory of language use will ever be in a position to replace the Formalist argument. The lack of such a theory in part explains both the longevity of the poetic/nonpoetic dichotomy and the ongoing mutual exclusiveness of poetics and linguistics.

It is worth noting in this regard, however, that those linguistic theories that do concentrate on language use or that do not recognize the Saussurian dichotomy likewise cannot accommodate the poetic/ordinary split in any of its variants. The functional linguistics of M.A.K. Halliday is an important case in point. Nevertheless, it must be confessed that the poetic/nonpoetic language opposition is still alive and well, especially in Paris, where ordinary language is getting more "ordinary" all the time. Here are some recent formulations to complement those already cited:

> Literature, as we know, exists precisely as an effort to say what ordinary discourse cannot and does not say. . . . It is only by virtue of this difference from everyday discourse that literature can come into being and exist. (Todorov, 1970:27, translation mine)

> What poetic discourse communicates is what practical discourse [*le langage véhiculaire*] does not communicate. (Delas and Filliolet, 1973:191, translation mine)

Roland Barthes, in his recent book, *The Pleasure of the Text* (*Le*

Plaisir du texte), calls it a "scientific scandal" that no grammar of spoken French exists, but he nevertheless observes with assurance that:

> Here [in the "language of the People" (*la classe populaire*)], all magical or poetical activity disappears: the party's over, no more games with words: an end to metaphors, reign of the stereotypes imposed by petit bourgeois culture. (Barthes, 1973:38)

From Britain, Winifred Nowottny's version echoes the passage from Levin (1962) quoted earlier and matches it in oversimplification:

> A verbal structure is literary if it presents its topic at more than one level of presentation at the same time, or alternatively, if one and the same utterance has more than one function in the structure of meaning in which it occurs. (Nowottny, 1962:2, quoted in Fowler, 1971:114)

David Lodge urgently revives the old "rape of the lexicon" argument:

> The writer's medium differs from the media of most other arts in that it is never virgin. Words come to the writer already violated by other men, impressed with meanings derived from the world of common experience. (Lodge, 1966:47)

The concepts of a "poetic language" and hence of a linguistically autonomous literature can remain intact as long as the scope of linguistic aesthetic investigation is limited to works known to *be* literature. Once this scope is established, the notion of "literary properties" can be expanded, as it was by some Russian Formalists, to include aesthetic structures of a type more global and abstract than can be described within the framework of structural linguistics. It was thus that, in applying their method to prose fiction, the Formalists gave the idea of "device" a much broader application than a strict commitment to structural linguistic units of analysis would have permitted. And they did so without feeling any loss of "specificity." In their analyses of prose fiction, devices like parallelism, foregrounding, or estrangement do not have to be describable in terms of morphemes, syllables, or sentences. All our "structuralisms" derive from this simple and intuitive upward extension of the methodological parallel with linguistics. That the formal method did detach itself so easily from its structural linguistic underpinnings is proof once again of how insubstantial and metaphorical those underpinnings are. Èjxenbaum seems to recognize this fact, albeit vaguely, when he notes that around 1923 "the original connection of the Formal method with linguistics slackened considerably" (Èjxenbaum, 1926:27). More important for the moment, however, is the fact that as the need to claim substantive support from linguistics weakens, the contrast with "ordinary language" loses its importance too. In Formalist prose fiction theory, the concept of ordinary language as the kind of aesthetic degree zero of language onto which poetic structure is imposed gets replaced by a new category called "language material." The underlying structure of literary narrative is a *fabula*, or story line, made up of brute "language material" which is then shaped and elaborated by means of literary devices into a *sjužet*, or plot (see, for example, Šklovskij, 1921).

The direction taken by Formalist prose fiction theory bears out the claim I have been making about the role linguistics actually plays in Formalist poetics: the stronger one's belief in the linguistic autonomy of literature, the less one's need for linguistic proof of it and hence the less one's need for a "nonpoetic" or "ordinary language" category. Likewise, the stronger one's belief in the ordinariness of ordinary language, the easier it is to overlook evidence to the contrary.

Perhaps because of their closer association with linguistics, a number of Prague School poeticians did pay some attention to evidence from extraliterary discourse, recognized the incompatibility of the binary opposition with that evidence, and tried to account for the irrefutable presence of poetic devices in extraliterary utterances. But in almost every instance, the impossibility of allowing for the "poeticalness" of nonliterary utterances without abandoning the idea of a linguistically autonomous literature gives rise to vagueness and contradiction. For example, in his article "The Functional Differentiation of the Standard Language" (1932), Bohuslav Havránek tries to counteract the excessive rigidity of a poetic/nonpoetic dichotomy by subdividing language into a multiplicity of "functional dialects": conversational, workaday, scientific and poetic. "It is impossible and incorrect," he warns, "to try to raise any one functional dialect or style to the status of a criterion for the others" (Havránek, 1932:12). Three pages later, however, he does just that in order to salvage the simple binary opposition. "There is," we read, "an essential difference between the first three functional dialects listed, which are always used to communicate something (have a communicative function), and between poetic language, which is not primarily communicative." Mukařovský postulates this same essential difference in "Standard Language and Poetic Language" (1932): "Foregrounding is of course common in the standard language, for instance, in journalistic style, even more in essays. But it is here always subordinate to communication: its purpose is to attract the reader's (hearer's) attention more closely to the subject matter expressed" (1932:22). Oddly enough, Mukařovský argues at the same time that this same feature, foregrounded subject matter, is not a ground for excluding prose fiction from the realm of poetry:

> It could of course be countered that in some works of poetry, or rather in some genres, only the "content" (subject matter) is foregrounded, so that the above remarks do not concern them. To this it must be noted that in a work of poetry of any genre there is no fixed limit, nor, in a certain sense, any essential difference, between the language and the subject matter. (Mukařovský, 1932:26)

What makes the subject matter of prose fiction "poetic," unlike that of journalism, is its fictitiousness, its lack of truth value:

> The subject matter of a work of poetry cannot be judged by its relationship to the extralinguistic reality entering into the work. ... The question of truthfulness does not apply in regard to the subject matter of a work of poetry, nor does it even make sense. ... The status of subject matter is entirely different in case of communicative speech. There a certain relationship of the subject matter to reality is an important value, a necessary prerequisite. (p. 26)

But even shifting the grounds on which poeticality is defined does not save the argument here, since fictitiousness plays an important role in extraliterary discourse, too. This is a point I shall be discussing shortly in connection with Richard Ohmann's restatement of Mukařovský's argument.

The point to be made here is that both Mukařovský's and Havránek's attempts to make the Formalist idea of poeticalness as a textual property compatible with evidence from extraliterary discourse succeed only by way of a built-in tautology: extraliterary utterances can be poetic but not really poetic, because after all they are not works of literature. I propose to analyze in detail two more recent articles in which the same circularity is evident: Jakobson's "Closing Statement: Linguistics and Poetics" (1960) and Edward Stankiewicz's "Poetic and Non-poetic Language in their Interrelation" (1961). Both are attempts to extend the concept of poeticalness to include certain aspects of extraliterary utterances; and in both, as in the two examples above, the weaknesses of the "poetic language" argument immediately surface as soon as "ordinary language" is treated not as a vacuous dummy category but as a real body of data.

Jakobson and Stankiewicz attempt to allow for evidence from outside literature in essentially the same way—by weakening the poetic/ nonpoetic dichotomy into a continuum, that is, by substituting the binary difference of kind by a difference of degree. To say that non-literary utterances are merely "less poetic" than literary ones seems acceptable enough on the surface. But even this concession poses a fundamental threat to the belief that intrinsic textual properties constitute "literariness." Consequently, both Jakobson and Stankiewicz, like Havránek and Mukařovský, take pains to allow for poeticalness outside literature without negating that belief, on whose acceptance the entire discipline of poetics seems to depend. Both attempt somehow to neutralize the poetic properties of non-literary discourse, allowing that such discourse can be poetic but not in the same way as works of literature. In short, both writers end up maintaining a difference of kind and denying it at the same time.

The attempt to deal directly with "ordinary language" produces another set of ambiguities in these two papers that I think are important to the literary critic. In both articles, as in Mukařovský's discussion, prose literature is dealt with in terms as equivocal as those used to describe nonliterary discourse. This is not a coincidence, obviously. Once ordinary language is actually admitted into the corpus of poetics, it is no longer possible to overlook the fact that prose literature is not systematically distinguishable as literature on the basis of textual properties that structuralist linguistics can recognize. Verse, however, does remain so distinguishable and thus becomes the sole domain in which a direct connection between literariness and linguistic form can be maintained. In other words, the blurring of the poetic/nonpoetic dichotomy raises the problem of empirical verification that, as I have suggested, the binary opposition was designed to avoid in the first place, the problem that apparently led the Russian Formalists to substitute "language material" for "ordinary language" when it came time to talk about prose fiction.

Once verification does become a problem, once poetics is required to make good its connection with linguistics, such empirical evidence for "immanent poeticality" as can be supplied by structural linguistics has to bear a great deal more weight. Consequently, verse acquires an exaggerated importance in these two papers, while the status of prose becomes utterly ambiguous, as it did for Mukařovský. It is probably because of this ambiguity that the word "literature" is substituted in both papers by the less conventional term "verbal art." Jakobson's statement in the 1960 paper, for example, that "poetics deals primarily with the question 'What makes a verbal message a work of art?'" (Jakobson, 1960:350) contrasts with his 1921 formulation of the same point: "The object of study in literary science is not literature but 'literariness,' that is, what makes a given work a literary work" (Jakobson 1921:8). "Literariness" and "literature" are perhaps uncomfortable terms for the linguistic poetician of the 1950s and 1960s. "Verbal art," as we shall see, acts for Jakobson and Stankiewicz as a handy lexical wedge inserted between what *is* literature and what poetics can *identify* as literature.

Stankiewicz begins his article by rejecting a poetic/nonpoetic distinction based on either grammatical deviance or an emotive/referential dichotomy and concludes that "there is no clear demarcation line between poetic and nonpoetic language." He proposes that "the analogue of a line be replaced by the analogue of two poles: i.e., a 'marked' more explicit pole of poetic language and an 'unmarked' or less explicit pole." In other words, the binary distinction would be replaced by a continuum along which utterances could be ranked according to their poeticality. This concession is short-lived, however. In the very next sentence, the possibility of an exclusive distinction is revived: "It consequently follows . . . that the primary domain of poetic studies is the 'marked' pole, which subordinates all functions of language to the poetic function and on which the features of poetic discourse are maximally organized and condensed," the marked pole being identified as lyric poetry. Here, while the notion of maximal organization supports the idea of a continuum and suggests poetry is differentiated only by degree, the idea of subordination of all functions to the poetic function points to a clear difference of kind. The difference of kind asserts itself more and more strongly as the argument proceeds. Stankiewicz acknowledges that poetic devices like rhyme, rhythmic organization, punning, and parallelism occur in nonpoetic discourse, yet he regards them only as "similar to those which occur in works of poetry" and not identical to them as the continuum analysis would imply. Poetic devices outside literature "are of particular interest since they *reflect* the formal properties of language and its poetic *potentialities*" (emphasis mine). No explanation is offered for why poetic devices outside poetry should be only reflections or potentialities, "similar" to their counterparts within poetry. In accordance with the continuum analysis, the transition from ordinary language to poetic language is described initially as a "shift of emphasis . . . from external information to the organization of the message itself." This "shift" is more radically labeled a few sentences later as "a transformation of the non-poetic linear sequence into a poetic pluridimensional sequence." A little later, the "transformation" becomes a "metamorphosis": "when it is filtered through the pluridimensional prism of poetry, ordinary language undergoes a metamorphosis" the result of which Stankiewicz describes in Kenneth Shapiro's words: "The 'word' of ordinary language, which has a communicable sense, becomes the 'non-word' of poetry, having no such sense at all." Thus, by way of a continuum, a shift of emphasis, a transformation, and a metamorphosis, we come once again face to face with an opposition: the word and the nonword. As the argument proceeds, verse ceases to be related to nonverse and even, it seems, to language itself: "The relationship of levels is far less conspicuous in linguistic systems than in verse"; "The interaction between constants and tendencies . . . is in verse far more transparent than it is in language."

Stankiewicz's treatment of prose fiction exhibits the same tendency to convert the difference of degree into a difference of kind. Genres are initially claimed to differ "only in degree of poetic condensation and internal organization." The epic genre is later described as allowing "*switching* to non-poetic discourse" (emphasis mine). No criteria are offered to help us determine when this switch has occurred in a text, that is, at what point poetic devices in a novel cease to be poetic devices and become only "similar" to them.

Stankiewicz's inability to prevent his proposed continuum between poles from turning back into the binary opposition he appears to reject goes hand in hand with another set of ambivalences, which concern the aesthetic impartiality of poetics. At the outset of his paper, Stankiewicz reaffirms the traditional tenet that "the study of poetic language must . . . be detached from the concept of values." But like many of his predecessors, Stankiewicz finds it difficult to maintain this detachment. "Everyday language," we are told, "transmits *merely* information about the outside world" (emphasis mine). We are to understand that "the maximalization of the poetic function in lyrical poetry does not imply . . . any value judgment as to priority of the genres," in spite of the fact that the poetic function, with its lyrical interiorization and condensation, constitutes "the essence of verbal art." Within Stankiewicz's own framework, it is difficult indeed to accept as "detached from the concept of values" a view of narrative fiction as the genre most lacking in the "essence of verbal art" and "most clearly connected with [the 'mere'] external reference" of ordinary language. In sum, both poeticality and value are assigned by Stankiewicz according to certain vague and predefined attributes of lyric poetry, criteria that are, of course, arbitrary from the point of view of literary theory and that make for an unsatisfying representation of all nonverse discourse, literary or otherwise.

The model of language Jakobson proposes in his 1960 paper likewise seeks to avoid a binary poetic/nonpoetic split and has the additional advantage of defining the poetic function independently of any genre. It thus does not in principle require a special status for lyric poetry. I refer to Jakobson's well-known projection principle and the six-point functional model of language on which it is based. Before going on with my critique of his paper, I would like to make clear that, to the extent that I hold Jakobson to his linguistics here, my criticisms of him are onesided. "Linguistics and Poetics" is an important and instructive paper. Indeed, had it been presented as an opening rather than a closing statement at the Indiana Style Conference, there would have been good reason for the conference to adjourn itself then and there. It is precisely because of the enormous scope of his discussion that Jakobson's paper so well reveals the bankruptcy of those traditional structural linguistic assumptions he does maintain.

For Jakobson, there are six factors which constitute any speech event:

	context	
addresser	message	addressee
	contact	
	code	

Any verbal message selects one of these six factors as its primary focus, and this focus determines the primary function language is serving in the given message. There are thus six possible functions language can serve, corresponding to the six aspects of the speech event:

	referential	
emotive	poetic	conative
	phatic	
	metalingual	

A message that the addressee focuses on himself is an emotive one, that is, one in which language is being used mainly in its emotive function. Messages that focus on context are using language mainly in its referential function. In messages like "Do you read me?" that focus on the contact, the main function is said to be phatic. A message like "What does metalingual mean?" exploits the metalingual function in focusing on the code. A message predominantly focused on itself is a poetic one. A given utterance may make use of several or perhaps even all of these functions, but one function will always be seen to predominate. Function in turn determines form: "The verbal structure of a message depends primarily on the dominant function." In other words, a text's intrinsic properties are the manifestations of its function. Concomitantly, a text's function can be deduced by analysis of those properties. This tenet, on which the descriptive power of Jakobson's theory obviously depends, gives rise to some important difficulties in the model. For one thing, the notion of "verbal structure" does not seem to mean the same thing for all six functions. To put it more formally, there seems to be no one set of linguistic properties in terms of which the six functions are distinguished and related. The referential, emotive, and metalingual functions seem to be distinguished from each other in terms of subject matter. Utterances with these functions carry information about the "context," the addresser's inner state, or the code, respectively. The phatic function, on the other hand, is defined contextually by the speaker's intention to "establish, prolong or discontinue communication." To define conative utterances Jakobson proposes a logical criterion, that imperatives lack truth value, in addition to the criteria of grammatical surface structure and referent. On the other hand, there are some important types of verbal structure for which the model does not attempt to account. Although the conative function does distinguish imperatives from other speech act types, the equally important difference between interrogatives and declaratives is nowhere reflected in the model, and the relation between interrogatives and imperatives is likewise unexpressed.

The poetic function is distinguished in the model not by its subject matter, its lexicon, its truth value, its speaker's intent, or its grammatical form but by a criterion of a rather more fundamental order. The "empirical linguistic criterion of the poetic function" is its unique effect on the axes of selection and combination, "the two basic modes of arrangement used in verbal behavior." This effect is expressed in the famous projection principle: "The poetic function projects the principle of equivalence from the axis of selection into the axis of combination." Jakobson makes the same claims for the poetic function as did Stankiewicz in his continuum analysis. Poeticality is a matter of degree, depending on the extent to which the poetic function participates in the grammatical and lexical organization of the message. In works of "verbal art" it is dominant.

But by the very nature of the projection principle, the difference of degree tends to resolve itself into a difference of kind, just as it did for Stankiewicz. The projection principle, if it is strictly interpreted, places the poetic function in rather special relation to all the other functions taken together. On the one hand, the poetic function requires the participation of at least one other function in order to give rise to a message at all. On the other hand, without the participation of the poetic function, the other functions or any combination of them presumably produce utterances in which the principle of equivalence remains in its "usual" place, in the axis of selection. The poetic function transforms this configuration. When it dominates, it produces "a *total re-evaluation* of the discourse and of all its components whatsoever. . . . In poetry any verbal element *is converted* into a figure of speech" (emphasis mine). The choice of words here is unmistakably similar to Stankiewicz's. Poetic devices occurring in speech outside literature are "latent manifestations of the poetic function" for Jakobson, just as they were "potentialities" for Stankiewicz. They retain some of their poeticality: "The *adaptation* of poetic means for some heterogeneous purpose does not conceal their *primary essence*" (emphasis mine). But they apparently don't retain all of it: in poetry, "The internal nexus between sound and meaning changes from latent into patent."

As in Stankiewicz's argument, it remains unclear how this change from latency to patency, from nonpoetry to poetry, is to be observed in a text. While Jakobson provides a definition of verbal art as those utterances dominated by the poetic function and an "empirical linguistic criterion," namely the projection principle, for determining when the poetic function is present, he does not provide any criteria for determining when presence has reached the point of dominance. Yet we need such criteria if we are to answer Jakobson's question "What makes a verbal message a work of art?" in terms of the poetic function. Stankiewicz's response to this problem was to select certain supposed attributes of lyric poetry, namely versification, condensation, interiorization, and lack of referentiality as the indicators of a maximalized poetic function. Jakobson focuses on only one of these, versification. Though he never says so overtly, Jakobson apparently takes the claim that "the verbal structure of a message depends primarily on the dominant function" to mean in the case of the poetic function that verse is a necessary condition of a poetic dominant. This condition by no means arises directly from the projection principle, for no constraints are stated on the grammatical domain of its application. A versification requirement would have the effect of a rule saying that in a poetic message, the projection principle must have applied at least at the syllabic level in such a way as to produce verse. Such a rule would, of course, make prose literature problematic, as did the notions of condensation, interiorization, and so on in Stankiewicz's analysis.

Consequently, Jakobson's statements on the subject, too, are ambivalent. He no sooner states the projection principle than, a sentence later, he identifies poetry with verse: "In poetry the syllable is equalized with any other syllable of the same sequence. . . ." Prose is described mainly in terms of its lack of these syllabic equivalences. It is "verseless composition . . . where parallelisms are not so strictly marked and strictly regular as 'continuous parallelism' and where there is no dominant figure of sound." In spite of this seemingly reduced organization at the level of phoneme, word, and syllable, prose is not altogether excluded from the domain of verbal art. A compromise is attempted: "The prosaic variety of verbal art" represents a "transitional linguistic area . . . between strictly poetic and strictly referential language." But it is an unacceptable compromise, first because it is not at all obvious that prose has a greater debt to referentiality than verse and second because this statement contradicts the claim that all verbal art is characterized by the dominance of the poetic function.

This ambivalence vitiates what is, from the point of view of literary theory, one of the greatest theoretical advantages of Jakobson's model, the fact that it explicitly rejects any ranking of genres according to poeticalness. It thus avoids Stankiewicz's unsatisfactory maneuver of assigning poetic primacy to the lyric. The poetic function for Jakobson is dominant in all genres, and "the particularities of diverse poetic genres imply a differently ranked participation of the other verbal functions along with the dominant poetic function. Epic poetry . . . strongly involves the referential function of language; the lyric . . . is intimately linked with the emotive function; poetry of the second person is involved with the conative function." Since Stankiewicz refuses to accept an "emotive theory of poetic language" on the grounds that no criteria are available for measuring the "emotional charge of poetry" (as if such criteria were available for measuring "interiorization"), he cannot relate genres in this way and thus ends up assigning reduced poeticality to the entire epic genre on the basis of its dependence on "external reference." For Jakobson, on the other hand, the referentiality of a narrative text evidently poses no threat to poeticality unless the narrative text is composed in prose, in which case referentiality does compromise the dominance of the poetic function, creating the "transition area."

Ultimately, in both Jakobson's and Stankiewicz's analyses, prose fiction ends up in the same unhappy place: not quite within verbal art and not quite outside it. Jakobson is aware, of course, that prose presents a problem to poetic theory. Indeed, his metonymy/metaphor distinction is, I believe, the only major contribution to prose fiction theory made by any Prague School poetician. But Jakobson's own model is powerless to correct the deficiency, for it needs the versification requirement. Without such a requirement, the projection principle quite literally can't distinguish a poem from a grocery list or alphabetical order in the phone book from alliteration.

Though he leaves the status of prose literature unclear, Jakobson does try to confront a second difficulty arising from a versification criterion. Because of the central place he accords versification, texts that are verse but are not literature are as problematic for Jakobson's analysis as texts that are not verse but are literature. Jakobson readily notes that "verse actually exceeds the limits of poetry," which is to say that versification cannot be a sufficient criterion for a poetic dominant. Jakobson offers the following account of non-literary verse, or, as he calls it, "applied verse":

> Mnemonic lines . . . (like 'Thirty days hath September'), modern advertising jingles and versified medieval laws . . . or finally Sanscrit scientific treatises in verse which in Indic tradition are strictly distinguished from true poetry (kāvya) —all these metrical texts make use of the poetic function without, however, assigning to this function the coercing, determining role it carries in poetry.

If we hold Jakobson to his linguistics and particularly to his idea of the relation between a message's function and its properties, we are entitled to infer that this configuration of functions proposed for applied verse can be derived by observation of the texts. In terms of the projection principle, the claim just quoted would mean that while applied verse texts have the necessary poetic organization at the syllabic level (which prose lacked), the projection principle has not dominated their organization at other levels of their "verbal structure." If this is the case, some systematic way of measuring this lack in terms of the axes of selection and combination must be appended to the projection principle and must be testable against the available examples of versified laws, advertising jingles, and so on. Jakobson offers no such measure and would doubtless have considered it a waste of time to look for one at the level of surface structure. If we do look for a generalized way of distinguishing poetry from applied verse, those criteria that do suggest themselves—speaker's intent, fictionality, intended audience, factual accuracy, or simply tradition—have nothing to do with the principle of equivalence and the axis of selection, and indeed they are not factors which textual analysis can necessarily reveal at all. Clearly, if poetry and applied verse *can* be distinguished linguistically, it will not be in terms of the projection principle.

The point here is not to argue whether advertising jingles are poetry but to show that a definition of verbal art in terms of the projection principle and the poetic dominant does not provide a basis for excluding them, though Jakobson does exclude them. Nor do I wish to argue that Jakobson's specific observations about how language is functioning within verse literature are false. On the whole, they are true. As I hope I have shown, the failure lies in the attempt to use those observations as a basis for distinguishing texts that are not held to be literature from those that are. In other words, although the projection principle and the ideas of dominance and focus on the message *can* be profitably and appropriately used to address the question "What makes a verbal work of art a verbal work of art?" they cannot provide an answer to the question Jakobson poses: "What makes a verbal message a verbal work of art?" As Karl Uitti observes, "As a category, 'poetry' possesses for Jakobson some kind of arbitrary status derived from its own ostensible nature; his ultimate 'definition' of poetry is not clear" (1969:233). In spite of his aim to do justice to "ordinary language," Jakobson's methodology, like that of his Formalist and structuralist predecessors, works successfully only within literature, where the distortive relation it implies between literature and nonliterature remains in the background. Let me repeat that this failing becomes apparent here only because Jakobson, unlike his predecessors, is willing to confront extraliterary utterances directly.

Chapter Two

Natural Narrative

What Is "Ordinary Language" Really Like?

> Let us only listen to common
> people's speech!
> What a lot of automatically
> occurring slips of the tongue
> there are, of barbarisms,
> solecisms, of anacoluthons!
>
> Vladímir Skalička, "The
> Need for a Linguistics
> of 'La parole' "

> Il se fait plus de figures en
> un jour de Halles qu'en un
> mois d'Académie.
>
> French Proverb

In the previous chapter, I tried to show that structural poeticians for the most part never tested their assumptions about ordinary language at all and that those who do try to account for poetic phenomena in extraliterary data draw from that data conclusions (like the latency/patency distinction) that support the assumptions of their predecessors but that the data themselves do not bear out. I propose to turn now to the work of a linguist who has approached the aesthetics of nonliterary discourse from outside poetics and whose results provide a vital corrective to the views of "ordinary language" arising from structural poetics. I refer to the eminent American sociolinguist William Labov whose work on the oral narrative of personal experience may well be the only body of data-based research dealing with aesthetically structured discourse which is not, by anybody's definition, literature.

Much of Labov's research over the past ten years has been devoted to documenting dialect variations in American English and above all to exploring the ways in which those divisions reflect and reinforce a speaker's place in the class hierarchy of the larger speech community. He has concentrated especially on those dialects of American English considered by most Americans to be not only nonstandard but also substandard. In his first book, *The Social Stratification of English in New York City* (1966), Labov showed that phonological variation in the speech of New Yorkers could not be systematically specified independently of the social pressures acting on the speakers in the given speech situation. This was an important realization for linguistics since it provided support for building information about social context into the grammar.

Labov's interest in oral narrative stems mainly from a study of Black English Vernacular (BEV), "that relatively uniform dialect spoken by the majority of black youth in most parts of the United States today, especially in the inner city areas" (Labov, 1972:xiii). The project, which resulted in the volume of essays titled *Language in the Inner City* (1972), was originally undertaken to find out whether dialect differences had anything to do with the consistent reading problems of inner city black children. It was conducted in Harlem. As he analyzed the phonological and grammatical differences between BEV and Standard English, Labov made an important observation:

> The major reading problems did not stem from structural interference in any simple sense. . . . The major causes of reading fail-

ure are political and cultural conflicts in the classroom, and dialect differences are important because they are symbols of this conflict. We must then understand the way in which the vernacular culture uses language and how verbal skills develop in this culture. (Labov, 1972:xiv)

BEV speakers had trouble reading not because they lacked verbal skills (the contrary proved to be the case) but because the verbal skills they had were of no use in school. All this seems a far cry from aesthetics, and it is true that Labov's interest in "verbal art" rose from his research quite indirectly. I quote here Labov's own description of this development. The passage is long but worthwhile as an introduction to my own discussion to follow:

> In the course of our studies of vernacular language, we have developed a number of devices to overcome the constraints of the face-to-face interview and obtain large bodies of tape-recorded casual speech. The most effective of these techniques produce *narratives of personal experience*, in which the speaker becomes deeply involved in rehearsing or even reliving events of his past. The "Danger of Death" question is the prototype and still the most generally used: at a certain point in the conversation, the interviewer asks, "Were you ever in a situation where you were in serious danger of being killed, where you said to yourself— *'This is it'?*" In the section of our interview schedule that deals with fights, we ask "Were you ever in a fight with a guy bigger than you?" When the subject says "Yes" we pause and then ask simply, "What happened?" The narratives that we have obtained by such methods form a large body of data on comparative verbal skills, ranging across age levels, classes and ethnic groups. Because they occur in response to a specific stimulus in the interview situation, they are not free of the interactive effect of the outside observer. The form they take is in fact typical of discourse directed to someone outside of the immediate peer group of the speaker. But because the experience and emotions involved here form an important part of the speaker's biography, he seems to undergo a partial reliving of that experience, and he is no longer

free to monitor his own speech as he normally does in face-to-face interviews. (1972:354–55)

Labov was fascinated by the high degree of verbal virtuosity displayed by many of his informants in these narratives and by the high value placed on that virtuosity by the vernacular speech communities. This interest and the fact that, despite cultural differences, the narratives had great structural similarities led him to attempt a structural description of the oral narrative of personal experience as a speech act. The results of his study are found in two papers, "Narrative Analysis: Oral Versions of Personal Experience" (1967), written in collaboration with Joshua Waletzky, and "The Transformation of Experience in Narrative Syntax," in *Language in the Inner City*. (Unless otherwise specified, all subsequent references are to the latter article.) Before presenting Labov's analysis of these narratives, let me offer two contrasting examples, both taken from Labov's data. The first is a story told by a middle-aged white male speaker from Martha's Vineyard:

(1)

I never believed a whole lot in licking. I was never—
with my children, and I never—when it was with my animals,
dogs; I never licked a dog, I never had to. A dog knew
what I meant; when I hollered at a dog, he knew the—what
5   I meant. I could—I had dogs that could do everything
but talk. And by gorry, sir, I never licked 'em.
   I never come nearer bootin' a dog in my life. I
had a dog—he was a wonderful retriever, but as I say he
could do everything but talk. I could waif him that way,
10   I could waif him on, I could waif him anywhere. If I
shot a crippled duck he went after it; he didn't see it
in the water, he'd always turn around look at me, and I'd
waif him over there, if the duck was there, or if it was
on the other side of where we're on, I could waif him
15   straight ahead, and he'd turn and he'd go. If he didn't
see me, he'd turn around, he'd look at me, and I'd keep
a-waifin' him on. And he'd finally catch sight of him,

and the minute he did, you know, he would beeline and
get that duck.

20   I was gunnin' one night with that dog—we had to
use live decoys in those days—a fellow named Jack Bumpus
was with me; I was over at a place called Deep Bottom,
darker than pitch. And—uh—heard a quackin' off shore.
And I said to Jack, "keep quiet. There's one comin' in."

25   And uh—finally Jack said to me, "I think I see 'im." I
said, "Give 'im a gun. Give 'im a gun. Try it."
So he shot, and this duck went for the shore with
his wings a-goin' like that for the shore. Went up on the
shore. Well this dog never lost a crippled duck on shore,

30   he'd take a track just the same as a hound would take a
rabbit track. And I sent him over. I said, "Go ahead."
So he went over there. And—gone a while and come
back and he didn't have the duck. And that was unusual—
I said, "You git back there and get that duck!" And he

35   went back there; and he stayed a little while longer,
longer than he did the first time, and he come back and
he didn't have the duck.
And I never come nearer shootin' a dog. By gorry,
I come pretty near. "*You git back there and get that*

40   *duck!*" And that dog went back there, and he didn't come
back. And he didn't come back. By gorry, we went over
there—I walked over there, and here he was; one of my
tame ducks that I had tethered out there had got the
strap off her leg, and had gone out there, and when

45   this fellah shot he hadn't hit the duck. The duck
came to the shore, he hadn't hit the duck; but the
duck was scared and come for the shore. My dog was
over there, and he had his paw right on top of that
duck, holdin' him down just as tight as could be, and—

50   by gorry, boy, I patted that dog, I'll tell you if I
had ever walloped that dog I'd have felt some bad. He
knew more 'n I did; the dog knew more than I did. He
knew that was that tame duck; he wasn't gonna pick him
up in his mouth and bring him, you know. He was just

55   holdin' him right down on the ground.
                                        (Labov, 1967:14-15)

The second is a fight story told by a black adolescent male from
Harlem referred to as Larry:

(2)

An' then, three weeks ago I had a fight with this other dude
outside. He got mad 'cause I wouldn't give him a cigarette
Ain't that a bitch? (Oh yeah?)
Yeah, you know, I was sittin' on the corner an' shit, smokin'
5   my cigarette, you know. I was high, an' shit. He walked over
to me:
    "Can I have a cigarette?"
He was a little taller than me, but not that much. I said:
    "I ain't got no more, man."
10 'Cause, you know, all I had was one left. An' I ain't gon'
give up my last cigarette unless I got some more. So I said:
    "I don't have no more, man."
So he, you know, dug on the pack, 'cause the pack was in my
pocket. So he said:
15   "Eh, man, I can't get a cigarette, man? I mean—I mean
we supposed to be brothers, an' shit."
So I say:
    "Yeah, well, you know, man, all I got is one, you dig it?"
An' I won't give up my las' one to nobody. So you know, the
20 dude, he looks at me, an' he—I 'on' know—he jus' thought
he gon' rough that motherfucker up. He said:
    "I can't get a cigarette."
I said:
    "Tha's what I said, my man."
25 You know, so he said:
    "What you supposed to be *bad* an' shit?"
So I said:
    "Look here, my man, I don't think I'm bad, you understand?
But I mean, you know, if I had it, you could git it. I like
30 to see you with it, you dig it? But the sad part about it,
you got to do without it. That's all, my man."
So the dude, he 'on' to pushin' me, man.
(Oh, he pushed you?)
An' why he do that? *Everytime somebody fuck with me*, why

35   they do it? I put that cigarette down, an' boy let me tell you. I
      beat the shit outa that motherfucker. I tried to *kill* 'im—over
      one cigarette! I tried to *kill* 'im. Square business! After I got
      through stompin' him in the face, man, you know, all of a
      sudden I went crazy! I jus' went crazy. An' I jus' wouldn't stop
40   hittin' the motherfucker. Dig it, I couldn't stop hittin'
      'im, man, till the teacher pulled me off o' him. An' guess
      what? After all that I gave the dude the cigarette, after
      all that. Ain't that a bitch?
      (How come you gave 'im the cigarette?)
45   I 'on' know. I jus' gave it to him. An' he smoked it, too!
                                                    (Labov, 1972:356-58)

Labov's (1972) analysis of these "natural narratives," as they are
commonly called, will seem self-evident to literary critics, and it is
for precisely this reason that I want to outline it here. Labov defines
narrative as:

> one method of recapitulating past experience by matching a ver-
> bal sequence of clauses to the sequence of events which (it is
> inferred) actually occurred. . . . Within this conception of nar-
> rative, we can define a *minimal narrative* as a sequence of two
> clauses which are *temporally ordered:* that is, a change in their
> order will result in a change in the temporal sequence of the origi-
> nal semantic interpretation. (p. 360)

Narrative clauses are clauses with a simple preterite verb or, in
some styles, a verb in the simple present. Here is an adult "danger
of death" narrative which consists of four such ordered clauses:
(This and all further examples in this chapter are taken from Labov's data.)

(3)   Well, this person had a little too much to drink and he at-
       tacked me and the friend came in and she stopped it.

Narratives like (3), which consist only of narrative clauses, are not very interesting, nor are they very common. A fully developed natural narrative, according to Labov, is made up of the following sections:

1. abstract
2. orientation
3. complicating action
4. evaluation
5. result or resolution
6. coda

"A complete narrative," he concludes, "begins with an orientation, proceeds to the complicating action, is suspended at the focus of evaluation before the resolution, concludes with the resolution, and returns the listener to the present time with the coda" (p. 369). I shall summarize briefly Labov's description of the six sections:

Complicating action and *resolution* are, of course, the core of the narrative. The former begins with the first narrative clause in the speech act; the latter usually ends with the last such clause.

The *abstract* is a short (usually one or two sentence) summary of the story that narrators generally provide before recounting the story proper. The abstract "encapsulates the point of the story." In narrative (1) above, the single sentence "I never come nearer bootin' a dog in my life" has this function; in narrative (2), lines 1–2 are the abstract.

The *orientation* serves to "identify in some way the time, place, persons, and their activity or situation" and occurs immediately before the first narrative clause, as a rule. The orientation often includes "an elaborate portrait of the main character" as in (1), whose narrator describes at length the prowess of his retriever before going on to the situation orientation (11. 20–22). In (2), some information is already available in the abstract, and the orientation section (11. 4–5) gives a more detailed picture of the situation, Syntactically, orientations often contain many past progressive verbs "sketching the kind of thing that was going on before the first event of the narrative occurred or during the entire episode."

The *coda's* general function is to "close off the sequence of complicating actions and indicate that none of the events that followed were important to the narrative." In addition to this mechanical function, "a good coda . . . leaves the listener with a feeling of satisfaction and completeness that matters have been rounded off and accounted for." Labov notes a number of forms codas can take. Sometimes they consist of a single sentence like "And that was that"; sometimes they "bring the narrator and the listener back to the point at which they entered the narrative," as does this coda, which closes out a story in which the teller was saved from drowning:

> (4) And you know, that man who picked me out of the water? He's a detective in Union City, and I see him every now and again.

and this coda to a fight story:

> (5) Ever since then I haven't seen the guy 'cause I quit. I quit, you know. No more problems.

In narrative (1) above, the narrative proper ends at "just as tight as could be" (1. 49) and the coda, starting with a pause and the phrase "by gorry," echoes the abstract ("If I had ever walloped. . . .") and provides an additional explication and recapitulation of the story's climax. In narrative (2), the fight story ends with the teacher's intervention, and the coda, beginning with "Guess what?" (1. 41), contains additional information about the ultimate effects of the events, as in (5) above. The narrator of (2), like that of (1), echoes the abstract in the coda, here by repeating the line "Ain't that a bitch?"

Evaluation is considered by Labov to be "perhaps the most important element in addition to the basic narrative clause." By evaluation, Labov means "the means used by the narrator to indicate the point of the narrative, its raison d'être: why it was told and what the narrator was getting at." He elaborates:

> There are many ways to tell the same story, to make very different points, or to make no point at all. Pointless stories are met (in English) with the withering rejoinder, "So what?" Every good narrator is continually warding off this question; when his narrative is over, it should be unthinkable for a bystander to say, "So what?" Instead, the appropriate remark would be "He did?" or similar means of registering the reportable character of the events of the narrative. (p. 366)

> To identify the evaluative portion of a narrative, it is necessary to know why this narrative—or any narrative—is felt to be tellable; in other words, why the events of the narrative are reportable. Most of the narratives cited here concern matters that are always reportable: danger of death or of physical injury. These matters occupy a high place on an unspoken permanent agenda. . . . The narrators of most of these stories were under social pressure to show that the events involved were truly dangerous and unusual, or that someone else really broke the normal rules in an outrageous and reportable way. Evaluative devices say to us: this was terrifying, dangerous, weird, wild, crazy; or amusing, hilarious and wonderful; more generally, that it was strange, uncommon, or unusual—that is, worth reporting. (p. 371)

The evaluation of a natural narrative is usually concentrated in one section immediately preceding the resolution. However, as Labov notes, evaluative devices are generally strung throughout the entire narrative, forming what he calls "a secondary structure." Labov's discussion of evaluation is long, and I shall only partially summarize here his preliminary typology of the evaluative devices used by his informants. Again, the examples are Labov's.

A. *Evaluative commentary*

The narrator interrupts the progress of the narrative with a statement reaffirming the tellability of the story or assessing the situation. Such commentary may be

1. External: The narrator himself asserts the point of the story as in statements like "it was quite an experience" or "it was the strangest feeling" and so on.

2. Internal: The evaluative statements are embedded in the story. The narrator may

a. present the statement as having occurred to him at the time in the story, e.g., "I just closed my eyes, I said, 'O my God, Here it is!' "

b. present the evaluation as statements addressed by himself to another character. Larry's evaluation, addressed (in rhymed couplets, no less) to his adversary (11. 28–31) is an example of this type.

c. attribute evaluative remarks to a witness or neutral observer in the story as in this example, referring to a knife wound: "And the doctor says, 'Just about this much more' he says, 'and you'd a been dead!' "

(a) to (c), you will notice, involve progressively deeper embedding of the evaluation in the story. As Labov notes, the more deeply embedded the evaluation, the more effective it is.

B. *Sentence-internal evaluation devices*

1. Intensifiers: These are devices superimposed or added onto the basic narrative syntax without affecting the unmarked (simple past) form of the narrative verb phrase. Examples:

a. gestures.

b. expressive phonology such as lengthened vowels ("a loooong time").

c. repetition; there are many examples in (1) and (2).

d. ritual interjections like "Well, sir," "By gorry," and so on.

2. *Comparators:* These are devices which involve the use of some verb phrase construction other than the simple past of the narrative clause. They include negatives, futures, modals, questions, commands, comparatives, and others.

The category called Comparators merits some explanation. Labov observed that complex auxiliary constructions tended to be concentrated in the evaluation sections of natural narratives, and he concluded upon analysis that most, if not all, verb constructions that depart from the simple past tense in natural narrative can be shown to be performing an evaluative role. The Comparators do so by referring to hypothetical events that are then compared to the observed events. Comparators, in other words, "draw upon a cognitive background considerably richer than the set of events which were observed." Negatives, for example, talk about what didn't happen but could have; futures allude to what could happen but hasn't yet; modals refer to hypothetical events; questions and commands are attempts to produce future events and function often as disguised threats in narratives, implying future consequences (see, for example, narrative (2) above). Generally speaking "a comparator moves away from the line of narrative events to consider unrealized possibilities and compare them with events that did occur." Labov uses the following evaluation taken from a schoolboy's narrative of a fight with "the baddest girl in the neighborhood" to exemplify the evaluative role played by complex auxiliary structures:

(6) So I says to myself, "There's *gonna* be times my mother won't give me money, because we're·a poor family and I *can't* take this every time she *don't* give me any money." So I say, "Well, I just *gotta* fight this girl. She *gonna hafta* whup me. I hope she *don't* whup me (emphasis mine).

The passage contains four negatives, four futures, and three modals, all involving speculation about hypothetical events or situations which are compared to the present state of affairs. In the resolution of the story which follows, the simple narrative syntax is restored:

> (7)   I hit the girl, powww! I put something on it. I win the fight.

Larry's fight narrative above (11.7–12 and elsewhere) is similarly organized. The grammatical comparative of course always performs an evaluative function, as do similes and metaphors. Interestingly, such overt comparisons are found mainly in the syntax of older, more highly skilled narrators like that of (1) (see for example, 11. 7, 30, 52).

One of the most striking aspects of Labov's model, as I suggested earlier, is its self-evidence. I think it is self-evident for two reasons. First, the oral narrative of personal experience is a speech act exceedingly familiar to us all, regardless of what dialect we speak. We all spend enormous amounts of conversational time exchanging anecdotes, though these may only occasionally involve fights or danger of death. Most speakers of English have a distinctive speech style for this type of narration with special intonation and in many cases special grammatical constructions not used in other contexts.[1] We are all perfectly aware of the "unspoken agenda" by which we assess an experience's tellability. We know that anecdotes, like novels, are expected to have endings. We know that for an anecdote

---

1. For example, adverbial constructions like "down we fell" or "over it went" are apparently exclusively narrative. In many languages, including North American English, speakers often switch to the present tense for narration or alternate between present and simple past, as in "so yesterday he comes into my office and I told him he was fired." Many North American English dialects use irregular first person forms like "I says," "I comes," "I runs" exclusively for narration. Needless to say, these phenomena are much in need of study, but their very existence strongly supports the hypothesis that, independent of any literary considerations, narration must be identified as a speech act in its own right.

to be successful, we must introduce it into the conversation in an appropriate way, provide our audience with the necessary background information, keep the point of the story in view at all times, and so on. And as with any speech situation, literary or otherwise, we form firm judgments all the time about how "good" an anecdote was and how well it was brought off by its teller; in fact, we are expected to express this judgment as soon as an anecdote ends. We recognize narrative expertise when we hear it, and when narrative speech acts fail, we can almost always say why: the experience was trivial, the teller longwinded, or we "missed the point." Should anyone be in doubt about any of these points, I would urge him to spend an hour some day listening to real "everyday language," watching for narratives and for people's responses to them.

The second reason Labov's analysis seems so obvious is that his subdivision of the narrative into six main components corresponds very closely indeed to the kind of organization we are traditionally taught to observe in narrative literature. Every high school student knows that novels and plays have an introduction, a gradual rising action, a climax followed by a swift dénouement and resolution with the option of an epilogue at the end. That novels and natural narratives both have a structurally similar "narrative core" is not so surprising, since both are attempts to render experience. But their similarities go beyond the minimal narrativity of causal and chronological sequence on which recent structural analysis has focused its attention.

Like natural narratives, novels[2] as a rule have an orientation sec-

---

2. Here and throughout, I use the term "novel" as a convenient short form for literary narrative in general, that is, for the class of literary utterances which include novels, novellas, short stories, and narrative poems. Obviously, the structural similarities I am pointing out between natural narratives and novels do not hold for all novels, especially today. Nevertheless, as I point out in chapters five and six, the label "novel" always entitles us to bring to bear on a novel many of the same expectations we bring to bear on natural narratives.

tion which precedes their first narrative clause and serves to identify the time, place, and opening situation. Here is an example, the opening passage of Henry Miller's *Plexus* (1963):

> In her tight-fitting Persian dress, with turban to match, she looked ravishing. Spring had come and she had donned a pair of long gloves and a beautiful taupe fur slung carelessly about her full, columnar neck. We had chosen Brooklyn Heights in which to search for an apartment, thinking to get as far away as possible from everyone we knew, particularly from Kronski and Arthur Raymond. Ulric was the only one to whom we intended giving our new address. It was to be a genuine *"vita nuova"* for us, free of intrusions from the outside world.
>
> The day we set out to look for our little love nest we were radiantly happy. Each time we came to a vestibule and pushed the doorbell I put my arms around her and kissed her again and again. Her dress fitted like a sheath. She never looked more tempting. Occasionally the door opened on us before we had a chance to unlock. Sometimes we were requested to produce the wedding ring or else the marriage license.
>
> Towards evening we encountered a broad-minded, warm-hearted Southern woman who seemed to take to us immediately.

I trust most readers find nothing particularly unusual about this passage as a way of beginning a novel. Except for the fact that its style is that of written discourse, it also has a great deal in common with the way natural narratives begin. Miller's novel opens with two paragraphs of orientation; a new paragraph is used to introduce the book's first narrative clause ("we encountered"). The first paragraph of orientation gives us the place (Brooklyn Heights), the season (spring), the activity underway (looking for an apartment), and the significance of that activity to the participants (the *vita nuova*). It also gives a portrait of the main character. The second paragraph narrows the time scope to a single day and describes in general terms the activities immediately preceding the first complicating action. Though this orientation does not furnish the ravishing woman's name or any explicit information about the narrator or any of the other people mentioned, it allows (and intends) us to deduce that the narrator is a man who is in love with the ravishing woman; his use of the phrase *vita nuova* tells us he is probably a man with a humanistic education.

As this passage suggests, it is common in novels for the orientation to be set apart by a paragraph or a space in the text, or even to be made an independent textual unit such as a prologue, an opening chapter, or a preface. Thomas Hardy's *The Return of the Native* (1878), for example, opens with an orientation chapter titled "A Face on Which Time Makes but Little Impression" and devoted exclusively to a description of the landscape of Egdon Heath on "a Saturday afternoon in November." The human characters and complicating action do not arrive until the second chapter, aptly titled "Humanity Appears Upon the Scene, Hand in Hand with Trouble."

Because their length is less limited than in natural narratives, the orientations of novels can vary widely in length and scope. The orientation of George Eliot's *Silas Marner* (1861), for example, is extremely complex. It begins with a very general description:

> In the days when the spinning-wheels hummed busily in the farmhouses—and even great ladies, clothed in silk and thread-lace had their toy spinning-wheels of polished oak—there might be seen in districts far away among the lanes, or deep in the bosom of the hills, certain pallid undersized men, who, by the side of the brawny country-folk, looked like the remnants of a disinherited race.

Only gradually does the orientation focus in on a specific setting (the village of Raveloe), time ("the early days of this century"), and main character (Silas Marner). The portrait of Marner himself fills several pages and includes a flashback, itself a complete narrative, used to explain how Marner came to Raveloe. The second chapter of the novel devotes several pages to the description of Raveloe and Marner's life there, and finally, nearly twenty pages into the book, the narrative proper begins: "About this time an incident happened which seemed to open a possibility of some fellowship with his neighbours."

In Charlotte Brontë's *Jane Eyre* (1847), by contrast, the orientation begins much closer to the story:

> There was no possibility of taking a walk that day. We had been wandering, indeed, in the leafless shrubbery an hour in the morning; but since dinner (Mrs. Reed, when there was no company, dined early) the cold winter wind had brought with it clouds so sombre, and a rain so penetrating, that further out-door exercise was now out of the question.
>
> I was glad of it: I never liked long walks, especially on chilly afternoons: dreadful to me was the coming home in the raw twilight, with nipped fingers and toes, and a heart saddened by the chidings of Bessie, the nurse, and humbled by the consciousness of my physical inferiority to Eliza, John, and Georgiana Reed.

The first narrative clause in this novel occurs in the fourth paragraph (" 'What does Bessie say I have done?' *I asked*" [emphasis mine].) The orientation of *Jane Eyre* is not only shorter than that of *Silas Marner* but also, like the orientation of *Plexus*, it is a good deal less complete. Apart from what this orientation tells us directly, we are able to deduce that the "I" of the passage is a child, who is apparently staying with a family not his or her own and who is very unhappy about it. Nevertheless, a good deal of information is lacking. In logical terms, the speaker of this passage has presupposed that he shares a good deal more information with his hearer than he actually does. This is a common mistake made by natural narrators. In novels, however, we do not perceive it as a mistake. Adult readers are fully accustomed to dealing with this sort of beginning. In fact, we even have a special term for them, the *in medias res* opening. Notice though, that the fact that we have a special term for literary narratives which begin without complete or explicit orientation suggests that we perceive such narratives to be *marked* with respect to fully oriented narrative.[3] We do not have a special term for narrative beginnings like that of *Silas Marner*. Intuition bears out such a claim. Readers of *Plexus* and *Jane Eyre* take it that the author has intentionally avoided a complete and explicit orientation section. The fact that we respond this way further suggests that complete and explicit orientation is the unmarked or expected case for novels as well as for natural narratives.

The fact that a novel begins *in medias res* does not mean that it is not oriented at all with respect to the reader. It means only that some or all of the orientative information is interwoven with the narrative information or is implied rather than asserted. Consider the opening of Albert Camus's novel *The Fall* (1956):

> May I, *monsieur*, offer my services without running the risk of intruding? I fear you may not be able to make yourself understood by the worthy ape who presides over the fate of this establishment. In fact, he speaks nothing but Dutch. Unless you authorize me to plead your case, he will not guess that you want gin.

In spite of the complete absence of an orientation section, the reader of this novel knows by the third sentence that one and probably both of the characters are adult males, that they have no prior acquaintance, that the setting is a bar, probably in a Dutch-speaking country, in which case one or both of the characters is a foreigner. Moreover, the reader knows Camus intends him to draw these in-

---

3. The distinction between the "marked" and "unmarked" case of a phenomenon is used in linguistic analysis to distinguish between the standard or expected member of a paradigm and the nonstandard or noncanonic case: "It is frequently the case that of two units in contrast . . . one will be positive or *marked* the other being neutral or *unmarked*. . . . When this situation holds, it is usually the case that the unmarked form is more general in sense or has a wider distribution than the marked form." (Lyons, 1969:79). For example, in English nouns, the plural is *marked* by *s*, the singular being the *unmarked* case.

ferences. In other words, the fact that his text has no orientation section does not mean that Camus did not intend to orient his narrative. Though he intends to momentarily disorient his reader, he has carefully provided him with enough information to orient the goings-on by deduction. And lest the reader find the disorientation too uncomfortable, Camus obligingly corroborates some of the deductions a few lines later, when he has the still unidentified speaker tell his still unidentified interlocutor that "his [the bartender's] business consists in entertaining sailors of all nationalities in this Amsterdam bar, which for that matter he named—no one knows why—*Mexico City*."

Similarly, readers of *Plexus* and *Jane Eyre* legitimately assume that in one way or another Miller and Brontë will provide them in short order with the further information they need. As I shall be discussing in the next few chapters, there are very specific reasons why this assumption is a safe one in a literary context and a much less safe one in a spontaneous speech context and why, in consequence, authors of literary works are much freer than natural narrators to make use of delayed or inexplicit orientation. The point to be made here is that both natural and literary narrators are considered to be under the same obligation to orient their narrative and that in the unmarked case, the orientation takes the same form in both types.

A novel's coda may consist of the single word "Fin" or some typographical symbol such as three asterisks, which, like Labov's sentence, "And that was that," merely signals the end of the narrative and the end of the speech act. Novels of course do not need such a verbal or typographical indication, since the end of the text visibly and palpably signals the end of the story (unless other volumes follow, in which case this fact must be made clear at the end of the text). Frequently, however, novels have elaborate codas that, like those of natural narratives, explain, recapitulate, and evaluate the story's outcome, inform us of the ultimate consequences of the story, provide supplemental narrative information, extend the story into the future so as to "bring the narrator and the listener back to the point at which they entered the narrative," and generally "leave the listener with a feeling of satisfaction and completeness that matters have been rounded off and accounted for" (Labov, 1972: 365). *Jane Eyre* provides us with an example typical of many mid-nineteenth-century novels. In the second to last chapter of the book, Jane Eyre and Mr. Rochester are at last reunited, and the chapter's final sentence, "We entered the wood and wended homeward," signals the resolution of the plot. The final chapter of the book is an elaborate coda, beginning with the sentence, "Reader, I married him." Since neither the wedding itself nor the events leading up to it are described, the reader understands that this sentence is intended to provide supplemental information about the ultimate effects of the resolution, like the lines "An' guess what? After all that I gave the dude the cigarette" in the coda of narrative (2) above. Janes Eyre then goes on to tell us how her union with Mr. Rochester was evaluated by the story's other main characters, information designed to leave us as happy with the outcome as Jane herself is. Then we read:

> My tale draws to its close: one word respecting my experience of married life, and one brief glance at the fortunes of those whose names have most frequently recurred in this narrative, and I have done.
>
> I have now been married ten years.

As the verb aspect indicates ("have been married," not "had been" or "was"), the narrator is now speaking from the point of view of her own present time, having brought the reader "back to the point at which they entered the narrative" as do the natural narrative codas quoted in (4) and (5) above. From this time perspective, Jane Eyre sketches the ultimate fates of the main characters. Finally, to leave her readers with the strongest possible "feeling of satisfaction that matters have been rounded off and accounted for," she ends the book on a decidedly conclusive note by quoting St. John River's words:

> "My master," he says, "has forewarned me. Daily he announces more distinctly,—'Surely I come quickly!' and hourly I more eagerly respond,—'Amen; even so come, Lord Jesus!' "

And that, for Jane Eyre, is that.

The coda of Herman Melville's story "Bartleby the Scrivener" (1853) is likewise explicitly set off from the narrative resolution:

> "His dinner is ready. Won't he dine today, either? Or does he live without dining?"
> "Lives without dining," said I, and closed the eyes.
> "Eh!—He's asleep, ain't he?"
> "With kings and counsellors," murmured I.
>
> There would seem little need for proceeding further in this history. Imagination will readily supply the meagre recital of poor Bartleby's interment. But ere parting with the reader, let me say, that if this little narrative has sufficiently interested him, to awaken curiosity as to who Bartleby was, and what manner of life he led prior to the present narrator's making his acquaintance, I can only reply, that in such curiosity I fully share—but am wholly unable to gratify it. Yet here I hardly know whether I should divulge one little item of rumour, which came upon my ear a few months after the scrivener's decease.

In this passage, the narrator and a food vendor have just found Bartleby dead, and their dialogue resolves the plot. "Murmured I" is the last narrative clause. The narrator signals the beginning of the coda by leaving a space in the text and taking up a stance outside the story, as Jane Eyre did with the sentence "Reader, I married him." He announces specifically that further narrative detail is unnecessary (something all codas imply anyway) and then offers some additional information (the "little item of rumour") intended to further our understanding and appreciation of the story. The rumor in question is that Bartleby was once a clerk in a Dead Letter Office. The peculiar relation of such a job to Bartleby's personality gives the narrator the opportunity for further evaluative musings. Finally, to round off the text, he appends a conclusive evaluative statement, "Ah, Bartleby! Ah humanity!" which is reminiscent both of Jane Eyre's finale and of the final "Ain't that a bitch" which concludes narrative (2) above.

As these examples indicate, novelistic codas, like orientations, are often set apart as a textual unit. And as in the codas of natural narratives, they frequently involve a change in temporal perspective (compare Jane Eyre's "I have now been married for ten years" with the coda in (5) above, "Ever since then I haven't seen the guy") and a rhetorical finale. The lengthy coda that makes up the final chapter of *The Great Gatsby* (1925) is similarly introduced by a change in temporal perspective, "After two years I remember the rest of that day," and ends with one of literature's most famous summings up: "So we beat on, boats against the current, borne back ceaselessly into the past." The final chapter of *Plexus*, also a coda, has these same features.

Just as novel readers are accustomed to dealing with *in medias res* beginnings, so they easily take in stride novels that have no coda and, in many cases, no plot resolution. We refer to such novels as "open-ended." But here again, the existence of a special term suggests a marked case, and intuition bears out the suggestion. We usually feel a novel without a coda has left us dangling, that the author has deliberately avoided leaving us with the "feeling of satisfaction" he assumes we expect. As with orientations, then, novels in the unmarked case have codas in the same way and for the same reasons as do natural narratives.

At first glance, the abstract of a natural narrative does not seem to have a literary correlate at all. We do not usually think of novels as beginning with a "short summary of the point of the story" just prior to the orientation. But they do. The abstract of a novel is, minimally, its title, which is given a special page of its own just before the orientation and which is always taken by readers to be a relevant and important clue to what the author considers the main point or theme of his narrative. Titles also serve, of course, as devices for referring to works, and so do the abstracts of natural narratives. When we want to evoke an anecdote, we give an abstract of it. We say things like "tell him about the time you wouldn't give the guy a cigarette" or "what was the one you told about your cousin in Tokyo?" In natural narrative, the abstract often functions as an invitation to the hearer to commit himself to playing the role of narrative audience. Abstracts like "you know, the very same thing happened to me once in Mexico" are intended to provoke from the hearers a ritual statement like "You're kidding" or "Oh yeah? What happened?" that ratifies the speaker's request to tell his story. This "Oh yeah? What happened?" response was built into Labov's interviewing technique and appears quite clearly in the opening exchange of narrative (2) above. In the very same way, titles and subtitles in literary works are there to invite people to commit themselves to the audience role. Anyone who has scanned a shelf trying to decide what to read next knows how decisive this invitation is, as does anyone who has been misled by a title. Early novelists, perhaps less sure of their readership, often reiterate this invitation at intervals throughout the book; they divide their text into chapters and head each one up with an abstract of its own. For example, chapter two of Smollett's *Adventures of Roderick Random* (1748) is introduced by a tantalizing summary which reads:

> I grow up—am hated by my relations—sent to school—neglected by my grandfather—maltreated by my master—seasoned to adversity—I form cabals against the pedant—am debarred access to my grandfather—hunted by his heir—I demolish the Teeth of his Tutor.

The similarity between this now archaic novelistic device and Labov's oral abstracts is impossible to ignore.

Titles and subtitles clearly differ from oral abstracts in that they are definitive. But this difference has to do with the difference between spoken and written discourse, not with a difference in function. It is interesting to note that when a novel title is conventionally abbreviated, the abbreviation often seems to reflect a judgment about what is the central point of the story. Thus Prévost's *Histoire du Chevalier des Grieux et de Manon Lescaut* has been shortened to *Manon Lescaut* and not *Le Chevalier des Grieux*; *Pamela or Virtue Rewarded* became *Pamela*, while *Julie ou la nouvelle Héloïse* became *La Nouvelle Héloïse*.

A novel's abstract can be much more elaborate than a mere title, however. Consider the opening passage of Melville's "Bartleby the Scrivener" (subtitled "A Story of Wall Street"):

> I am a rather elderly man. The nature of my avocations for the last thirty years has brought me into more than ordinary contact with what would seem an interesting and somewhat singular set of men, of whom as yet nothing that I know of has ever been written:—I mean the law-copyists or scriveners. I have known very many of them, professionally and privately, and if I pleased, could relate divers histories, at which good-natured gentlemen might smile, and sentimental souls might weep. But I waive the biographies of all other scriveners for a few passages in the life of Bartleby, who was a scrivener the strangest I ever saw or heard of. While of other law-copyists I might write the complete life, of Bartleby nothing of that sort can be done. I believe that no materials exist for a full and satisfactory biography of this man. It is an irreparable loss to literature. Bartleby was one of those beings of whom nothing is ascertainable, except from the original sources, and in his case those are very small. What my own astonished eyes saw of Bartleby, *that* is all I know of him, except, indeed, one vague report which will appear in the sequel.
> Ere introducing the scrivener, as he first appeared to me, it is

fit I make some mention of myself, my *employés*, my business, my chambers, and general surroundings.

The second paragraph of this passage (and of the story) explicitly announces the beginning of the orientation. The first paragraph is an extension of the abstract. Here, Melville's narrator tells us in more detail why his subject matter is worth our attention (scriveners are "interesting" and "singular," nothing has ever been written about them, and Bartleby is the "strangest" of them all) and why he is particularly and uniquely competent to deal with that subject matter (he has worked in "more than ordinary contact" with scriveners, he is an "original source" about Bartleby, there are no other sources, and so on). He also informs us of his competence to deal with his subject matter in writing. He tells us he could write the biographies of many scriveners and lets us know more generally that he is an educated man, presumably a lawyer, placed high enough to have *employés* and chambers, and a man who reads enough to know that scriveners are an unusual literary subject. Through these remarks, the narrator solidifies the newly made contract between himself and his reader and reassures his audience that they have not erred in giving him their attention. Such remarks are common in natural narratives, too. The stock phrase "I wouldn't have believed it if I hadn't seen it with my own eyes" is often used by natural narrators in their abstracts to stress their own credibility and the worth of their upcoming story. Similarly, it is perfectly appropriate for a natural narrator to start off with a statement like "well, I've been in a lot of places and I've met a lot of people, but I never knew anybody like this guy in Algiers." Notice that such a remark could be used either as a way of requesting ratification to tell a story (i.e., of inviting the "oh yeah?") or as an extension of the abstract after permission has been granted. In the latter case, its job, as in the Melville passage, is to seal the narrator/audience contract, to reassure the audience the story will be worth their attention, and to build up suspense.

In novels whose speaker is claiming to reproduce a story someone else told him, his abstract almost invariably includes information about how he came by the story and what judgments he makes about its credibility. This is exactly what we do in conversation when we introduce an anecdote we have heard from somebody else and that we narrate in the third person. Third-person anecdotes are always prefaced by statements like "this friend of mine told me the funniest story at hockey practice last night" or "I just got a letter from my cousin. She's on a trip to Japan and wait till I tell you what happened to her in Tokyo." To this we may wish to add assessments of the story's veracity. We can say things like "Crawford said his dad told him something like that happened in the war. I don't know if I believe him, though—he always exaggerates" or "if it hadn't 'a been Bill who told me this, I wouldn't 'a believed it." In a common novelistic variant of this same procedure, the source of the second-hand narrative is not oral but written—manuscripts discovered in a dusty attic, packets of faded letters, and so on. Novels of this type usually open with a preface, fictional editor's note, or foreword explaining the source of the materials, the speaker's assessment of their veracity, and his reasons for making them public. Cervantes's *Don Quixote* (1605), Defoe's *Moll Flanders* (1722), Hesse's *Steppenwolf* (1927), and Cela's *Family of Pascual Duarte* (1942) are just a few examples of novels using such devices.

As for Labov's evaluation devices, there is scarcely any need to elaborate on their similarity with those used in literary narrative to control the reader's attitude and point of view. We are all familiar with author interruptions instructing us what judgments we should form (Labov's external evaluation), with the long passages of internal monologue as the hero pauses to reflect on his situation, with the dialogues assessing a state of affairs from several viewpoints, and with the pronouncements of authority figures on whose judgments we are invited to rely. As in Labov's data, it is in novelistic passages like these that we find the highest concentration of comparative constructions, complex auxiliaries, metaphors, and so on. All the evaluative devices Labov described in natural narrative are there in literary narrative, and they perform the same function in both types. Here are a few examples, presented according to the same classification used earlier (pp. 47–48) to outline the evaluation devices of natural narrative:

A. *Evaluative commentary*

1. *External* Speaker comments directly on the events:

> Was I very gleeful, settled, content, during the hours I passed in yonder bare, humble school-room this morning and afternoon? Not to deceive myself, I must reply—No; I felt desolate to a degree. I felt—yes, idiot that I am—I felt degraded. (*Jane Eyre*)
> I look and I see this thing flying along and mention it to Dave who takes one brief look and says "Ah it's only the top of a radio tower"—It reminds me of the time I took a mescaline pill and thought an airplane was a flying saucer (a strange story this, a man has to be crazy to write it anyway). (Jack Kerouac, *Big Sur*, 1962)

2. *Internal*

   a. Comments presented as occurring to the speaker at the time:

   > And as I sat there brooding on the old, unknown world, I thought of Gatsby's wonder when he first picked out the green light at the end of Daisy's dock. He had come a long way to this blue lawn, and his dream must have seemed so close that he could hardly fail to grasp it. He did not know that it was already behind him. (*The Great Gatsby*)

   b. Comments addressed by the speaker to another character: An example of this type occurs in the passage quoted above from "Bartleby the Scrivener." The narrator's remark, "With kings and counsellors," addressed to the food vendor, counts as an evaluative comment on Bartleby's death.

c. Comments attributed to an outside observer or authority figure:

> In the open yard before the Rainbow the party of guests were already assembled, though it was still nearly an hour before the appointed feast-time. But by this means they could not only enjoy the slow advent of their pleasure, they had also ample leisure to talk of Silas Marner's strange history, and arrive by due degrees at the conclusion that he had brought a blessing on himself by acting like a father to a lone motherless child. (*Silas Marner*)

B. *Sentence-internal evaluation*

1. Intensifiers Type (a) is impossible in written discourse. The other three types are exemplified in this passage from *Big Sur*:

> But you look up into the sky, bend way back, my God you're standing directly under that aerial bridge with its thin white line running from rock to rock and witless cars racing across it like dreams! From rock to rock! All the way down the raging coast!

In addition to lexical intensifiers ("*way* back," "*directly* under," "*all the way* down") this passage uses interjection ("my God") repetition ("from rock to rock") and expressive phonology, here signaled by the exclamation point.

2. Comparators Verb constructions juxtaposing one object or state of affairs with another:

a. Overt comparison:

> A less truthful man than him might have been tempted into the subsequent creation of a vision in the form of resurgent memory;

a less sane man might have believed in such a creation; but Silas was both sane and honest. (*Silas Marner*)

b. Negatives, futures, modals:

> This was true. But there was this of a kind of pride: he had never tried to enter the big house, even though he believed that if he had, Sutpen would have received him, permitted him. "But I ain't going to give no black nigger the chance to tell me I can't go nowhere," he said to himself. "I ain't even going to give Kernel the chance to have to cuss a nigger on my account." (William Faulkner, "Wash," 1934)

Here, the phrase "never tried" evokes a possible world in which Wash "does try," and the conditional construction which follows ("if he had," etc.) explores possibilities within this hypothetical world. The exploration continues in the character's own mind, in the future tense, where he rejects the possibility of his giving some other character the possibility of denying him the possibility of entering the big house. The entire passage serves to examine the complexity of Wash's situation in the society of the story. Similar devices are used in the *Gatsby* passage quoted above, where the narrator hypothetically reconstructs Gatsby's one-time view of the future (his "dream") and juxtaposes it to the true state of affairs ("he did not know," etc.).

The Faulkner passage just quoted also gives us examples of external evaluation ("This was true" and so on), internal evaluation ("he said to himself"), intensifiers ("even"), and repetition ("received him, permitted him," "give the chance").

In sum, even this brief comparison is enough to show that literary and natural narrative are formally and functionally very much alike. Put another way, all the problems of coherence, chronology, causality, foregrounding, plausibility, selection of detail, tense, point of view, and emotional intensity exist for the natural narrator just as they do for the novelist, and they are confronted and solved (with greater or lesser success) by speakers of the language every day. These are not rhetorical problems that literary narrators have had to solve by inventing a poetic language; they are problems whose solutions can readily be adapted from spoken to written discourse.[4]

Perhaps the best proof of this pudding is the frequency and ease with which the natural narrative speech situation is reproduced and imitated in narrative literary works. The natural narrative speech situation has provided a framework for innumerable literary works, from Chaucer's *Canterbury Tales* (ca. 1380) through Diderot's *Jacques le fataliste* (1796), James's *Turn of the Screw* (1898), Conrad's *Lord Jim* (1900), and João Guimarães Rosa's *Devil to Pay in the Backlands* (1956). Conrad and Faulkner are two of the best-known modern writers to use the natural narrative framework. An even greater number of literary narratives contain natural narratives embedded in dialogue and functioning either as digressions, as in Cervantes's *Don Quixote* (1605) and Sterne's *Tristram Shandy* (1760), or as a way of bringing the reader up to date on events which have happened offstage, as in Emily Brontë's *Wuthering Heights* (1847).

What is important about the fact that literary narratives can be analyzed in the same way as the short anecdotes scattered throughout our conversation? To begin with, it casts grave doubt on the Formalist and structuralist claims that the language of literature is formally and functionally distinctive. Narratives of personal experience belong to our most casual, ordinary, everyday, conversational, prosaic mode of speech. They are the smallest of small talk. Yet they conform scarcely at all to the views of extraliterary language implied by the poeticians I have been quoting. In fact, they quite clearly

---

4. It is worth noting that the two syntactic features taken by Käte Hamburger in *The Logic of Literature* as unique to "epic fictional" discourse, namely verbs of mental process attributed to third persons and present tense adverbials with past tense verbs, also occur in natural narrative, at least in some common narrative styles.

contradict those views. They are entirely amenable to the kinds of analysis the poeticians have devised for literary utterances, whereas their composition cannot be explained at all in terms of maximally efficient communication, dummy constructions, or single-layered construction. Even the versification criterion loses force, given the climactic use of rhymed couplets in Narrative (2) (11. 29–31).

If it weren't for the fact that his data are not literature, Labov's analysis could have provided valuable linguistic support for the Formalists' ideas about the aesthetic organization of narrative. Šklovskij's *fabula/sjužet* distinction is very similar to Labov's distinction between narrative core and the "secondary structure" of evaluation on which the effectiveness of the narrative depends. Labov's "intensifiers" and "comparators," which call attention to the subject matter by suspending the progress of the narrative, are all, in structuralist terminology, foregrounding devices. In "Art as Technique" (1917), Šklovskij provides us with a list of such devices when he speaks of "ordinary or negative parallelism, comparison, repetition, balanced structure, hyperbole, the commonly accepted rhetorical figures, and all those methods which emphasize the emotional effect of an expression" (pp. 8–9). It is impossible not to notice the extent to which this list overlaps with Labov's catalogue of evaluation devices. Ordinary and negative parallelism, comparison, and repetition are all specifically mentioned by Labov. Hyperbole is one type of what Labov calls intensifiers; balanced structure is another way of talking about parallelism and repetition. In the later terminology of Jakobson, all parallelisms, comparisons, and repetitions as well as many intensifiers would be described as manifestations of the projection principle. Labov's claim—that the more deeply an evaluation is embedded in the narrative the more successful it is—would be explained by Šklovskij in terms of greater or lesser motivation. In short, if aesthetic objects are, as Šklovskij says, objects created by means of techniques designed to "emphasize the emotional effect of an expression," then natural narratives are such objects, and it no longer makes any sense to speak of an opposition between the laws of poetic and everyday languages.

Even the later, weakened version of the poetic language hypothesis offered by Mukařovský, Havránek and others cannot account for the oral data. In this version, recall, extraliterary utterances may possess a certain degree of poeticality, but the poetic function will always turn out to be subordinate to some other function; only in literature is the predominant function that of focusing on the message. But except for the fact that they are not literature, natural narratives clearly fall within the category of self-focused messages as described by the structuralists. They are not utterances whose chief function is to transmit information. Oftentimes, the "information" content is given in the abstract, but the story goes on anyway. To declare natural narratives formally and functionally opposed to or even distinct from their literary counterparts is to render them thoroughly inexplicable.

Unless we are foolish enough to claim that people organize their oral anecdotes around patterns they learn from reading literature, we are obliged to draw the more obvious conclusion that the formal similarities between natural narrative and literary narrative derive from the fact that at some level of analysis they are utterances of the same type. And, let me repeat, their identity goes beyond minimal narrativity. From the point of view of structural poetics, this claim implies a redefinition of the relation between literary and nonliterary uses of language. It means that most of the features which poeticians believed constituted the "literariness" of novels are not "literary" at all. They occur in novels not because they are novels (i.e., literature) but because they are members of some other more general category of speech acts. In other words, the "poeticality" or aesthetic organization of novels cannot be directly identified with or derived from their "literariness" and cannot, therefore, be used to define them as literature. The same can be said, I believe, of all the devices and features that for the structuralist poeticians made up the "poetic language" underlying poetic utterances.[5] I will elaborate on this claim shortly, but before leaving Labov behind, I would like to call attention to another point on which his work offers an important corrective to structural poetic analysis.

If, as Labov's data indicate, aesthetic organization does not arise directly from an utterance's being literature, where does it come from? Or, to put it another way, if we cannot use our knowledge that a text is literature to motivate our claims about its poeticality, how are we to motivate such claims? This is obviously a question that did not concern Labov, since he was not dealing with literature at all, but his answer to it is implicit in his methodology. Reconsider narrative (3) quoted above and repeated here for convenience:

> (3)   Well, this person had a little too much to drink and he at-
> tacked me and the friend came in and she stopped it.

The narrative core is there, but as an anecdote (3) is a horrible failure. It has no abstract, coda, evaluation, or orientation. (The first clause could be construed as either narrative or orientative. Labov treats it as a narrative clause, but even if it is an orientation, it is decidedly rudimentary and colorless.) If we had to assign (3) a place on Stankiewicz's poetic/nonpoetic continuum, we would surely locate it at the nether extreme. It has no "poetic" properties. And that is probably about all Stankiewicz would have to say about this utterance. But there is a good deal more to say. The following dialogue immediately precedes (3) in Labov's interview (A = interviewer, B = informant):

> (8)   A: Were you ever in a situation where you were in
> serious danger of being killed?

---

5. I believe this argument can be extended to lyric poetry as well, though I have not undertaken to prove it in this study. Here and throughout, I have chosen to concentrate on narrative discourse, partly because it turns up so frequently as the fly in the poetic language ointment; occasionally, however, I have made suggestions as to how the lyric fits into the schema I am proposing.

B: Yes.
A: What happened?
B: I don't really like to talk about it.
A: Well tell me as much about it as you can?

                                          (Labov, 1967:16)

Labov comments:

> The suppression of full narrative structure [in (3)] is plainly
> motivated by the explicit reluctance of the narrator to identify
> persons and places. Here as in many of the critical issues dis-
> cussed below, it is essential to preserve the context of the narra-
> tive. Because such originating context is often missing and cannot
> be reconstructed in traditional folk tales, it is more difficult [i.e.,
> in the case of the folk tale] to relate analysis to the originating
> function. (Labov, 1967:32)

Narrative (3) does not have any orientation, abstract, coda, or
evaluation because the narrator does not *want* to foreground his
subject matter; he does not want anyone to focus on his message.
He refuses his interlocutor's invitation to tell the story and consents
only to answer the latter's question in the most minimal way possible by stating the complicating action and the resolution. Now
this information about the context is crucial to our understanding
of the way language is functioning in (3), but it is in no way deriv-
able from the intrinsic analysis of (3). The speaker in this case is
using language "antipoetically," and though this fact largely determines the syntax of his utterance, it cannot be discovered by observation of the utterance. If this utterance had been addressed, for
example, to a policeman called to the scene of the fight, uttered by
the straight man in a comedy show, if it were intended ironically,
or if it were the abstract of an anecdote to follow, we would have to
analyze its function differently. Obviously, there are contexts in
which evaluative narrative is not appropriate. Recording secretaries
do not interpolate in the minutes their astonishment at what the

chairman said next. Television courtroom dramas like *Perry Mason* find an important source of comic relief in the naive witness who, unaware of the difference between telling a story and testifying, starts out giving his own highly evaluative version of events, only to be coldly advised by the judge to "stick to the facts" or "just answer the question." The situation in (3) is just the reverse: an evaluative narrative is called for, but the speaker does not cooperate.

Structural poeticians as a rule frowned on the use of the kind of contextual information we need to analyze (3) correctly—information, that is, about the speaker's intent, his relation to the hearer, his attitude to his utterance, and so on. Such information, being "mentalistic" and not empirically verifiable, belonged to what Èjxenbaum called "speculative aesthetics." In formalist or intrinsic criticism, every statement has to be referred back to "the text itself," the assumption being, of course, that poeticality inheres in the text and that if language is functioning poetically in an utterance, this fact will be evident from the "unordinary" linguistic properties of that utterance.

Labov, by contrast, argues on several occasions that the grammatical surface structure of an utterance is not enough. He warns, for example, that "to identify the evaluative portion of a narrative, it is necessary to know why this narrative—or any narrative—is felt to be tellable" (1972:370). In fight narratives, he points out, tellability depends on an "*unspoken* permanent agenda" of topics (emphasis mine). Certain types of evaluatives cannot be identified by their grammatical properties: "In fight narratives there are many ritual utterances (such as the Black English Vernacular expression 'And there it was') which do not contain any overt markers of emphasis ... yet a knowledge of the culture tells us that these apparently unexpressive utterances play an evaluative role" (p. 380). Labov's entire analysis is stated not in terms of characteristics utterances manifest but in terms of devices speakers use to produce effects in hearers. He introduces his discussion of comparators by asking a question that is simple yet more revealing than any we could expect from an intrinsic critic:

> Why *should* narratives require syntactic complexity? Why should the auxiliary contain anything but simple preterits and quasi-modals? If the task of the narrator is to tell what happened, these will serve very well. What use has he for questions, or what reason does he have to speak of the future, since he is dealing with past events? Why should the auxiliary contain negatives? What reasons would the narrator have for telling us something did not happen, since he is in the business of telling us what did happen? (p. 360)

Poetics' answer to Labov's "whys" would have been "because it is literature." But of course in Labov's case it isn't literature, and a much more powerful explanation is required. Labov in effect translates the rather opaque question "Has the poetic function dominated the verbal organization of this message?" into the broader and more meaningful questions "What is the speaker trying to do in forming this discourse?" and "What does the hearer do when he receives it?" It is the answers to these questions which motivate Labov's statements about the formal properties of his data. His analysis, in other words, is context-dependent, anchored in the circumstances surrounding the utterance. This fact about Labov's methodology suggests a solution to the problem his data raise for poetics. His data make it impossible to attribute the aesthetic organization of prose fiction to "literariness," but his methodology shows us what we can attribute it to: the nature of the speech situation in which the utterance occurs, in which the speaker and his audience are engaged. The formal and functional similarities between literary and natural narrative can be specified in terms of similarities in the speech situation and their differences identified in terms of differences in that situation. We can discuss them, for example, as similar ways of displaying and contemplating experience, which differ in their manner of composition and transmission. Thus the point of departure gets shifted from the message (to use Jakobson's terms) to the addresser, the addressee, and the context. Notice that such a shift eliminates the circularity of defining literature in terms of poeticality and poeticality in terms of literature (or message in terms of function and function in terms of message).

The degree to which contextual statements such as Labov's were repugnant to structural poeticians is well revealed by the pains they usually take to avoid them. Almost invariably, by a kind of verbal sleight of hand, they convert contextual information about a work's effect on the reader or its author's intention into attributes of the text itself. When Èjxenbaum describes Šklovskij's principles of estrangement and palpableness of form, for example, he feels obliged to justify the obviously perceptual, reader-oriented basis of those two concepts by making perception a textual property: "It should be evident that *perception* figures here not as a simple psychological concept (the perception of individual human beings) but as an element of art itself, since it is impossible for art to exist without being perceived" (Èjxenbaum, 1926:12). The well-known term dominant" was frequently used to convert author intention into an aspect of the text, too: the dominant is the "focusing component" which "specifies the work" (Jakobson, 1935:82). The overriding tendency to disguise all notions of intention, perception, and value by converting them into textual attributes has a conspicuous stylistic effect on almost all formalist and structuralist writings. They are a grammarian's goldmine of agentless passives, statives, reflexives, and attributives, all with conspicuously nonhuman subjects. Some samples (emphasis mine):

> *Poetry may employ* the methods of emotive language but only for *its own purposes*. (Jakobson, quoted in Èjxenbaum, 1926:26)

> New form *comes about* not in order to express new content but in order to replace old form. (Šklovskij, quoted in Èjxenbaum, 1926:29)

Verse itself a system of values . . . it *possesses* its own hierarchy. (Jakobson, 1935:82)

Poetic language imposes on the discourse some structure in addition to that which *derives* from [ordinary language]. (Levin, 1962:18)

The *intentions of a poetic work* are often closely related to philosophy. (Jakobson, 1935:83)

In the degree to which care *is exercised* in the selection and arrangement of the individual units . . . the text *is elevated* from the status of a . . . non-poetic text to a text *exhibiting* certain characteristics of style. (Levin, 1962:60)

The style is familiar to us all. In a sense, the view of poetic language implied by these quotations is as impoverished as the view of ordinary language lying behind them. Literary composition appears as a kind of self-motivated automatic writing dependent only incidentally on the participation of human beings. The poetic text, which "forms itself" and "orients itself" according to its own intentions and values, is every bit as mechanistic, as divorced from the reality of human communication as the "ordinary" utterance that "transmits merely information about the outside world."[6] Spitzer, by contrast, simply declares, "Whoever has thought strongly or felt strongly has innovated in his language" (1948:15).

The idea that poetic language could and ought to be studied intrinsically came of course from structural linguistics. It reflects what Roger Fowler describes as "the belief current among that generation of linguists that their discipline was defined by a set of analytic . . . *discovery procedures*; and relatedly, that linguistic description consisted of the induction of structure, of patterns of abstract units which were inherent in the linguistic materials under consideration"

---

6. As absurd as it may seem now, this view of poetic language did have psychological reality at the time it was conceived, at least for the surrealists, who made it the basis of their own "formal method" of literary composition, aptly called "automatic writing."

(1971:5). The assumption that the "verbal structure" of an utterance inheres in that utterance and is fully discoverable from it without further information from the context places a formidable constraint on the descriptive power of a grammar, especially when coupled with the structural linguistic model of "verbal structure" in which the upper limit of analysis is a kind of sentence-internal linear parsing based on selection and combination. Within such a model, a distinction between literature and nonliterature, if it existed at all, could only exist context-free at the level of grammatical surface structure. It is this restriction that, as we saw earlier, prevents Jakobson from making full use of his model of the speech situation and that, as we have also seen, Labov does away with entirely.

The tendency to exclude reader, author, and context from poetic analysis has been a rallying point for critical opposition to structural poetics and to structural analysis in general. M.A.K. Halliday and Michael Riffaterre have repeatedly emphasized the inability of structural poetics to provide a relevance criterion for poetic analysis, that is, a criterion which can distinguish those features of a text which have stylistic relevance from those which do not. Since "there is no such thing as an intrinsically stylistic device," Riffaterre argues (1959:172), an analysis which lacks an explicit relevance criterion remains strictly arbitrary and impossible to evaluate. For Riffaterre, it is the reader's intuitions, or more accurately, the collective intuitions of a number of readers, that must form the base for such a criterion. According to Riffaterre, stylistically relevant features will be those "elements which limit the freedom of perception in the process of decoding" (1959:158). In a later article Riffaterre extends his objection to structural analysis in general, whose error, he claims,

> is that it fails to recognize one essential condition of the actual literary phenomenon (that is, the contact between text and

reader): the perceptibility condition. Perceptibility, in fact, seems to be the only important aspect of Russian formalist theory which has not been explicitly adopted by French formalism. (Riffaterre, 1971:276, translation mine)

For Riffaterre, the problem of relevance and verifiability is only compounded when the level of analysis is moved to underlying or latent structures that have no surface textual realization. Objecting to "this misleading concept of *latency* which the formalist definition of structure contains within it," he restates the reader's case: "If there is latency, it is a latency encoded in order to (1) reveal that there is something to discover and (2) indicate how the discovery is to be made" (1971:285, translation mine). Halliday similarly objects to the notion of latency on the grounds that any "prominence" (foregrounding) will appear motivated if it relates to our interpretation of the work (1971:339). Halliday proposes a relevance criterion based on reader's intuition and comparison of the given text with appropriate norm texts. Enkvist, Spencer, and Gregory (1964) similarly call for a context-dependent description of style.

These contextual approaches, though they differ a great deal from each other, can all be seen as attempts to restate the problem of linguistic aesthetics at the level of language use, where it belongs and where it is stated from the outset by Labov. The need for such a restatement has been recognized with increasing urgency by critics over the last five years. Karl Uitti objects that "unless ... some loopholes in either linguistic or literary analysis are left allowing one to deal relevantly with the experiential fact of confrontation between text (and/or author) and reader, the reality of language or of the poetic experience will be necessarily shunted aside and quite possibly other kinds of understanding themselves vitiated (1971: 114). In a similar vein, Hendricks argues that "the emphasis needs to be shifted from considerations of poetic language to considerations of texts. Strictly speaking, there is no such thing as poetic language, there are only poems" (1969:17). Fowler also notes the error of locating poeticality at the level of *langue*, pointing out that "the sense in which there is a gap between the "normal language' and any distinctive text is the same for all texts: there is the grammar and what you do with the grammar" (1971:73). For Fowler, the linguistic analysis of literature is "an attempt to make explicit part of the process of reading by the use of terms and concepts which have psychological reality ... through being appropriate to the reader's individually internalized yet culturally shared grammar of the language" (p. 69).

P's Expansion of Sp-Act Theory from sentence-level to discourse-level — not acceptable to some s-a-theorists.

Chapter Three

The Linguistics of Use

> I gotta use words when I talk to you
> But if you understand or if you don't
> That's nothing to me and nothing to you
> We all gotta do what we gotta do
>
> T. S. ELIOT,
> *Sweeney Agonistes*

Labov is only one of a growing number of American and British linguists who have focused their attention in the last few years on "what we do with the grammar," and the outlines of a theory of language use are beginning to emerge. With the exception of Halliday, linguists working in this area have so far scarcely attempted to discuss literary discourse, but there is no question that their theory is ultimately obliged to provide *some* account of what we are doing when we are reading or producing literary works. Whether the account of the literary use of language that satisfies linguistics will in the end prove to be of interest to literary studies is of course open to question. The fact remains that linguistics is perhaps for the first time equipped to offer a description of literary discourse that answers the need for a contextually based approach to texts and that at the same time bridges the gap between literature and nonliterature, and thus between linguistics and poetics. The very least such a description can provide is an important corrective to the theories of "poetic language" that have dominated linguistic aesthetics in this

79

century. The particular theory whose implications I intend to explore is known as speech act theory and has been developed over the last fifteen years by the British ordinary language philosophers Austin, Searle, Strawson, Grice, and others.[1] Speech act theory offers, I think, a useful and interesting way of treating the kind of contextual information which gives Labov's approach to natural narrative its superior explanatory power.

For speech act theoreticians, "speaking a language is engaging in a (highly complex) rule-governed form of behavior" (Searle, 1969: 12). To make an utterance is to perform an act. A person who performs a speech act does at least two and possibly three things. First, he performs a *locutionary act*, the act of producing a recognizable grammatical utterance in the given language. Second, he performs an *illocutionary act* of a certain type. "Promising," "warning," "greeting," "reminding," "informing," or "commanding" are all kinds of illocutionary acts.

There have been numerous attempts to classify illocutionary acts according to the kind of communication they represent, that is, the way in which the speaker is using the language. Searle (1973), for example, proposes that illocutionary acts be classified into five basic categories:

1. *representatives:* illocutionary acts that undertake to represent a state of affairs, whether past, present, future, or hypothetical, e.g. stating, claiming, hypothesizing, describing, predicting, telling, insisting, suggesting, or swearing that something is the case

2. *directives:* illocutionary acts designed to get the addressee to do

---

1. It is important not to identify the "ordinary language" of British ordinary language philosophy with the "ordinary language" of structuralist poetics. The former is conceived in opposition to formal logic, the latter in opposition to "poetic language." The philosophers take ordinary language to be their subject matter, while the subject matter of poetics is poetic language. Nevertheless, as I shall suggest shortly, it is not a coincidence that the two areas of endeavor should share this troublesome term.

something, e.g. requesting, commanding, pleading, inviting, daring

3. *commissives*: illocutionary acts that commit the speaker to doing something, e.g. promising, threatening, vowing

4. *expressives*: illocutionary acts that express only the speaker's psychological state, e.g. congratulating, thanking, deploring, condoling, welcoming

5. *declarations*: illocutionary acts that bring about the state of affairs they refer to, e.g. blessing, firing, baptizing, bidding, passing sentence.

Finally, a speaker who performs an illocutionary act may also be performing a *perlocutionary act*; that is, by saying what he says, he may be achieving certain intended effects in his hearer in addition to those achieved by the illocutionary act. By warning a person one may frighten him, by arguing one may convince, and so on.

To perform a speech act correctly, however, it is not enough merely to utter a grammatical sentence. Speech acts, like all behavior, are correctly or felicitously performed only if certain conditions obtain. The illocutionary act of promising, for example, is only felicitously carried out if the speaker is able to fulfill the promise, sincerely intends to do so, and believes that what he is promising to do is something the hearer would like him to do. (This latter condition is what distinguishes promising from threatening.) Promising, in other words, depends on more than just saying the sentence "I promise to do X," and speakers of the language know it. These conditions on which the felicity of a speech act depends are called *appropriateness conditions* or *felicity conditions*. They represent rules which users of the language assume to be in force in their verbal dealings with each other; they form part of the knowledge which speakers of a language share and on which they rely in order to use the language correctly and effectively, both in producing and understanding utterances. An account of the appropriateness conditions for the illocutionary act of asking a question, for example, would include the following statements:

1. speaker does not know the answer
2. speaker believes it is possible hearer knows the answer
3. it is not obvious that hearer will provide the answer at the time without being asked
4. speaker wants to know the answer

A speaker who utters a question implies that these conditions have been met, and the addressee assumes the speaker has implied this. If the conditions have not been met, the speaker's question is inappropriate or infelicitous. Searle (1969) proposes that appropriateness conditions be classified as either preparatory, essential, or sincerity conditions. Conditions (1) to (3) above would be preparatory conditions, condition (4) is the sincerity condition. The essential condition is the definition of a question as an undertaking to elicit information from the addressee. Similarly, the illocutionary act of making a statement carries the following appropriateness conditions:

1. speaker believes p (where p is the proposition being asserted)
2. speaker has evidence for the truth of p (or reasons for believing p)
3. it is not obvious to both speaker and addressee that the addressee knows p (or does not need to be reminded of p)
4. speaker has some reason for wanting addressee to know p (or to remember p)

Each of the five main categories of illocutionary acts mentioned above encompasses a wide range of illocutionary acts, which can be differentiated from each other in terms of their appropriateness conditions. Thus, pleading, commanding, and requesting are all directives, but they differ according to the relationship that must exist between speaker and addressee. The illocutionary act of commanding, for example, has an appropriateness condition requiring that the speaker be in a position of authority; for pleading, the addressee must be in authority; for requesting, either speaker and addressee must be peers, or the addressee must have some measure of authority.

Suggesting, insisting, and hypothesizing (that something is the case) are all illocutionary acts belonging to the class of representatives, but they differ in that in each case the speaker is expressing a different degree of belief or commitment toward the truth of what he is representing. These distinctions would likewise be stated as appropriateness conditions. Concluding, replying, and disagreeing are all representatives, but they differ in that they each express a different relationship between what is being said and prior discourse. Many declarations have appropriateness conditions requiring that the speaker be endowed with institutional authority to perform the act in question, as with marrying, excommunicating, or sentencing someone to prison.

As speakers of the language, we rely at every moment on our knowledge of appropriateness conditions, both when we produce utterances and when we decode utterances of others. It is our knowledge of appropriateness conditions that lets us know, for example, that the sentence "You must have another piece of cake," uttered by our hostess at a tea party, is an invitation and not a command (R. Lakoff, 1972); that the sentence "Could you take out the garbage?" in spite of its interrogative form is not a question about our physical capacities; or that in most contexts, there would be something odd about the sentence "Thank you for the hideous sweater."

From a linguist's point of view, appropriateness conditions are a crucial component of the grammar of a language, even though they represent aspects of an utterance which are not part of the explicit verbal structure. The appropriateness conditions for questions, for example, will form part of a linguist's description of what a question is along with his description of the explicit syntactic and phonological configurations given to questions. In this regard, speech act theory supplies an important corrective to the overwhelming concentration on syntax and phonology which has accompanied Chomskyan linguistics. If, as Chomsky claimed, the goal of linguistics is to describe what a speaker knows about his language that enables him to produce and understand new utterances (his competence), such a description must specify not only our knowledge of grammatical rules but also our "ability to handle possible linguistic structures appropriately in specific contexts, that is, what Hymes (1971) has called our 'communicative competence' " (Traugott, 1973:6). This contextual knowledge is exactly what appropriateness conditions express. The post-Chomskyan linguistic movement known as generative semantics, developed since about 1968 by G. Lakoff, R. Lakoff, C. Fillmore, and many others, has undertaken to devise formal linguistic models based on this expanded notion of competence and has relied a great deal on the approach taken by speech act theory.[2]

As is probably already clear, many appropriateness conditions are shared by large numbers and classes of illocutionary acts. All directives, for example, have a preparatory condition to the effect that the addressee must be able to carry out what is being asked of him. Some appropriateness conditions apply even more generally. No illocutionary act can be felicitous if the addressee does not speak the lanuage in question, is out of earshot, or is otherwise incapable of understanding the utterance. Appropriateness conditions would specify that utterances performed in such contexts are infelicitous. It is both impractical and counterintuitive to view appropriateness conditions such as these as separate rules attaching to specific illocutionary acts; rather, they are to be construed as rules for language use of a more general kind (cf. Searle, 1969:69).

Similarly, there are many cases in which it is impractical and coun-

---

2. For the literary scholar, Elizabeth Traugott's article "Generative Semantics and the Concept of Literary Discourse" (*Journal of Literary Semantics*, 1973) is the best introduction to generative semantics and its implications for literary studies.

terintuitive to view appropriateness conditions as applying only at the level of the sentence. Searle claims that "the characteristic grammatical form of an illocutionary act is the complete sentence (it can be a one-word sentence)" (1969:25), and indeed, speech acts have been discussed mostly in terms of single-sentence utterances. Nevertheless, it is clear that the appropriateness conditions for explaining, thanking, or persuading, for example, must at some level of analysis be seen as applying to explanations, thankings, or persuadings that are many sentences long. This is an issue to which few speech act philosophers (and few linguists) have addressed themselves, and to which I will be returning in the next chapter. For the moment, we need only say that in cases of multisentence utterances that have a single point or purpose, there will be appropriateness conditions that, by virtue of that overall purpose, apply across the entire utterance. An individual sentence within such an utterance will be subject to these larger appropriateness conditions as well as to the sentence-level ones that apply to it alone. In other words while we must be able to treat any single sentence as a single speech act, subject to a given set of appropriateness conditions, we must also be able to view appropriateness conditions as applying at the level of discourse. At this level, for example, the contrast I mentioned earlier between telling a story and testifying in court is the result of contrasting appropriateness conditions. The court requires that the witness *not* evaluate the events he recounts; the appropriateness conditions on natural narrative require that he do so. In addition, the appropriateness conditions for natural narrative require that the speaker tell a complete narrative (with complicating action and resolution) and that he orient it adequately with respect to his audience. Thus, example (3) in chapter two, if analyzed as a natural narrative, would fail to fulfill the conditions requiring adequate orientation and evaluation. But if analyzed as an answer to a request (the interviewer's request to "tell me as much about it as you can"), the appropriateness conditions requiring orientation and evaluation would not apply, and (3) would be viewed as perfectly felicitous.

In sum, speech act theory provides a way of talking about utterances not only in terms of their surface grammatical properties but also in terms of the context in which they are made, the intentions, attitudes, and expectations of the participants, the relationships existing between participants, and generally, the unspoken rules and conventions that are understood to be in play when an utterance is made and received.

There are enormous advantages to talking about literature in this way, too, for literary works, like all our communicative activities, are context-dependent. Literature itself is a speech context. And as with any utterance, the way people produce and understand literary works depends enormously on unspoken, culturally-shared knowledge of the rules, conventions, and expectations that are in play when language is used in that context. Just as a definition of explaining, thanking, or persuading must include the unspoken contextual information on which the participants are relying, so must a definition of literature.

One of the most obvious kinds of contextual information we bring to bear in confronting a literary work is our knowledge of its genre. As Traugott (1973) notes, genres and subgenres can to a great extent be defined as systems of appropriateness conditions. Thus elegies, for example, presuppose that someone has died and that the dead person was known to the speaker of the poem. Unless otherwise indicated, we assume the "you" of an elegy refers to the dead person and that the death in question was a human one, hence the (obviously intentional) inappropriateness of an elegy to the death of a mad dog. Fairy tales and fables allow for supernatural events and objects but have rather strict rules about what kinds of supernatural events may occur and how they may come about. It is very likely that these conventions, too, can be formulated as appropriateness conditions.

More generally, appropriateness conditions provide a way of building into the description of an utterance the contextual norms which Riffaterre, Halliday, and the others were seeking, so that style in any kind of discourse can be represented as the context-dependent phenomenon it is. Each aspect of an utterance's context can be formulated as a subset of appropriateness conditions interacting with all the others. With respect to a given literary work, we may be called upon to study "the complex interplay of appropriateness conditions of the language of the author's time, of the genre of literary discourse, of the world the author sets up, and of the interplay between these and our expectations at this point in time when we are attempting to establish a theory of the author's work" (Traugott, 1973:20). By the same token, many kinds of literary deviance can be described as violations of specific appropriateness conditions.

Notice that by treating literary works as speech acts of a certain type that occur in a speech situation of a certain type and that presuppose certain knowledge shared by the participants, a speech act approach to literature overcomes the main fault I found with structural poetics, namely the necessity of associating "literariness" directly with formal textual properties. Speech act theory lets us say meaningfully and legitimately what I think any theory of literary discourse is obliged to say, that, as Richard Ohmann puts it, "Our readiness to discover and dwell on the implicit meanings in literary works—and to judge them important—is a consequence of our knowing them to *be* literary works, rather than that which tells us they are such" (1971:6). Ohmann offers this statement to refute Beardsley's (1958) definition of literature as "discourse with important implicit meaning." With a context-dependent linguistics, the essence of literariness or poeticality can be said to reside not in the message but in a particular disposition of speaker and audience with regard to the message, one that is characteristic of the literary speech situation. This view has considerably more explanatory power than the view that asks us to regard "poetic resources" as "concealed in the morphological and syntactic structure of the language" (Jakobson, 1960:375). Clearly, it is the reader who focuses on the message in a literary speech situation, not the message that focuses on itself. Likewise it is the speaker, not the text, who invites and attempts to control or manipulate this focusing according to his own, not the text's, intention. Finally, once we are able to make explicit the speech situation itself, we are in a position to account for something Šklovskij noted but could not explain, the fact that "a work may be (1) intended as prosaic [i.e., 'ordinary'] and accepted as poetic, or (2) intended as poetic and accepted as prosaic" (1917: 8). As hearers and readers, we are free to lend our aesthetic attention to any text at all. In principle, there is no utterance on whose message (or "implicit meaning" or "style" or "poetic structure") we may not choose to focus.

Finally, and perhaps most important of all, a speech act approach to literature enables and indeed requires us to describe and define literature *in the same terms* used to describe and define all other kinds of discourse. It thus does away with the distortive and misleading concepts of "poetic" and "ordinary" language. Speech act theory views a person's ability to deal with literary works as part of his general "ability to handle possible linguistic structures in specific contexts." Similarities between literary and nonliterary utterance types (such as the similarities between natural and literary narrative discussed earlier) can be linked quite naturally to similarities in the linguistic context and the communicative purposes of the participants. Their differences can be specified in the same terms. In such a description, then, the relations holding between the many kinds of literary discourse and the many kinds of nonliterary discourse are no different in kind from the relations holding between any two speech act types. In short, a speech act approach to literature offers the important possibility of integrating literary discourse into the same basic model of language as all our other communicative activities. The remainder of this study can be taken as an attempt to explore this possibility and to lay some groundwork for a context-dependent theory of literature.

The first attempt to apply speech act theory to the literary speech situation was made by Richard Ohmann in his 1971 article, "Speech Acts and the Definition of Literature," an article that is of prime importance to anyone interested in the linguistics of literature. Ultimately, the argument Ohmann presents falls down, but its failure is a most instructive one and merits our close attention.[3]

The "literature" Ohmann aims to define in his paper corresponds to the traditional category "imaginative literature" (novels, stories, poems, plays) in what he calls its "non-honorific" sense, which includes all such works regardless of quality. Ohmann's definition of this category of utterances rests on his observation that the appropriateness conditions outlined by Austin (1962) for illocutionary acts do not seem to apply to statements made in works of literature. Of a declarative sentence in a lyric poem, for example, we cannot meaningfully ask whether the person making the assertion was qualified to do so, whether he believed what he said and made the statement under appropriate circumstances, whether objects are referred to correctly and really exist, whether all relevant information has been included, and so on. Ohmann concludes that these appropriateness conditions fail to apply to literary utterances because the latter do not have any illocutionary force. They are "quasi-speech-acts":

> The writer *pretends* to report discourse, and the reader accepts the pretense. Specifically, the reader constructs (imagines) a speaker and a set of circumstances to accompany the quasi-speech-act, and makes it felicitous (or infelicitous—for there are

3. Ohmann has changed his position somewhat in his more recent but equally important publication, "Speech, Literature and the Space Between" (*New Literary History*, 1974), to which I also refer here. I have chosen to focus on the 1971 paper, however, because of the continuity it demonstrates with structuralist poetics and because it represents a position which many critics would be tempted to adopt vis-à-vis the status of literature in a theory of speech acts.

> unreliable narrators, etc.). . . . *A literary work is a discourse whose sentences lack the illocutionary forces that would normally attach to them. Its illocutionary force is mimetic.* By "mimetic" I mean purportedly imitative. Specifically, a literary work *purportedly imitates* (or reports) a series of speech acts, which in fact have no other existence. By so doing, it leads the reader to imagine a speaker, a situation, a set of ancillary events, and so on." (Ohmann, 1971:14)

As Ohmann suggests, his definition is mainly an elaboration of the very old observation that the poet nothing affirmeth; however, in Ohmann's view, that observation acquires a great deal of explanatory power when it is restated in speech act terms. For Ohmann, it is the suspension of normal illocutionary force that allows speech acts to be "exhibited" in literary works and that underlies our tendency, when reading literature, to "focus on the message," to attend to implicit or secondary meaning, or to respond emotively to the text:

> Since the quasi-speech-acts of literature are not carrying on the world's business—describing, urging, contracting, etc.—the reader may well attend to them in a non-pragmatic way, and thus allow them to realize their emotive potential. In other words, the suspension of normal illocutionary forces tends to shift a reader's attention to the locutionary acts themselves and to their perlocutionary effects. (p. 17)

The speech act analysis, Ohmann claims, adds "concreteness and precision" to the traditional critical claims that literature is play, presentational symbolism, or rhetoric, that it is essentially dramatic, mimetic, or world-creating, and that it is autonomous.

Many literary critics will find Ohmann's observations about literature entirely acceptable. It is true that authors of fictional literary works are not bound by the appropriateness conditions for the speech acts they invent. It is true that literary works are speech acts which are on exhibit. Literary works indeed do not "carry on the world's business" in the same way many other kinds of speech acts do, and this fact does encourage us to respond aesthetically and

emotively to literary texts. However, if we are to use these characteristics to define literature, they must be shown to be unique to literature. And they are not.

The basic criterion on which Ohmann's definition depends is
fictivity, and his definition could only stand if it were true that all
and only the fictive utterances in a language were literature. Mukařovský, you will recall, posited this same criterion when he was looking for a distinguishing literary feature of prose fiction. Ohmann
acknowledges that such a definition of literature would have to include "jokes, ironic rejoinders, parables and fables within political
speeches, some advertisements, and many other such," but he is not
much troubled by these intruders since they "actually *are* very close
to being literature." Poeticians have always been comfortable ad-
mitting jokes and fables into literature, but our daily discourse is
full of other kinds of fictive speech acts that I am sure would cause
even Ohmann to hesitate. For example, in addition to hyperbole,
teasing, "kidding around," imitations, and other verbal play, hypotheses of any kind are as immune to Austin's appropriateness conditions as any poem. The "scenarios" in the Oval Office, the hypothetical situations used in mathematical problems and philosophical
arguments, assumptions made "for the sake of the discussion," speculation about "what he'll do next" or "what might have happened
if only. . . ." are all fictional, as indeed are imaginings, plannings,
dreams, wishings, and fantasizings of almost any kind. It is "suspended illocutionary force" in Ohmann's sense that distinguishes
teasing from insulting, irony from deceit, devil's advocating from
real advocating, and hypotheses from claims. A conventional re-
ductio ad absurdum argument is, by Ohmann's own criteria, every
bit as "mimetic" a speech act as a novel. If fictivity were indeed the
distinguishing characteristic of literature, we would have to describe
such speech acts as these *in terms of* their similarity to works of literature. But why should we? This would be nothing short of absurd,
like describing apples in terms of oranges without reference to the

category "fruit." Does it not make more sense to say that our ability to conceive and manipulate hypothetical worlds or states of affairs, possible or impossible, real or unreal, and to mediate between those worlds and our own is part of our normal cognitive and linguistic competence? And the capacity to use that imaginative faculty in aesthetically and rhetorically effective ways is also a part of our normal linguistic competence. The technique of juxtaposing possible states of affairs to the given situation by means of the "comparators" was, you will recall, an important evaluation device used by Labov's narrators.

Labov's data show that the kind of narrative rhetoric that we tend to think of as exclusively literary does not in fact derive from an utterance's being literature, and the same is clearly true for fictivity or, as Ohmann puts it, the suspension of normal illocutionary force. Labov's data make it necessary to account for narrative rhetoric in terms that are not exclusively literary; the fact that fictive or mimetically organized utterances can occur in almost any realm of extraliterary discourse requires that we do the same for fictivity or mimesis. In other words, the relation between a work's fictivity and its literariness is indirect. The same is true of all the characteristics of literature that Ohmann (and most proponents of fictivity theories of literature) claims to derive from the suspension of illocutionary force.

Let me offer an example. On several occasions, Ohmann uses Truman Capote's *In Cold Blood* (1965) as an example of a discourse in which normal illocutionary forces are *not* suspended, meaning the book is not to be defined as literature.[4] In the case of *In Cold Blood*, Ohmann claims, "It makes sense to ask all of the questions implied by Austin's rules." Of any assertion in Capote's book then, I can meaningfully ask questions like the following: Do

---

4. *In Cold Blood* is, in Capote's own words, "a true account of a multiple murder and its consequences."

these people and places really exist? Does Capote know what he is talking about? Is he telling the truth? Is all the relevant information included? Now, it is meaningful to ask these questions in the sense that I could appropriately address them to Mr. Capote, whereas I could perhaps not appropriately have asked Emily Brontë (or Ellis Bell) for Heathcliff's middle name. Notice, however, that when I read *In Cold Blood*, I do not have the answers to these questions, nor do I have access to them, nor do I need them to execute my side of the speech act felicitously. I have only Capote's claim that all the pertinent conditions have been met, and I accept his claim automatically, in the same way I accept the "pretense" of the fiction writer the way Ohmann describes it. For this reason, Capote's claim that his utterance does indeed have "normal illocutionary force" does not affect my participation in the speech act in the way Ohmann's analysis predicts. It does not prevent me from focusing on the message, noticing secondary meanings, and generally attending to the utterance in the "non-pragmatic" way Ohmann describes for literature. In fact, my position with respect to Capote's report is necessarily almost exactly the same as that of Ohmann's fiction reader (except for the *quasi*, of course): "The reader constructs (imagines) a speaker and a set of circumstances to accompany the quasi-speech-act and make it felicitous." Obviously, this reconstructive imagining is as much a part of my role when I read *In Cold Blood* as when I read *Emma*. Pragmatically speaking, I have no more knowledge of the situations reported and the reporting circumstances in the former case than I do in the latter, and Capote knows it. Unless I am otherwise acquainted with Capote or his characters, the events and the speaker of *In Cold Blood*, like those of *Emma*, do not exist for me outside the text. The only difference for me between the two speech situations is my knowledge in the first case that Capote intends me to believe his story really happened, and the only effect this has on my reading experience is perhaps an intensification of certain perlocutionary effects—the same perlocutionary effects Conrad tries to capture by having Marlow tell us *Lord Jim*.

Should we classify *In Cold Blood* as literature, then? This would hardly solve the problem, for the claims I have been making with regard to *In Cold Blood* apply identically to natural narratives, too. Narrative (2) quoted earlier was nonfiction to you only because I said that Labov said that his informant said it was true. It was part of our job in reading that narrative to reconstruct mentally both the circumstances surrounding the fight and the circumstances under which the informant told his story to the interviewer, at least insofar as such reconstruction was necessary to make the narrative speech act felicitous. And we did so automatically. Nor is such reconstruction or filling in peculiar to our dealings with written texts. "Making felicitous" is equally part of our role in decoding natural narratives in natural oral situations. Thus, natural narratives do not become infelicitous when they concern people and places the audience has never heard of. Without the slightest hint of infelicity, I can recount an anecdote I heard from someone else whose name I can't remember to an audience I don't know about events I didn't witness that happened somewhere I've never been. And all the time I am talking, those in my audience who do not know me will be busy not just filling in my narrative, but making assessments about me, my background, my social class, my personality, and my reliability, just as we do with the first person narrator of a novel.

In short, in at least some types of nonfictional, nonliterary discourse, the answers to Austin's questions can be unavailable to the audience without vitiating the speech act, and the procedures of inference and reconstruction that we use to fill in those answers are the same as those available for the quasi-speech acts Ohmann discusses. Thus, while Ohmann is quite correct in pointing out that the opening sentence of Jane Austen's *Pride and Prejudice* (1813)— "It is a truth universally acknowledged that a single man in possession of a fortune must be in want of a wife"—is taken by the audi-

ence to be ironic rather than plain false (infelicitous), he is wrong
in attributing this interpretation to the fact that "the making of the
statement is an imaginary illocutionary act." The irony would not
disappear if that sentence were to occur in the abstract of a natural
narrative, a "real" not a "quasi-" speech act,[5] and the sentence
would function in such an abstract in the same way it does in the
novel, as a "tip-off to the fact that the . . . narrator of the story is
being ironic" (Ohmann, pp. 14–15). In short, it is not the "quasi-
ness" of quasi-speech-acts that "leads the reader to imagine a speaker,
a situation, a set of ancillary events, and so on." It is not the quasi-
ness which gives literature its world-creating capacity. Nonfictional
narrative accounts are world-creating in the same sense as are works
of literature and, say, accounts of dreams. After all, the actual world
is a member of the set of all possible worlds. If we accept Ohmann's
claim that "a literary work creates a world . . . by providing the
reader with impaired and incomplete speech acts which he com-
pletes by supplying the appropriate circumstances" (p. 17), we must
be prepared to regard a good deal of what we say to be impaired and
incomplete in this way. Alternatively, we must describe our reconstructive role in terms of some more general principles governing
the way we interpret all new utterances. Granted, we do use this
capacity to make felicitous, "impaired" speech acts like conversations overheard in restaurants and discussions we join *in medias res.*
Speech situations like these can be regarded as genuinely impaired
or incomplete, but it seems absurd to construct a theory in which
these adjectives apply across the board to entire domains of perfectly acceptable and indeed highly conventional discourse. More-

---

5. In an oral context, some rewording would be in order, obviously. But it
is not hard to imagine an opener like "Look, dearie, if he's single and he's got
money, it's a sure thing he's in the market for a wife." Depending on the context, such a remark could be intended to be either "straight" or ironical. That
only one interpretation is possible in Austen's case will be explained in chapter
five.

over, it is not the quasi-ness of quasi-speech-acts that accounts for our focus on the message. In fact, such focus is as crucial to *In Cold Blood* or to Labov's danger-of-death narratives as it is to *Emma*. In all three cases, it is the whole point of the utterance, it is what we are supposed to do. As a glance at today's best-seller lists can show, nonfictional narratives—memoirs, survival stories, travel tales, and the like—are as much a part of the public's literary preference as fiction. I think this claim would hold for nearly any literary period.

In sum, those characteristics of the literary speech situation which Ohmann attributes to a work's being a quasi-speech-act are actually characteristics of the real speech acts that the literary works "purportedly imitate." In failing to recognize this fact, Ohmann falls into the same trap as his formalist and structuralist predecessors: his definition of a linguistically autonomous literature can stand only at the expense of nonliterary discourse. As I suggested before, a definition of literature which impoverishes and misrepresents nonliterature equally impoverishes and misrepresents literature. Again, unless we are willing to view "non-quasi" utterances like Capote's or Labov's data as imitations of literature, we have to describe the speech situation obtaining in the two types of discourse at least in part without reference to literariness or fictionality.

There is an even simpler reason for rejecting a fictivity criterion for literature: the line between fiction and nonfiction is often extremely unclear. Within literature, writers can explicitly lay claim to degrees of historical accuracy, as in *romans à clef* or in novels based on a *fait divers* such as Defoe's *Robinson Crusoe* and Mauriac's *Thérèse Desqueyroux*. We believe that Wordsworth's "Lines Composed a Few Miles Above Tintern Abbey," were composed there, though it wouldn't trouble us much if they weren't. In general, we take lyric poems to be renderings of a personal experience unless invited to think otherwise. We have a category called the historical novel for works claiming a high degree of factual accuracy or "non-quasi-ness."

On the other side of the line, in real-life narrative, we have a high tolerance indeed for exaggeration, embellishment, and even certain kinds of implausibility. We do not have to believe that dialogues "reported" by Capote actually occurred, or that Labov's informant quoted above (p. 48) really did "close [her] eyes and say 'Oh my God, here it is.'" Similarly, with regard to the lengthy evaluative passage quoted in (6) above (p. 49), Labov says, "Of course it is unlikely that all of this internal dialogue took place between the time the girl said powww! and the time that he [the speaker] hit her back, but listeners are willing to accept this dramatic fiction" (Labov, 1972:372). Probably we expect from oral narrators of personal experience about what we expect from the narrators of historical novels like *The Agony and the Ecstasy:* a reasonable facsimile of the events.

On the other hand there are contexts where it is appropriate for the fiction/nonfiction line to remain completely undefined. This is often the case for jokes. The stand-up comedian who starts out "I went into Macy's the other day. . . ." or the toastmaster at a wedding who begins "I remember one day when Bill was about sixteen. . . ." makes no commitment whatever to the truth of his anecdote. If it is implausible enough, the audience will infer that it is fictive, but it is entirely appropriate in such contexts for the fictivity question to remain undecided. The question of veracity simply doesn't seem to matter that much when the point of the utterance is understood to be pleasure. Apocryphal anecdotes are a similar example. In labeling them apocryphal, we suspend any commitment as to their truth. Possibly we take such utterances to be without intended future consequences, so that the speaker's truth commitments lose importance. (This is not to say, of course, that such utterances never have consequences, especially unconscious or second-order ones, such as reinforcing stereotypes.) Contrast the examples above with the case of narrative reconstruction in the courtroom, where truth commitments are central. In court, even hearsay is inadmissible, and the reliability of a witness is a matter of central importance. If the statement that the reader of literature is "neither contractually nor morally implicated nor in any way bound by the act in which he participates" (Ohmann, 1974:56) is true at all, it is true of the nonfictional *In Cold Blood* as well, and is thus not directly related to fictivity. Conversely, there are contexts in which it is entirely possible for the speaker of a fictive utterance to be bound by truth commitments. If I construct a hypothetical case in order to reduce someone else's argument ad absurdum, my proof can fail if it depends on an argument I know to be false outside the fictional world of my example.

Finally, there are cases in which people legitimately disagree as to whether an utterance is fiction or nonfiction. Epics and myths, which are understood as historical fact in the culture which engendered them, are often treated as fiction in other cultures. Within our own culture, all of us have at some point had to take a stand on the truth value of the Book of Genesis.

Just as Mukařovský's faulty conception of ordinary language allowed him to use fictivity as the distinguishing poetic feature of prose fiction, so Ohmann's tendency to overestimate the importance and well-boundedness of fictivity derives from a faulty conception of what constitutes "normal illocutionary force." Despite his recognition that literariness cannot be identified with textual properties, Ohmann's view of nonliterary discourse ultimately differs very little from that of his predecessors. Utterances with normal illocutionary force are "pragmatic," they "carry on the world's business." Readers of literature are without their "conventional responsibilities."

As I have said before, as long as nonliterary discourse is viewed in this way, literature will always appear to be generically distinct. Any adequate theory of speech acts, whether or not it includes literature in its scope, will have to make room within the notion of "normal illocutionary force" for the many kinds of discourse that do not carry on the world's business and yet which do make up a large part of our verbal behavior. It is as unenlightening as it is easy to regard fictional, world-creating, self-focused, or pleasure-oriented utterances as abnormalities of one kind or another. And it is downright absurd to view our ability to create and understand such utterances in a wide range of contexts as an eccentric by-product of our "normal" linguistic capacities, outside our "conventional responsibilities" as users of the language. The objection clearly holds for literature as well. The real lesson speech act theory has to offer is that *literature is a context, too,* not the absence of one, as Ohmann and so many others imply. Ohmann's analysis leads him to the astonishing conclusion that "the reader [of literature] is an observer rather than a participant with elaborate conventional responsibilities. In this sense he comes to the work with esthetic detachment" (1972: 18). As in all the binary analyses we have seen, literature here becomes a nonspeech-act, unapproachable and inexplicable from outside the wall set up around it. Surely there is more to be learned from arguing the opposite of Ohmann's statement: our role in literary works presupposes aesthetic commitment, not detachment; the conventional responsibilities tied to this commitment are exceedingly elaborate; and that commitment and those responsibilities are what define the literary speech situation.

Chapter Four

The Literary
Speech Situation

Speech act theoreticians and sociolinguists have already worked out some general principles of discourse that can be used to characterize the literary speech situation and to account for many of the properties of literary discourse that poetics has traditionally held to be exclusively literary. On the basis of some of these principles, I propose now to take some preliminary steps toward integrating literary discourse into the general description of all our communicative activities. I will continue to concentrate on narrative discourse in its literary and nonliterary manifestations and, like Ohmann, I will be interested mainly in the larger, more general appropriateness conditions governing entire classes of speech acts rather than in those attaching to specific utterances.

1. On being an Audience

Let us first take up the question of nonparticipation, the point on which the literary speech situation would appear to differ most radically from spoken discourse. In discussing the role of the abstract in natural narrative, I have suggested that its main function is that of requesting ratification to tell the story, of inviting the hearer to commit himself to the role of narrative audience. Now, if we think about it, it is not usually the case in conversation for an interlocutor to ask permission to make a contribution or invite his hearer to listen to what he has to say. As a rule, this is not necessary, because conversation, like so many human activities, is organized by turns, with everybody's right to speak specified in advance. As a number of sociolinguists, notably Sacks, Schegloff, and Jefferson, have shown, the rules for conversation include a large number of rather subtle mechanisms for controlling the allocation of turns in a way satisfactory to all participants. According to Schegloff (1973):

> The basic shape of the turn-taking system allocates, in giving somebody a turn, the right to produce a single turn-construc-tional unit—that is to say, a single lexical, phrasal, clausal or sentential construction. Thereafter a variety of rules come into play, whereby the turn can shift, though, clearly, there are ways in which current speakers can get to produce more than a single one of those units and can pile up pretty sizable turns indeed. (p. 12)

Sacks et al. (n.d.) propose three general mechanisms by which shifting of turns is effected. First, the current speaker may select the next speaker, by asking him a question, for example. If he does not, then the first person to start talking acquires the right to a turn. If neither of these options occurs, the current speaker may continue. Obviously, the conversational harmony these rules suggest does not prevail in real life. Battles for the floor are a normal and significant part of conversation and, as Schegloff (1973) tries to show, we speakers possess some very specific verbal weaponry with which we wage such battles. The current speaker has an initial advantage in the competition for turns, for it is easier to hold the floor than to gain it. You just have to keep talking. Schegloff identifies a number of techniques available to current speakers specifically to extend the length of their turns as they approach what would otherwise be a possible completion point. A speaker may, for example, speed up his talk so that the pause at the end of a given sentence is not long enough to allow anyone else to start; he may prolong the sentence itself by adding clauses; he may fill in pauses with "uh" or other markers indicating intent to continue. This current speaker advantage is counterbalanced, as Schegloff shows, by techniques available to other participants who are trying to gain the floor. For example, as the current speaker approaches a possible completion point, a potential next-speaker can and frequently does overlap the beginning of his utterance with the end of the current speaker's, and having obliged the latter to stop, may then repeat that part of his turn which was overlapped and probably not deciphered. This technique of overlap and repetition is available at the beginning of a turn but not at the end (the current speaker cannot appropriately repeat the last half of his sentence). The technique thus offers an advantage to the potential next-speaker. In a variant of this procedure, the potential next-speaker overlaps his turn by echoing or anticipating what the current speaker is saying. Though the repetition and overlap technique is a form of interruption, it does not count as a conversational violation since it is used only when the current speaker is approaching a turn-completion point. Interruptions in the middle or at the beginning of a turn unit are much less legitimate, of course.

Given that there is a detailed set of rules for turn-taking that participants in a conversation tacitly assume to be in force, why should a speaker who wants to tell a story need to explicitly request permission to do so? Why can't he simply take a turn according to the normal procedures already in effect? One way of approaching this question is to examine other contexts in which speakers ask permission to perform a certain type of speech act. This is frequently the case with requests. In many languages a speaker can perform a request by asking permission to do so. In English, for example, we say "may I ask you to step out of the room for a moment?" or "could I trouble you for the salt?" or, even more indirectly, "would you mind if I asked you to stop off at the post office?" It is important to note that these request-to-request forms can only be appropriately addressed to one's equals, or to one's superiors in those contexts which permit us to make requests of superiors at all. (Usually we can make requests of superiors when no one other than the superior is able to grant the request.) The important point is that we cannot usually be this polite with our linguistic inferiors. Remarks like "could I trouble you for a piece of cheesecake?" or "would you mind if I asked you to bring me a fork?" are inappropriate if addressed to a waiter and would probably be interpreted as sarcastic, that is, intentionally inappropriate. Except for sarcasm, a speaker uses these request-to-request forms when he sees himself as imposing an unusual or unwanted obligation on the hearer (his equal or superior). He therefore imposes the obligation by asking permission to do so. The hostess who says "may I offer you a second cup of coffee?" is indicating, in accordance with the rules of politeness (see R. Lakoff, 1972), that her coffee is so bad that her offer can only be an imposition on her guest. Similarly, in conversation we frequently interrupt a current speaker by asking permission to "make a brief comment" or whatever. In this way, we gain a turn and at the same time acknowledge that we have thereby placed an undesirable obligation on a participant, namely the obligation to give up the floor when he would not otherwise have done so. In short, requests to perform a speech act of a certain type presuppose that said speech act is imposing an unwanted obligation on an equal or a superior.

But in what sense can a speaker who wants to tell a story that he believes will excite and interest his audience be said to be imposing on them an undesirable obligation? The answer, I suggest, is that such a speaker is asking permission to take a turn in the conversation whose length his audience will not be able to control by the normal turn-shifting techniques. In ratifying a speaker's request to tell a story, we (the hearers) agree to allow him an enormous advantage in the competition for turns. We waive our right to preempt the floor until the storyteller himself offers to give it up (with his narrative coda). Knowing as we do that stories can be prolonged more or less indefinitely, we leave the length of the teller's turn to his discretion.[1] We can, of course, interrupt to request clarification or details, but we do not thereby put an end to the storyteller's turn. More than nearly any other speech act, I believe, narratives, once begun, are immune to control by other participants in a conversation. Only in extremities of boredom do we interrupt a storyteller to ask him to "get to the point," and only with great rudeness can we restore normal turn-taking procedures (change the subject) or take our leave before he *has* reached the point.

Natural narratives, in other words, upset the usual balance of face-to-face conversation by obliging potential next-speakers to temporarily but indefinitely waive access to those conversational mechanisms that exist precisely to counterbalance the considerable advantage the current speaker already has in competition for the floor. No wonder the potential narrator feels obliged to ask permission (by means of his abstract) to take such a turn in the same way we ask permission to make requests or to interrupt in contexts in which we do not have clear authority. The storyteller is imposing an obligation on us, and he includes in his abstract a summary of the story or some other indication of its tellability at least partly as a way of showing us it will be worth our while to accept the imposition. Notice that we do not have to accept it. The request to narrate can be and often is turned down in conversation. Interlocutors may say without being inappropriate that you already told them about that or that they don't want to hear any more fight stories, or they may

---

1. It is worth pointing out that length seems to be the main variable in the case of the oral (folk) tale. Here, as Ong (1975) notes, the audience already knows the story, but does not know how long this telling of it will take. These facts will doubtless prove important in a description of the folktale situation. Moreover, these same conditions can hold in natural narrative situations too, suggesting that there may be no clear-cut distinction between folktale and natural narrative.

simply ignore the abstract altogether and move the conversation ahead. All these devices count as refusals for ratification to narrate, and we all use them from time to time in dealing with long-winded, narrative-prone acquaintances. Obviously the possibility of turning down a narrative request is not revealed in Labov's data because he is encouraging his informants to tell stories.

The imbalance of turn rights that I am suggesting exists in the storytelling situation also helps explain another fact about oral narratives, natural or otherwise: if allowed to occur freely, oral narratives tend to occur in series. In conversation, one anecdote tends to follow another, and a single speaker rarely gets to tell two in succession. Storytelling, in other words, tends to establish its own turn-taking procedure such that if one speaker has been given the luxury of an uninterruptable turn, so should the others. Many of our earliest novel-like literary texts, such as those by Chaucer and Boccaccio, are such stories in series.

The fact that storytellings, unlike other conversational contributions, require the consent of the nonspeaking participants and that the request for this consent is explicitly built into the formal structure of natural narratives suggests, I believe, a rather important generalization about what it means to be an audience. Natural narratives formally acknowledge that in voluntarily committing ourselves to play the role of audience, we are accepting an exceptional or unusual imposition. This claim, I believe, holds for voluntary audience roles in general and is crucial to our understanding of the appropriateness conditions bearing on many kinds of speech situations, including literary ones. I am claiming that in speech situations in which no one person is clearly in authority, the unmarked case (see footnote 3, p. 55) is that all participants have equal access to the floor and that among peers, an unequal distribution of such access is marked and brings with it a redistribution of obligations and expectations among the participants. This is a broad generalization, and it merits a good deal more analysis than I am able to give it here. It is clear, though, that equal-access-to-the-floor rules play an important role in many situations other than conversation. Such rules are considered crucial in decision-making gatherings of almost any kind, so that in many societies, including our own, the turn-taking rules for such gatherings are explicitly set down (in the "rules of order") and a presiding officer is appointed solely to enforce them. There are clear, pragmatic motives behind such procedures. Battles for the floor can easily paralyze conversation when disagreements arise. Hence, it is not surprising that speech situations that are specifically tailored to presenting and settling disagreements should possess some other less time-consuming mechanism—the chairman and his rule book—for guaranteeing the equitable allocation of turns. Understandably, speech situations that presuppose disagreement, notably debates of any kind, make particular use of strict equal access rules and time allotments. Notice that in such institutionalized speech situations, wherever there are rules prohibiting interruptions of a current speaker, there are also rules guaranteeing potential next-speakers a chance for a turn. In societies with egalitarian values the right to a turn, that is, freedom of speech, in part defines one's equality to one's fellow citizens.

What happens, then, when we give up our access rights to a fellow speaker, when we agree of our own free will to become an Audience? (I am using the capitalized "Audience" in this discussion to mean *voluntary* audience, as opposed to audiences who, by virtue of inferior status in the situation, have no floor rights to give up, e.g., employees addressed by their boss). For one thing, our expectations of the speaker increase, and his obligations to us likewise increase. He had better make sure, in other words, that his contribution is "worth it" to us. Boring lectures and bad jokes annoy us more than boring turns in conversation, because we expect more of lectures and jokes, and we expect more because we cannot without rudeness stop the speaker, correct him, have our own say, change the subject, or walk out before he has finished. At most we can indicate our displeasure by some nonverbal means like facial expression or body posture. Audiences in this sense are indeed captive, and speakers addressing Audiences are obliged to make the captivity worthwhile. Labov's oral narrators are under peer pressure not only to recount an experience worth hearing about, but to recount it in such a way that it is worth listening to. Furthermore, if Sacks et al. are right, there is another reason why speakers with unique floor control have a special obligation to make their contribution a good one. Sacks et al. argue that, apart from a conversation's content and interest, potential next-speakers are obliged to pay attention to the current speaker in order to find a chance to take a turn themselves and in order to make that turn appropriate to the context. Participants who accept the role of Audience, then, lose at least this one motivation for listening to the other's utterance. In parallel but ironic fashion, the speaker who gains an Audience likewise loses one motivation for making his contribution worthwhile, namely the fear of losing the floor; only the speaker's increased obligation to his Audience restores the balance, discourages him from abusing his monopoly and encourages the Audience to pay attention. In the case of natural narrative, this marked distribution of obligations and expectations that I am positing for speaker/Audience situations helps to explain the presence and composition of the abstract, the role of the coda, the pervasive rhetorical design of the utterance as a whole, its stress on "tellability," and the tendency for oral narratives to follow on one another's heels spontaneously.

The same analysis explains some facts about other speaker/ Audience situations too. For one thing, it accounts in detail for the rituals surrounding public speeches nowadays. Like natural narratives, public speeches also require that the special distribution of obligations and expectations be made explicit and be ratified by the participants before the speech takes place. While in natural narratives this ratification is worked out between speaker and potential Audience directly, on speech-making occasions it is carried out by a moderator or master of ceremonies, whose job is to mediate between Audience and speaker both before and after the speaker takes the floor in the same way a moderator controls equal access in meetings and debates. One of the moderator's jobs in introducing the speaker is to display the speaker's credentials, that is, the evidence that he is worth listening to, in the same way the natural narrator vouches for the tellability and veracity of his story in his abstract. The appropriateness conditions for what information the moderator may include in his introduction make it clear that he is presenting credentials and not just a biography. One cannot introduce a cabinet minister as a former cheeleader and prom queen unless the topic of the day is women's liberation.

After introducing the speaker, the moderator more or less simultaneously requests the floor on the speaker's behalf ("I now ask you to give your full attention to. . . .") and offers the speaker the floor on the Audience's behalf ("Take it away, Bill"). The Audience ratifies either or both of these actions by applauding, at which time the disillusioned have a last chance to slip out of the room. This applause plays the role of Labov's "Oh yeah? What happened?" The speaker thanks the Audience for its applause (i.e., permission) and for the privilege of having the floor. At the end of his speech he reiterates his thanks and the Audience applauds again, indicating the degree to which their nonparticipation has been "worth it" to them. Then the moderator verbalizes this judgment on behalf of the Audience, usually indicating fairly precisely why it has been "worth it": the speech was interesting, informative, educational, or entertaining. These remarks are obvious correlates of the "you're kidding!" which follows a successful danger-of-death narrative. Like the introduction, they are appropriate only if they relate to the intent of the speechmaker.

It is important to note that a speaker's having an authority over his subject matter which his Audience lacks does not erase his indebtedness when the Audience is a voluntary one. The storyteller knows something his Audience does not, yet he is indebted to them for consenting to listen. A lecturer or after-dinner speaker may be invited to talk because he is an "expert"; nevertheless, in our society at least, he is obliged by convention to treat his Audience as equals and thus to assume a debt to them precisely *because* they have chosen to attend. Such a speaker will very likely address his Audience as "my fellow X's." The voluntary aspect of the Audience role, in other words, serves to establish a peer relation between speaker and Audience whether or not one existed before, because the context assumes such a relation. Students attending compulsory lectures need not and should not be thanked by the professor for their attention; students voluntarily attending the same professor's public lectures do merit his thanks like anyone else in the Audience. This presupposed peer relation which obtains in fact or by convention between speakers and voluntary Audiences explains why we frequently accuse boring or unsatisfactory speakers of conceit or contempt for their Audiences. They are felt to have treated us as inferiors and thus to have claimed illegitimate authority over us. Failure to maintain this peer relation by talking "up" or "down" to one's Audience is the public speaker's worst sin. By the same token, attending a speech by a famous personage confers status on the Audience since for the time they are peers of the personage. "Getting" an obscure allusion in a literary work has the same effect.

I have said that in compensation for the asymmetrical distribution of turn-taking rights that prevails in speaker/Audience situations, the Audience is entitled to expect more of the speaker than they would if they were playing a participant role. "More" is a very unsatisfying way of characterizing nonparticipant as opposed to participant expectations; however, there does seem to be one area of speaker/Audience relations in which this increase in expectations is explicitly acknowledged. As a rule, in giving up floor rights, Audiences gain the right to pass judgment on the speaker's contribution. Conventionally, a space is allotted at the end of a performance in which the Audience is offered the floor for the purpose of addressing its judgment to the performer(s), and the performance is not over until this has occurred. A repertory of noises and gestures is available for indicating Audience judgments, including handclapping, knee-slapping, egg-throwing, foot-stomping, cheers, whistles, laughter, boos, hisses, and standing up. At public events, applause intensity is considered a very meaningful indication of Audience judgment. At Protestant church services, where applause would be unseemly, the minister customarily stations himself at the exit as the congregation files out expressly to expose himself to their verbal judgments of the sermon. At scholarly gatherings, the question period serves this function, among others. In the case of artistic performances and books, printed reviews are an important and obvious exercise of the Audience's right to judge. In addition, I have already mentioned the kind of approving commentary which follows a successful natural narrative and the dreaded "so what?" response to an unsuccessful one. Some such commentary invariably follows a natural narrative in conversation. Notice, however, that when no evaluative commentary occurs, a judgment is nevertheless understood to have been expressed, and a very damning one at that. The fact that silence itself counts as a judgment in speaker/Audience situations provides important support for the claim that the act of judging is presupposed to be an integral part of the speaker/Audience exchange. These evaluative rituals can be seen as a way of giving the erstwhile nonparticipants a "turn"; the fact that this turn is specifically set aside for judging indicates the degree to which the speaker addressing an Audience puts himself in jeopardy.[2] A performer who satisfies is said in English to have "acquitted himself." Notice too that this judging goes on whether or not the performer is

---

2. McCawley (1973) claims that the notion of "jeopardy" must be formally built into the semantic representation of verbs of judging like "criticize." Fillmore (1971) uses, albeit unwillingly, the concepts of "judge" and "defendant" in describing the role structure of verbs of judging.

present to hear it, as anyone knows who has listened in on the buzz of evaluative commentary with which departing Audiences fill the corridors of theaters and lecture halls. We seldom applaud films anymore, there being no live addressees to receive the applause, but we do invariably talk about them on the way home.

It may be that the act of expressing judgment, preferably in the performer's presence, is the Audience's way of reclaiming the peer status which it has voluntarily placed in jeopardy, or of counterbalancing the asymmetry of the speaker/Audience relation. By more or less formally building the judicial act into the performance itself, we create a different, delayed kind of symmetry to replace turn-taking. This identification of nonparticipation with judging extends beyond formal, institutionalized manifestations such as applause. In any face-to-face exchange, the nonparticipants can usually be relied upon to provide the current speaker with an ongoing evaluative commentary in the form of nods, facial expressions, grunts, and so on. Withdrawing these cues is one of the few ways we can (eventually) get a long-winded speaker to see that we want him to stop. Similarly, because nonresponse counts as negative response, we are often made uncomfortable in conversation by the presence of silent third parties who choose not to participate and who we feel are quietly passing judgment on everyone else while refusing to jeopardize themselves. Voluntary nonparticipation in conversation is labeled non- or anti-social. Perhaps because of the particularly silent and solitary nonparticipation the literary speech situation imposes, judging is felt to be a central part of the reader's role in literature. Indeed, it is only rather recently that we have begun to perceive literary studies as concerned with anything other than evaluation.

The role of Audience is, of course, one we play in a great many situations which are not verbal. In fact, it is a role we can play with respect to any human activity, and perhaps with respect to anything at all. Likewise, the marked distribution of rights, obligations, and expectations which characterizes verbal Audience roles applies to nonverbal performances, too. Anybody's behavior changes "dramatically" when he becomes aware that someone has chosen to pause and look on; such changes occur in many animals, too. And people do speak of being "let down" by the Grand Canyon. By the some token, all public spectacles, not just verbal ones, use institutionalized mechanisms for moderating and acknowledging the redistribution of floor rights, and enabling the Audience to express judgment.

At artistic spectacles like plays and concerts, a printed program performs some of the duties of the moderator or master of ceremonies. Theater programs present a list of the performers, and they may also include an abstract of the play, its historical background, verbal portraits presenting the credentials of the main actors, even details about the theater building itself. Part of the function of such a document is to display credentials, reinforce the potential Audience's expectation of pleasure, acknowledge the "honor of its presence," and forestall its impatience during the ambiguous interval between the time people take their seats (literally abandoning the floor) and the time the spectacle begins. A program is also intended to provide data which will help the Audience reach an enlightened judgment of the performance. At sports events, Audiences often receive a printed list of players, complete with statistical credentials (batting averages and so on). In some sports, the players request the floor (or field or ice) by lining up in the middle of it while the national anthem is played. The applause that follows, you will note, is not primarily addressed to the anthem but to the players, giving them permission to begin. Other sports make use of a moderator—the referee at boxing matches and the public address system announcer in racing sports, for example. Scoreboards assist the sports Audience in its evaluation of the proceedings and are supplemented on TV and radio by play-by-play commentary and instantaneous playbacks. As with artistic performances, Audience judgment is expressed through written as well as audiovisual means: sports reports are more akin to reviews than to news summaries. In sum, the point to be made is that this or any discussion of *speaker*/Audience relations will ultimately have to find its place in a more general account of *performer*/Audience relations, which will in turn be defined in relation to turn-taking relations.

To sum up the argument as it applies to verbal behavior, I am proposing that we recognize the speaker/Audience relation as one of the possible role structures that may obtain between the participants in a speech situation. This role structure is marked with respect to the unmarked situation among peers, in which all participants have equal access to the floor. Participants who become an Audience temporarily waive their access rights. The speaker who wishes to address an Audience must request and receive permission to do so; his request counts as an imposition on his interlocutors and thereby places him under obligation to them. For the Audience, ratifying the speaker's request for unique floor access counts as a favor done and entitles the Audience, first, to expect the speaker will repay them via the special quality of what he says during his special floor time and, second, to pass judgment on his success when his turn is over. The speaker's indebtedness and the Audience's right to judge persist even when the speaker has actually been invited to take the floor and when the other participants are present for the sole purpose of being an Audience. I have argued that this role structure can account for certain formal features of natural narratives and of the conventions surrounding public performances and that it accurately represents the attitudes of the participants in those situations. Just as the appropriateness conditions for conversation have to include a specification of the turn-taking system, so the appropriateness conditions for natural narratives, public speeches, and many other speech act types will have to specify the marked redistribution of rights, obligations, and expectations that suspension of turn-taking brings with it.

The analysis holds for literary speech situations, too, and must do so if it is to hold at all. Our role in the literary speech situation has the main formal characteristic I have been using to define an Audience: we knowingly and willingly enter a speech situation in which another speaker has unique access to the floor. The formal similarities I noted earlier between natural narrative and literary narrative are readily explained if we posit a similar disposition of speaker and Audience with respect to the message in both types. Titles, subtitles, chapter headings, and summaries, for example, perform the "request for the floor" role of Labov's abstracts and similarly correspond in function to the public speaking conventions just discussed. Readers of literary works usually feel that the writer is under obligation to make their attention worthwhile, and that they have the right to judge what he has done.[3] Hence, even though we are not imprisoned by a book the way we are by a lecture hall or an oral anecdote, we do not put down a bad book with indifference or neutrality but rather with annoyance, frustration, disappointment, and anger at the author. We throw it across the room. Nor are most writers unaware of their indebtedness to the Audience. The "dear reader" remarks common to eighteenth- and nineteenth-century novels, like the "my fellow X's" address of the orator, are readily interpreted as acknowledgments of the peer relation which holds between author and reader, of the sense of obligation the author feels as a result of that relation, and of his awareness of being in jeopardy. From the beginnings of literature to the present, iconoclastic works of literature have often come to us accompanied by prefaces, built-in self-defenses very much akin to the moderator's credentials list. If their role were purely discursive or commentative rather than defensive, prefaces would be as well or better placed at

---

3. Teachers of literature will note that these claims do not so readily apply to their students. The pedagogical situation assumes that the student of literature is not in fact a fully qualified reader and is therefore not entitled to full reader's rights. Possibly a person will always tend to view himself in this way if his only contact with literature takes place in the classroom.

the end of the book. But they aren't. And even writers who profess not to "give a damn what the public thinks" are usually careful if not eager to apprise us of this fact. Certainly, not caring what the Audience thinks is not the same as not wanting to be read and applauded. In short, the author's "authority" in a literary work, like the authority of the speechmaking "expert," does not suffice to put him in the clear with the reader.

Even these rudimentary similarities between literature and other speaker/Audience situations are enough to tell us that speaker and Audience are present in the literary speech situation, that their existence is presupposed by literary works, that they have commitments to one another as they do everywhere else, and that those commitments are presupposed by both the creator and the receivers of the work. Far from being autonomous, self-contained, self-motivating, context-free objects which exist independently from the "pragmatic" concerns of "everyday" discourse, literary works take place in a context, and like any other utterance they cannot be described apart from that context. Whether or not literary critics wish to acknowledge this fact—and they sometimes have not—a theory of literary discourse must do so. More importantly, like so many of the characteristics believed to constitute literariness, the basic speaker/Audience situation which prevails in a literary work is not fundamentally or uniquely literary. It is not the result of a use of the language different from all other uses. Far from suspending, transforming, or opposing the laws of nonliterary discourse, literature, in this aspect at least, obeys them. At least some of the expectations with which readers approach literary works cannot be attributed directly to the fact that the utterances are literary works or works of fiction but rather to more general appropriateness conditions governing speaker/Audience relations in the most familiar and commonplace speech contexts (to say nothing of activities not primarily verbal). To put it the other way round, the nonparticipant Audience role, which has been considered a key to literary response, is a familiar component of many other speech situations as well. The role is not part of the rhetoric of fiction but of the rhetoric of Audience-ship which is itself defined in relation to the rhetoric of conversation.

2.   Definitiveness, pre-paration, and pre-selection

The fact that we constitute a voluntary Audience is not the only reason we approach literary works with increased expectations of delight. Reconsider Ohmann's important observation that "our readiness to discover and dwell on the implicit meanings in works of literature—and to judge them important—is a consequence of our knowing them to *be* literary works, rather than that which tells us they are such." It seems to me that one of the most important things we know when we know an utterance to be a work of litera-ture is the fact that it got published and that most likely it was in-tended to be. A number of important reader assumptions follow from this fact. Unless otherwise indicated, readers of modern pub-lished works assume that the text was composed in writing and that it is definitive. This means, among other things, that its author had more time to plan and prepare his utterance than conversation al-lows and that he also had (and probably used) the opportunity to correct and improve on his utterance before delivering it over to the Audience. We are entitled to assume, then, that this text is free of gross randomness and errors and that it is, in its author's eyes, if not the best possible version of itself at least a satisfactory version, one which the author has chosen to give us having had the chance to deliberate. If an author has not had this chance to correct, deliber-ate, and choose his version—if, for example, he dies and a manu-script is published without his final approval—this fact *must* be made known to the Audience at the outset of the text, and we ad-just our expectations and responses accordingly. In approaching literary works, and printed discourse in general, I think we normally assume that this opportunity for deliberation makes it more likely that this utterance will be "worth it" to us.[4] It is partly for this reason that written compositions can make exceptional demands on their Audiences: they can be longer and more difficult to decipher than spontaneous, spoken discourse, especially if intended to be read rather than heard.

In addition to knowing that a published literary work was composed in writing and approved by its author, we know that before reaching us, that text has had to pass through a process of selection carried out by specialists whose job is to eliminate the least successful creations and ensure the distribution and preservation of the most successful. Nowadays, for better or worse, we have delegated this role to publishers and their professional readers and editors who, in some cases, are joined by government or church censors. After a work reaches print, its fate is in the hands of still other groups of selectors, whose judgment probably but not necessarily influences our literary decisions and expectations: critics, reviewers, librarians, the professors who set up college curricula, even the people who decide what reviews to quote on the covers of the paperback edition. These processes of selection and elimination play a central role in defining and bringing into being the institution we

---

4. To a certain extent, we are entitled to make the same assumption in approaching orally composed literature. Oral works are in part pre-pared, and refinement and correction are possible in a living oral tradition, given that a teller can repeat his performance many times. On the other hand, we consider it important to know that a work was orally composed—it does make a difference. Perhaps oral literature is the exception that proves my rule, since it would seem that here in the Gutenberg Galaxy, what seems to preoccupy us most about oral composition is the fact that it is not written, the knowledge that a speaker could produce something this long and this "good" without benefit of writing. In studying oral literature, modern critics tend to focus on those mechanisms that can be viewed precisely as ways of doing without writing: metric conventions, mnemonic devices, formulaic expressions, and the like. Furthermore, it seems that the only oral works which fall within the purview of conventional literary studies are those which were written down many centuries ago. Contemporary oral literature usually gets classified as folklore ("craft," not "art") and assigned to the domain of anthropologists.

call Literature, and, as I shall discuss in the next chapter, our knowledge of the selection process is one of the most important sets of presuppositions we bring to bear when we read a literary work. Publishers, editors, critics, and reviewers are our literary moderators, mediating between the writer who wishes to take the floor and the public which has a floor to give him. Like the master of ceremonies, these literary judges ratify the speaker on our behalf and request our attention on his behalf, with the obvious difference that the role of master of ceremonies is mainly symbolic, while that of editors, publishers, and critics is very real indeed. The emcee represents a selection and ratification procedure that has taken place elsewhere; publishers and critics carry out such selection and ratification procedures themselves.

In the literary speech situation, the book itself as *object* symbolizes this selection and ratification procedure: like the emcee's introduction, the theater program, or the poster announcing a lecture, the book not only informs us that the text was pre-selected but also provides us with information about how and by whom it was selected —its credentials, in short.[5] Thus, the names of a book's publisher, author, and collection count as credentials, which is one reason they appear at the front of the text; a hardback (as opposed to a paperback text) can function as a credential, as can the thickness of the paper, the size of print, or the price. Important also is the cover design, often used to supplement or elaborate on the title. A paperback displaying a naked woman in a pool of blood with a dagger in her heart, a caption "3,000,000 copies sold!" and a quotation like " 'Absolutely shocking!'—Time Magazine" tell us a lot about how this book was selected, and will arouse in us entirely different expectations than will an austere college edition with a plain cover and an

---

5. In the case of oral literature, the professional performer carries his own credentials. Aside from his personal reputation, the fact that he is a professional, one who is able to make his living at it, entitles the Audience to expectations analogous to those we have vis-à-vis a published work.

introductory note by a scholar. A work which has been ratified by a prestigious publishing house or journal is assumed to have won a keener competition over a wider field than a work published on a small scale. Data such as these play a significant role in conditioning our choice of what to read and our expectations of what we do read, though they are in most cases secondary in importance to the data about the book's genre, subgenre, and subject matter that we glean from the title page. These types of data—both typological and evaluative—are designed to bring together literary works and their intended Audiences, that is (in most cases), the Audiences most likely to appreciate them.[6] They are important data, because, unlike the Audience for the natural narrator, the Audience for an author is both undefined and expandable.

The effect of the selection process in individual reader/book encounters obviously varies enormously. Some readers find the interests of professional selectors to be largely at odds with their own; the label "Banned in Boston" will affect the gospel preacher, the porno fan, and the literary historian quite differently. Likewise, the content of the selection process differs for different varieties of literature. Nevertheless, I think two meaningful generalizations about the role of the literary selection process can be made. First, an individual reader will bring whatever background information he has about the judgments already passed on a given work and about the criteria involved to bear on his reading of the work and/or on his decision of whether to read a work. Second, with the exception of vanity press publications, every book bears with it at least the message that some professional judge, someone other than the writer himself, thinks that within its genre and subgenre the text is "worth it." By contrast, the would-be poet who peddles his creations on the

---

6. One might be tempted to revise the latter part of this sentence to read "the largest Audiences most likely to buy them." It is true that the relations between economics and taste are complex—but the two *are* related.

street corner, like the orators in Hyde Park, does without these institutionalized mediators. He must win his Audience personally, and he has little assurance indeed that his speech acts will reach the largest Audience most likely to appreciate them, nor do passers-by have much reason to expect such speech acts as these will be "worth it" to them. The institutionalized processes of publishing, reviewing, and advertising literary works are in part designed to eliminate such randomness, just as institutionalized turn-taking rules are used in meetings to make floor allocation equitable and efficient.

Needless to say, these selection procedures, like the procedures characterizing Audience-ship, are not peculiar to literature. They apply in one way or another to all published discourse, and our knowledge of them is part of the contextual information we bring to bear on printed works in general. Likewise, all printed texts bear with them the badges of their selection process. The tangible physical features that distinguish pamphlets, newspapers, magazines, journals, and books express (in a code which must be learned) a wide variety of differences in intended function, intended Audience, stringency of selection, range of subject matter, and so on. This is another case, then, where the rules that govern the literary speech situation are not unique to it but rather are general rules which apply in the literary speech situation by virtue of characteristics that situation shares with other speech situations. It is through such shared rules that we can identify and express the relationship of literature to other areas of discourse.

A speech act approach to literature will have to treat the literary pre-paration and pre-selection processes as part of what speech act theory calls the "conventional procedure" for making a literary speech act, and it will have to incorporate some account of those processes into a description of the literary speech situation. But it is true that passing through a selection process is part of the conventional procedure for making a literary speech act, it would seem to follow that an utterance which does not pass through this process (whether because it was not submitted or because it was rejected) is not a work of literature. Must we thus make the counter-intuitive claims that an unpublished novel is not a novel and an unpublished novelist is not a novelist? Within the approach I am advocating here, the answer to these questions must be neither yes nor no. The most obvious reason is that in any case where communication between speaker and intended addressee is dependent on a mediator, the speaker's utterance exists in a kind of limbo until the mediation is completed. If I write a letter to the editor and never send it, there is a sense in which I have written the editor and a sense in which I have not. If I send the letter and the editor has not received it yet, never does receive it, or does not read it, there is a sense in which I have written him and a sense in which I have not. Pragmatically, my communicative aim has not been achieved, though my letter was and still is a letter. In describing such a situation, a speaker would have to say "I wrote the editor, but. . . ." Analogously, there is something odd about an exchange such as:

A: I called Bill today.
B: Oh? What did he say?
A: He wasn't home.

A might have been expected to say either "I tried to call Bill" or "I called Bill, but. . . ." In the same sense, it would seem that an unratified and untransmitted literary work is "a literary work, but. . . ." Within speech act theory, little attention has so far been given to the question of delayed and mediated communication; however, the approach is easily flexible enough to accommodate such cases.

As I shall discuss in chapter five, the plain fact that the literary speech situation conventionally presupposes pre-paration and pre-selection explains a great deal about how readers respond to and cooperate with works of literature. For the moment, however, I should like to look at some other implications that these facts have for the theory of literary discourse. One of these is that it does not really make sense to attempt, as did the Formalists and structuralists, to describe or define literature in terms that are "detached from the concept of values" (the phrase, you will recall, is Stankiewicz's). In approaching their subject this way, the Formalists and structuralists were seeking a way of defining literature, first, without reference to the academic aesthetic canon of their day (which they, with the avant-garde, had rejected), and second, without reference to "speculative aesthetics" (which they, as literary scientists, had rejected). Their aim was to use and define the term "literature" in what Ohmann (1971) has called a "non-honorific" sense, in which the category "literature" includes, if I may borrow Ohmann's phrase, "the sum of all actual (and perhaps possible) literary works" (1971:1). In its "honorific" or normative sense, only works of particularly high quality can merit the label "literature." For obvious reasons, the nonhonorific sense is the one that has traditionally been used by critics who wish to view literature as an autonomous, empirically definable body of data upon which a theory may be built and who wish to make nonnormative (value-free, objective, or empirical) statements about its properties, the way linguists make statements about sentences.

Now the honorific sense of the term "literature" is a legitimate one if it is understood to refer to a set of literary works that have passed a filtering process carried out by a specific group of people, namely scholars or intellectuals, according to standards associated primarily with the academy. This is the selection process that designates "classics." The nonhonorific sense then refers to a set of literary works that includes both those that have passed through this filtering process and those that have not (either because they were rejected or because they were not considered). But the difference between these two sets of literary works (and thus between the two senses of the term "literature") does not and cannot entitle us to conclude that the nonhonorific literature exists apart from values

or that it can be discussed "detached from the concept of values."
Strictly speaking, there is nothing nonhonorific at all about the
"sum of all actual (and perhaps possible) literary works." Because
they have gone through a qualitative selection process, all actual
works of literature present themselves as literature in an honorific
sense, and all are read as literature in such a sense. The class of possible literary works (which is the class of all possible utterances) will
not *become* full-fledged literary works until they have been ratified
by the community by passing through the relevant selection process.
Put another way, every work of literature is intended by its author
to be a good one of its type, one that could get published, acclaimed,
and widely read (or bought). Every pornographic novel is meant to
be a good one of its kind, though not all literate citizens are expected
to enjoy pornography. Even the writer who is only in it for the
money won't be in it for long unless he does what he does well by
some public standards.

In short, the very notion of literature is a normative one. As we
saw in the case of Stankiewicz, critics who try to define literature
without reference to human values and preferences easily end up
presupposing values and preferences—inevitably their own. But
there is clearly no one set of values in terms of which literature can
be defined. We all know that literary values, and the selection criteria which reflect them, differ from culture to culture, from period to
period, and from genre to genre. But within a single culture, period,
and genre, there are many subvarieties of literature that reflect the
many uses to which literature is put and the many groups of people it
serves. A theory that recognizes only one set of literary values cannot deal with all the kinds any better than a theory which recognizes
no literary values.

The existence of the literary selection process has a second implication for criticism. Once the role of selection is recognized, the
"special-ness" of literature, which poeticians have long been at pains
to demonstrate empirically, does not have to be proved at all. In

order to defend the claim that literary works are particularly worthy of our attention, one has no need to go in search of intrinsic qualities that "distinguish literary material from material of any other kind" and that make up literature's worth (which is after all what poeticians usually mean by "literariness" and "poeticality"). It is people, not properties, that "make a verbal message a verbal work of art"—people writing, editing, revising, reading, and judging. The specialness is in the context. Paul Goodman has put this point nicely from the poet's point of view:

> One could fantasize that the poetic tradition extends right back to the aboriginal language, and we never did forget how to talk it! But the realistic explanation is quite adequate: human beings are busy and ingenious; then consider the effects of the concerted effort of a gifted group over generations and centuries and indeed millennia, in devising and refining literary expressions not losing touch with one another. (Goodman, 1971:154)

Once we take into account the institutionalized aspect of literature, intrinsic definitions of literature become unnecessary and indeed suspect; statements like "the best example of the imaginative use of words is to be found in poetry" (Duncan, 1953:109) or "literature is an ideal form of communication because it has the most powerful examples of verbal skill" (Duncan, p. 93) are complete tautologies, given that literature is a category we have set up precisely to select and preserve the "best examples of the imaginative use of words" and "the most powerful examples of verbal skill." The commonplace belief that nonliterature is the arena where language gets corrupted, automatized, and conventionalized while in literature it becomes "purified" and "made new" derives precisely from a failure to recognize that literary selection conspires always to eliminate what a community takes to be the least interesting and least skillful verbal productions. "Making new" is as important a linguistic value outside literature as within—witness the rapid and constant turnover of slang, the popularity of the pun, and the high value placed on wit and humor of every kind in conversation. The difference is that out-side literature, the noninnovative, unimaginative speaker still has the right to a turn. In literature he does not, or at least he is not sup-posed to. When he does get a turn, we feel not only that he, the speaker, has failed but that the selection process has broken down as well. In responding to a work he considers a failure, a reader probably will ask not "How could anyone write such bunk?" but "How could such bunk get into print?" More generally, the exist-ence of literary selection makes it an oversimplification to view liter-ature and nonliterature as analogous bodies of data, as the poetic language argument requires. Access to the channel between the literary speaker and his intended public Audience is controlled by persons in addition to the speaker himself. In conversation, channel access is worked out directly between interlocutors.

3.   The Cooperative Principle and the rules for conversation

The processes of pre-paration and pre-selection that the literary speech situation presupposes have important consequences for the next set of "ordinary language" rules whose applicability to litera-ture I propose to explore. I refer to H. P. Grice's concepts of the Cooperative Principle and conversational implicature, as outlined in his 1967 William James lectures titled *Logic and Conversation*. Like Searle and Austin, Grice is primarily a speech act philosopher rather than a linguist; however, his work, too, has great implications for linguistics, and his lectures have had an enormous impact in lin-guistic circles. Grice attempts to clarify and correct the traditional Austinian view of appropriateness conditions by relating the ones which hold for a particular speech act in a particular context to general rules governing all verbal discourse and indeed all goal-directed cooperative human behavior. Because of its generality, I believe Grice's approach to discourse holds promise for those of us interested in making a space for literature inside the theory of language use. I shall outline Grice's theory in the next few pages and then discuss the extent to which his model of conversation works for literature as well.

As his title suggests, Grice uses the term *conversation* to mean, roughly, "ordinary language" or "talk" as opposed in this case to formal logic (cf. footnote, p. 80). Grice is mainly concerned in *Logic and Conversation* with clarifying the distinction between meaning and use of utterances. In particular, he calls into question a tendency among speech act analysts to account for the inappropriateness of a given word or phrase in a given context by attaching appropriateness conditions to that word or phrase as aspects of its meaning or "sense." Grice aims to show that many cases of inappropriateness which have previously been analyzed as violations of conditions governing the applicability of a particular word or expression in question are actually best viewed as violations of other more general rules governing all discourse. Once these general rules are specified, he argues, many of the appropriateness conditions previously attached to individual words or phrases—as semantic features of the expression itself—will become unnecessary, and a simpler and more powerful grammar will result. Here is an example. It is true but inappropriate to say "it looks like a car to me" when "it" obviously *is* a car and I obviously know it. Pre-Griceans would account for this inappropriateness by stating an appropriateness condition to the effect that the expression "X looks like a Y" presupposes either that X is not a Y or that the speaker does not know whether X is a Y. Grice argues that the inappropriateness can actually be accounted for by a much more general rule of language use which requires that wherever possible one should give as much information as is required by the purposes of the talk exchange in which one is participating. Thus, if X *is* in fact a Y, then to say merely that it *looks like* a Y is to say too little—less than I know and less than I am required to say by the rules of conversation. It is important to note that such a rule would apply to all conversation regardless of its subject matter and consequently would apply independently of the specific word or phrase in question.

Similarly, it is true but usually inappropriate to say "Bill is in Oxford or in London" when I know for certain that Bill is in London. This fact, says Grice, "has led to the idea that it is part of the meaning of 'or' ... to convey that the speaker is ignorant of the truth-values of the particular disjuncts" (I, 10).[7] Rather, argues Grice, this inappropriateness, too, is accounted for by the general rule requiring that one give all the relevant information one has. If I knew where Bill was, I would say so unless, say, I had promised not to tell, in which case I must explain this fact or take responsibility for misleading my addressee. When I say "Bill is in Oxford or in London," my addressee understands that I am ignorant of Bill's whereabouts, but he understands that not because of something he knows about the *meaning* of "or" but because of something he knows about language *use*, namely, the "all-the-relevant-facts" rule. The same rule explains the inappropriateness of saying "X tried to turn on the lights" when X in fact succeeded in doing so and there was no reason to think he would not succeed. There is then no need to attach to the word "try" an appropriateness condition saying that "try" presupposes failure or difficulty.

The example with "or" that I have just quoted is an important one to Grice, for one of his particular interests in *Logic and Conversation* is to show that the divergence in meaning which philosophers have commonly believed to exist between ordinary language expressions like "not," "if ... then," "either ... or," and their counterparts in formal logic, "∼," "⊃," "∨," are not really differences in

---

7. Grice's lectures have not yet been published in their entirety, though a substantial excerpt has appeared in Cole and Morgan (1975). My own discussion of Grice is based on the unpublished manuscript of the lectures. In this and following page references I have used a roman numeral to indicate the number of the lecture, followed by an Arabic numeral indicating the page number within the lecture text.

meaning but in use. Once the rules for the use of ordinary language are isolated, Grice contends, the devices of formal logic and of ordinary language can be seen to have the same meaning. Obviously, his argument is intended to refute the philosophical position (commonly associated with Bertrand Russell) that ordinary language is loose, imperfect, metaphysically loaded, and altogether inadequate to philosophy and science, a position which holds that "the proper course is to conceive and begin to construct an ideal language, incorporating the formal devices [of logic], the sentences of which will be clear, determinate in truth-value and certifiably free from metaphysical implications; the foundations of science will now be philosophically secure, since the statements of the scientist will be expressible (though not necessarily expressed) within this language" (Grice, II, 2).

Grice's polemical interest—stating the case for ordinary language vis-à-vis the so-called "language of science" (formal logic)—seems curiously related to my present interest in stating the case for ordinary language vis-à-vis the so-called "language of poetry." It is worth noting that the idea of an "ordinary language" that was alien to the purposes of science achieved prominence about the same time as did the idea of an "ordinary language" alien to the purposes of literature—in the first three decades of this century. "Ordinary language," it seems, was too poetic for the scientists and too scientific for the poets. It is probably not a coincidence that "ordinary language" became the whipping boy of two apparently opposed factions at once.

In any quarter, skepticism about "ordinary language" (the term was used until recently only by the skeptical) is in the end skepticism about ordinary people, be they nonscientists or nonpoets. In both the new, improved "poetic language" of the futurists and the new, improved scientific language of the logicians we witness a movement toward increased artificiality and, more importantly, toward unrecognizability. Both the science and the literature of the academy become increasingly inaccessible linguistically to the speaker lacking special training, and this inaccessibility becomes the sign of their value. "Specialized" comes to equal "special"; the scientist's ideal audience is scientists, the poet's poets. The connection between this tendency toward specialization and the advent of mass literacy, mass education, and mass printing has often been pointed out. It would also be worth investigating the hypothesis that the "ordinary language" concept arose as a kind of residue left over from the seventeenth-century poetry-science split which reached an extreme at the beginning of this century. At any rate, it does seem that the fault Grice finds with the "scientific language" doctrine is the same one I have been finding with the "poetic language" doctrine, namely the mistake of positing a contrast based on intrinsic features of expressions when in fact the contrast, to the extent that it exists, is based on meaning-independent contextual features, that is, use. Grice aims to show how the rules for language use mediate between logic and conversation; I am concerned with examining the extent to which the same rules can mediate between literature and conversation, bringing to light the similarities and differences of the two verbal activities.

The all-the-relevant-facts rules I mentioned earlier is one of a set of exceedingly general rules Grice proposes as a framework for a theory of language use. I will outline the rest of his schema here. According to Grice, the fact that conversation normally exhibits some degree of coherence and continuity suggests that our conversational behavior is governed by "a rough general principle which participants will be expected (ceteris paribus) to observe, viz: 'Make your conversational contribution such as is required, at the stage at which it occurs, by the accepted purpose or direction of the talk-exchange in which you are engaged.' " (II, 7) Grice calls this the *Cooperative Principle*. He then proposes four sets of conversational "maxims" that we observe in observing the Cooperative Principle:

I. *Maxims of Quantity*
1. "Make your contribution as informative as is required (for the current purposes of the exchange)."
2. "Do not make your contribution more informative than is required." (Grice expresses some doubt about whether this maxim is needed.)

II. *Maxims of Quality*
Supermaxim: "Make your contribution one that is true."
Maxims 1. "Do not say what you believe to be false." 2. "Do not say that for which you lack adequate evidence."

III. *Maxim of Relation*
1. "Be relevant."

> Grice's note: "Though the maxim itself is terse, its formulation conceals a number of problems which exercise me a good deal; questions about what different kinds of foci or relevance there may be, how these shift in the course of a talk-exchange, how to allow for the fact that subjects of conversation are legitimately changed, and so on." (II, 8)

IV. *Maxims of Manner*
Supermaxim: "Be perspicuous."
Maxims: 1. "Avoid obscurity of expression." 2. "Avoid ambiguity." 3. "Be brief (avoid unnecessary prolixity)." 4. "Be orderly." There are possibly others.

These rules can be understood as large, very general appropriateness conditions that participants in a speech exchange normally assume to be in force. A participant in a speech exchange normally takes it for granted that his interlocutor shares a knowledge of the rules, is trying to observe them, and expects the same of him. I say "normally" because of course there are speech situations where participants will not assume the Cooperative Principle and maxims to be in effect. A soldier captured by the enemy, for example, will be expected to cooperate to the extent of giving his name, rank, and serial number, but beyond that he can be expected to try *not* to observe any of the conversational maxims. This kind of exception helps to prove Grice's rules. The soldier does not cooperate because he would much rather not be engaged in the speech situation at all.

Grice appends two important qualifications to the rule schema outlined above. First, like the turn-taking procedures discussed earlier, the maxims he is proposing can be seen to govern not just conversation but also any cooperative, rational human activity (two people fixing a car is his example). This fact suggests to Grice that talking is "a special case or variety of purposive, indeed rational behaviour" (II, 9), the implication being, apparently, that the Cooperative Principle may have a cognitive basis. Second, the list of maxims he offers is not intended to be complete:

> There are of course all sorts of other maxims (aesthetic, social or moral in character) such as "Be polite," which are also normally observed by participants in talk-exchanges. ... The conversational maxims, however, and the conversational implicatures connected with them are specially connected (I hope) with the particular purposes which talk (and so talk-exchange) is adapted to serve and is primarily employed to serve. I have stated my maxims as if this purpose were a maximally effective exchange of information; this specification is of course too narrow, and the scheme needs to be generalized to allow for such general purposes as influencing or directing the actions of others. (II, 9)

This caveat is important, clearly, if we are to make room within Grice's model for the full range of illocutionary acts possible in a given language. Obviously, there are a great many types, including natural narrative and literature, whose purpose is not a maximally effective exchange of information in the Gricean sense. Indeed, as the maxims stand, they represent those aspects of discourse which literature has often been felt to subvert. Finally, the maxims are anything but iron-clad. In fact, they are honored as often in the breach as in the observance. One of the main virtues of Grice's model is that it offers a way of describing the breaches as well, a matter of no small importance to the present undertaking. Before turning to breaches, however, some observations about the observance are in order. In the next section, therefore, I turn to the question of how the Cooperative Principle and maxims do apply to utterances whose accepted point or purpose is not a maximally effective exchange of information. Again the focus will be on literary and natural narrative. My point of departure is the question of relevance.

4.   Assertibility, tellability, relevance, and the "display text"

I claimed earlier that at some level of analysis, literary and natural narratives had to be analyzed as utterances of the same type. Using Grice's Cooperative Principle and maxims, I propose now to make a few more precise observations about what type they are and where their borders lie in relation to other utterance types. In particular, I would like to elaborate a little on Grice's maxim of Relation as it applies to declarative or assertive speech acts in the hope of moving toward an understanding of relevance in literary works and their extraliterary kin. As Grice observes repeatedly, the notion of relevance is extremely complex and greatly in need of clarification. It would be impossible to undertake a full-scale analysis of relevance at this time. My intent here is only to clarify some of the issues such an analysis will have to confront.

In the outline of speech act theory presented earlier, I noted that the appropriateness conditions on questions include a condition to the effect that "the speaker wants to know the answer"; analogously, one of the appropriateness conditions for imperative utterances says that "the speaker wants the addressee to do X." Both questions and imperatives, then, presuppose, among other things, that the speaker has a very specific motive. His point is to generate a specific action on the part of the hearer.[8] The fact that questions and imperatives share this same point (generating action) is usually considered grounds for identifying them as speech acts of the same basic type (Searle's "directives"). Questions are requests or commands to *tell* something, imperatives request or demand us to *do* something. This presupposed purpose determines what counts as a "relevant" question or command. For example, I cannot appropriately ask you a question whose answer you cannot be expected to know; I cannot give you an order which you are clearly unable to carry out. On the other hand, except in pedagogical situations, I cannot appropriately ask you a question whose answer I already know, and except for rhetorical questions, I cannot ask you a question whose answer is patently obvious to both of us. Nor can I appropriately order you to do something which you would clearly do anyway. In Grice's argument appropriateness conditions such as these do not need to be attached independently to the illocutionary acts of requesting, commanding, or questioning, as they commonly have been. Once we are given the definition of an imperative or question (a definition which would include the speaker's intent to get the addressee to do something), such conditions follow naturally from the larger conversational maxim of Relation and will be specified by relation to it.

Assertions, it is usually argued, contrast with imperatives and questions in that they are concerned with getting the addressee to believe or know or think something rather than to do something.[9] As

---

8. Actually, Grice argues that imperatives are intended to produce in the hearer the intention to perform a specific action, not the action itself.

9. Here and throughout, I define "assertion" in the broad sense as any indicative statement or remark. Actually, Grice argues that assertions are attempts to get the addressee to recognize that the speaker is thinking that X, from which the addressee will normally pass to thinking that X himself.

with questions and commands, this presupposed purpose determines the relevance criteria for assertions. Thus, in addition to an appropriate condition requiring that a speaker believe his assertion to be true (Grice's maxim of Quality), many analyses attach a condition to "verbs of saying" to the effect that the speaker must believe that the addressee may not know or may not remember that which is being asserted. Another, perhaps weaker, version of this condition says that for an assertion to be appropriate, it must not be obvious to both speaker and hearer that what is being asserted is true. Or, put another way, an assertion will be inappropriate unless there is a real or supposed chance of its being false. Thus, a remark like "Sister Martha is wearing her habit today" will probably be inappropriate if Sister Martha has never been known to wear anything but her habit. This condition in its various formulations is usually called the Assertibility Condition or the Nonobviousness Condition. As with questions and imperatives, Grice argues that such an Assertibility Condition need not be stated independently for verbs of saying, because it follows naturally from the maxim of Relation in conjunction with the definition of an assertion as an attempt to get someone to think something.

To say that assertions must be (a) true and (b) not obviously true clearly does not exhaust the relevance rules for assertions, nor has anyone claimed it does. For example, in addition to being true and nonobvious, assertions usually must relate somehow to the discourse in progress and to the addressee(s). Just as I cannot appropriately ask someone something he cannot possibly know, so I cannot appropriately tell someone something he cannot possibly understand or be interested in. An assertion that is both true and nonobvious will still be pointless if it has no real or supposed relation to the interests of the hearer. This aspect of relevance in assertions has been for the most part ignored by speech act theoreticians,[10] largely because in dealing with assertions, they have focused

---

10. Searle (1969), for example, states only a single sincerity condition for assertions, namely, the condition "speaker believes that p." It seems to me that

on assertions that are answers to questions and that therefore presuppose both the hearer's ignorance and his interest. But, although we spend most of our talking time making assertions, answers to questions are only a small fraction of these. I would like to examine another kind.

Consider the totally unspectacular remark, "Bill went to the bank today." I could make this remark relevantly and appropriately in answer to a question such as "where's Bill?" Or I could volunteer this remark if I were addressing, say, a person who had lent Bill money and was anxious to collect, or anyone else whose expectations or future actions might be affected by Bill's going (or not going) to the bank. If Bill might have been expected to show up with me for lunch, I could volunteer this remark as a way of letting everyone else at lunch know not to expect Bill today. In this case, I anticipate the question, "Where's Bill?" In all these contexts, in asserting "Bill went to the bank today," I am giving my interlocutors a piece of information which will usefully correct their knowledge and expectations of the world as regards Bill. But there is another kind of circumstance under which I can volunteer a remark like "Bill went to the bank today." Suppose Bill is a miser, notoriously mistrustful of banks and known to keep his money at home stuffed in a sock. In this case, the information that Bill actually went to the bank is downright spectacular and can be volunteered for that reason alone. It is news; it can be displayed. In such a context, I would probably signal that I was offering the information as a display by giving my assertion the stress and intonation of an exclamation, "*Bill* went to the *bank* today!" and I might preface it with a remark like "you're not going to believe this, but...." I would expect my addressee's response to be some exclamation of surprise like "you're kidding!"

---

making an assertion which one supposes to be of no interest to the hearer counts as a form of insincerity, just as making a question without wanting to know the answer counts as insincerity. Whether or not hearer-relevance in assertions is stated as a sincerity condition, it must be stated somewhere. The hearer's ignorance is simply not a sufficient relevance criterion for assertions. As will appear shortly, it is not always a necessary criterion either.

or just "No!" In this context, my statement that Bill went to the bank is not only assertible (as defined by the Assertibility Condition) but also *tellable* (in the Labovian sense). In other words, not only is it *possible* that Bill would not have gone to the bank, it is *exceedingly likely* that he wouldn't have and problematic that he did. In the context I have just described, what makes my assertion a relevant one is precisely the presupposed unlikelihood and problematicalness of the state of affairs I am representing. This kind of display-producing relevance, which I will refer to as "tellability," characterizes an important subclass of assertive or representative speech acts that includes natural narrative, an enormous proportion of conversation, and many if not all literary works. It contrasts sharply with the kind of relevance we expect of assertions made in answer to or in anticipation of a question, these being paradigm examples of what Grice means by a "maximally effective exchange of information." Assertions whose relevance is tellability must represent states of affairs that are held to be unusual, contrary to expectations, or otherwise problematic; informing assertions may do so, but they do not have to, and it is not their point to do so. Both types are used to inform, but they inform for different reasons. In making an assertion whose relevance is tellability, a speaker is not only reporting but also verbally *displaying* a state of affairs, inviting his addressee(s) to join him in contemplating it, evaluating it, and responding to it. His point is to produce in his hearers not only belief but also an imaginative and affective involvement in the state of affairs he is representing and an evaluative stance toward it. He intends them to share his wonder, amusement, terror, or admiration of the event. Ultimately, it would seem, what he is after is an *interpretation* of the problematic event, an assignment of meaning and value supported by the consensus of himself and his hearers.

Traditional grammar has at least in part recognized two such classes of assertions by distinguishing between statements and exclamations. Exclamatory assertions are by definition assertions that display states of affairs, presenting them for their tellability. (I exclude here exclamations like "you don't say!" which are used to acknowledge the tellability of a previous remark.) Thus, as Elliott (1975:242) shows, exclamations are inappropriate unless they assert information that the speaker believes to be unusual or unexpected. For example, one cannot appropriately exclaim, "It isn't incredible what big feet he has!"[11] Exclamatory assertions must be tellable. On the other hand, they do not always have to be assertible in the sense prescribed by the Assertibility Condition. That is, they do not have to assert something the addressee doesn't know, though they certainly may do so. Thus, "have you ever grown!" or "you've had your hair cut!" are perfectly appropriate exclamations even though the addressee is presumably aware of such alterations in his appearance. Similarly, in most contexts, a remark like "boy it's hot!" is understood to assert information that is not new to the addressee. As these examples show, information does not have to be new to be tellable; it only has to be unusual or problematic.

The devices we use to make exclamations are precisely devices to indicate that the assertion is being made for its tellability. Exclamations have their own intonation and gestures and some idiosyncratic syntactic options like "what big X's you have!" Prefacing expressions like "this is/was incredible," "guess what?" or just "oh say," are markers of upcoming assertions whose point is display. The assertions that follow such markers may or may not be exclamations, but they will be assertions whose relevance is tellability. Robin Lakoff and George Lakoff have made some observations about the adverb "absolutely" which indicate that it, too, is a tellability marker. Here are some examples modeled on their data (G. Lakoff, 1971: 237):

---

11. This sentence could be uttered to express violent disagreement with a previous remark. In that case, however, its stress pattern (stress on "isn't") differs from that of the true exclamation (stress on "incredible"), as does its function.

1 (a) Harry's talk was absolutely fascinating
   (b) Harry's talk was absolutely interesting
   (c) Harry's talk was absolutely uninteresting

2 (a) I absolutely loved Harry's talk
   (b) I absolutely liked Harry's talk
   (c) I absolutely loathed Harry's talk

3 (a) Harry's talk was absolutely wonderful
   (b) Harry's talk was absolutely good
   (c) Harry's talk was absolutely terrible

Each set of sentences illustrates an evaluative continuum. In all three sets, the (a) and (c) sentences, representing the "tellable" extremes of the continuum, are clearly felicitous with "absolutely." The (b) sentences are felicitous only under three conditions: if they represent the positive extreme of the continua, in which case they would replace the (a) sentences; if the speaker is disagreeing with someone else's statement, in which case he will use the intonation pattern for disagreeing; or if the speaker expected Harry's talk to be a terrible disaster and is acknowledging that his expectations were contradicted. In this latter case, given the speaker's expectations, even the middle term of the continua becomes tellable. These facts seem to indicate that the role of "absolutely" is precisely to call attention to the tellability of the assertion. In most cases, to use "absolutely" in the (b) sentences is to signal the tellability of the untellable and thus to produce a contradiction.

Exclamatory assertions are only the most obvious cases of relevance by tellability. Probably the bulk of our casual conversation is made up of utterances built around information that has been introduced because it is new (i.e., assertible) *and* interesting (i.e., tellable) and that is under discussion because of its tellability. Let me stress here that in distinguishing between tellability and assertibility, I am distinguishing not between two types of information, but between two uses of information. That is, I am not trying to distinguish between information or states of affairs which are in fact unexpected and those which are not. Rather, I am distinguishing between information or states of affairs that are being verbally represented because they are felt to be unexpected and those that are being represented for some other reason. Suppose I lose a tennis match that everyone expected me to win. I come home after the match and immediately say, "I lost." The information is unexpected, and I know it, but I would scarcely want to call attention to this fact, let alone make it the point of my assertion. My sentence counts as an informing assertion made in anticipation of the inevitable question, "Did you win?" but it does not count as a displaying assertion. Narrative (3) above ("Well, this friend had a little too much to drink and he attacked me and the friend came in and she stopped it") is a similar example. More generally, negative assertions like "Bill didn't come" frequently assert information presupposed to be contrary to the addressee's expectations, but they do not always assert this information *because of* its unexpectedness. When they do, they are displaying assertions; when they do not, they are not. It will not be easy to formalize the distinction I am suggesting between assertions that are relevant because they are tellable and those that are relevant for some other reason; nevertheless, some such distinction will have to be acknowledged if we are to produce a description of relevance which accurately accounts for what gets said in conversation.[12]

In particular, such a distinction will be crucial to our understanding of natural narrative, for it, too, is an utterance type whose rele-

---

12. In speech act terms, I am claiming that Searle's (1969) maxim "no remark without remarkableness," used to explain the occurrence of adverbs like "voluntarily" and "carefully," does not follow directly from his Assertibility Condition, as he implies it does. Not everything that is assertible is remarkable. The information one gives in answer to a question has no obligation to be remarkable at all.

vance is tellability. As with exclamations, in natural narrative the speaker is interested not only in reporting states of affairs, but in verbally displaying them, in enabling his audience to join him in contemplating them, responding to them, evaluating them, and interpreting them. He creates and tables a verbal version of an experience, seeking his audience's imaginative, affective, and evaluative involvement and its support for his interpretation or its help in finding a better one (recall the repeated refrain "Why he do that?" in narrative (2) above). As with exclamations, natural narratives invariably deal with states of affairs that are held to be unusual and problematic, in need of experiential and evaluative resolution. Indeed, the "unspoken permanent agenda" of topics which Labov felt was presupposed by natural narrators is itself a kind of tellability index. Most people will agree that this kind of verbal rendering and display of experience is a fundamentally human activity, one that is crucial to our well-being in the world and that affords us endless pleasure. One of the most important ways we have of dealing with the unexpected, uncertain, unintelligible aspects of our lives is to share and interpret them collectively. Carrying out this re-creative, interpretive process is one of the most important uses we make of language.

However, we ultimately wish to characterize this verbal experience-displaying, experience-sharing activity (I have not begun to do so adequately), it is clear that literary works, or at least a great many of them, are also examples of it. Like the natural narrator, the speaker of a literary work is understood to be displaying an experience or a state of affairs, creating a verbal version in which he, and we along with him, contemplate, explore, interpret, and evaluate, seeking pleasure and interpretive consensus. As with natural narratives, we expect literary works to be tellable. We expect narrative literary works to deal with people in situations of unusual conflict and stress, unusual for the characters if not for us. Even in the absence of explicit plot, we tend to assume that lyric poems, for example, present and explore states of affairs, states of mind, or emotive experiences that are assumed to be unusual or problematic. Indeed, the lyric as speech act has often been compared to the exclamation. Broadly speaking, Labov's tellability agenda is much the same for literature as it is for conversation; in fact, that agenda is probably a fairly accurate indicator of what aspects or varieties of human experience a community holds to be wonderful, amusing, terrifying, unusual, and problematic, that is, in need of interpretation and evaluation.

To extend the concepts of tellability and display from exclamatory assertions to natural narratives and literary works is to claim that those concepts can be meaningfully applied to utterances of more than a single sentence, utterances whose individual sentences probably represent a wide variety of speech act types. More broadly, the question is whether and to what extent the terms and categories designed to describe language at sentence level can be applied at the level of discourse, that is, to utterances of more than a single sentence. (In some cases, the real question seems to be whether terms originally developed by sentence theory actually belong to discourse theory.) These are questions that no one has so far answered and that most linguists and language philosophers lamentably tend to avoid by choosing one-sentence examples. Ohmann, in the paper analyzed above, steers clear of this issue by treating the literary work as a series of sentences, each of which has suspended illocutionary force. The chief objection to such a linear, sentence-by-sentence approach to discourse is that it has no way of isolating those contextual features applying to the discourse or text as a whole—no way, that is, of making precisely the kind of generalization Grice is aiming at through his Cooperative Principle and the maxims. As I suggested earlier, there is clearly a level of analysis at which utterances with a single point or purpose must be treated as single speech acts, or "discourse acts," or "texts," if we wish. Some such upward extension of the speech act approach is necessary if, for example, we are to be able to say that the one-sentence utterance "Thank you for the hideous sweater" will be inappropriate in the same contexts for the same reasons as the two-sentence utterance "Thank you for the sweater. It is hideous." The appropriateness conditions for thanking clearly apply to the sentence "It is hideous" in this context, even though that sentence may by itself be a perfectly felicitous statement of belief. Similarly, of a fictive literary work or joke, we want to be able to make the generalization that the entire discourse is understood to be fictive from the outset, not that each of its sentences is independently (and inexplicably) labeled as fictive. As Charles Fillmore observes, there is no "clear boundary between sentence grammar and text grammar" (1974:V, 7).

I suggested earlier that in cases of multisentence utterances that have a single point or purpose, there will be appropriateness conditions which, by virtue of that overall point, apply across the entire utterance. Individual sentences within such an utterance will be subject to these larger appropriateness conditions as well as to the sentence-level ones that apply to them. In saying that literary works, natural narratives, and single sentence exclamations all lay claim to relevance by tellability, I am claiming that they all have the same basic point and that ultimately, it is to this point that their individual sentences will be understood to relate.

It is perhaps less clear whether we should be able to use the label "assertion" when discussing multisentence utterances like natural narratives or literary works. Such usage is justifiable if "assertion" is used in the broad sense of an utterance that undertakes to represent a state of affairs, or in the Gricean sense of an utterance designed to produce thoughts rather than actions. This category corresponds quite closely to the class of illocutionary acts Searle defines as "representatives." In fact, Grice's distinction between thought-producing and action-producing utterances corresponds to one of the criteria used by Searle in setting up the five classes of illocutionary acts outlined earlier, namely the question of whether an illocutionary act is world-changing or world-describing. Of Searle's five classes, only representatives are characterized as world-describing. These are very broad ways of classifying the uses of language. But to the extent that they do apply, it is clear that exclamations, natural narratives, and many if not all literary works fall into the class whose primary point is thought-producing, representative or world-describing.[13] Though one could use the term "assertion" to designate this entire class, to avoid confusion and unnecessary clashes, I will replace it in what follows with the more neutral term "text" and will refer to exclamations, natural narratives and literary works as "display texts" rather than "displaying assertions." It should be understood, however, that I assume display texts to belong by definition to the representative or world-describing class. Indeed, it would seem that the notion of tellability could only refer to utterances of this type. In some cases, the state of affairs (or world) being represented, the world we are intended to have thoughts about, is a fictive or hypothetical one that will overlap (or rather claim to overlap) to varying degrees with the real world. As I have already suggested, the fiction/nonfiction distinction is neither as clear-cut nor as important as we might think, at least not in the realm of the tellable. Our capacity for verbally displaying and evaluating experience and for finding pleasure in such displays applies equally to experience which is claimed to be real as to that which is not.

Any discussion of the role played by display texts in conversation will have to recognize at least two features of such utterances: their detachability from the immediate speech context, and their susceptibility to elaboration. These two features will likewise be important to a discussion of literary works as display texts. By detachability

---

13. It will be argued that literature is often or always didactic, that is, intended to have some world-changing or action-inducing force. I think it can be shown, however, that this aim has to be viewed as indirect in an analysis of literary speech acts, since its achievement depends on first achieving the representative aim. All exempla work this way and differ in this respect from direct persuasion.

from context, I mean two things. First, because their relevance is understood to derive from tellability, display texts can be introduced into conversation rather easily. They can be volunteered, as opposed to answering or anticipating a question, and they do not have to relate in any strict logical or topical way to prior discourse. To appropriately introduce a natural narrative or anecdote, a speaker need establish only the most tenuous links with previous discussion. Very often, a superficial lexical link is all that is offered or required, as in the familiar expression, "Speaking of X's, did I tell you. . . ." Even more weakly, we can say simply "that reminds me. . . ." In general, any vague equivalence will do. "News" in conversation has an even greater freedom of occurrence. By "news" I mean tellable events, physical or psychological, that have come about "since I saw you last." Like my example of Bill at the bank, news can be volunteered at almost any moment when the floor is up for grabs. To be relevant, it does not have to relate to prior discourse at all. Because of their detachability from prior discourse, display texts frequently serve to bring about changes of topic in conversation, as simple observation will show. In fact, they are the most important device we have for changing the subject. Interestingly, we often introduce information we think of as tellable by offering as news the event through which we obtained the information, as in "say, I read the oddest thing in *Time* the other day" or "you know, I was just thinking this morning. . . ." News is also the device we most commonly use for establishing topics of conversation in situations where the topic is not predefined. Thus greetings in a great many languages take the form of requests for the tellable. In English we say "what's new?" or "what's happening?" There are parallel expressions in French, Spanish, Portuguese, Greek, Swahili, and doubtless many others.

In addition to being highly detachable from prior discourse, display texts, unlike informing texts, do not have to relate to the concrete, momentary concerns of the addressee. They are not primarily aimed at correcting the addressee's immediate knowledge or expectations of his surroundings. (As I suggested earlier, this is probably the reason we so easily tolerate exaggeration, embellishment, and fictionalizing in natural narrative.) The only hearer-based appropriateness condition for display texts is that the hearer be able to recognize and appreciate the tellability of what is being asserted. The unusual has a wide appeal indeed; consequently, in addition to being adaptable to a wide variety of speech contexts, display texts are adaptable to a wide variety of audiences. To resurrect my earlier example, the fact that Bill the bank-hating miser went to the bank can be just as tellable to an audience that doesn't know Bill as to one that does, provided I furnish the necessary background information. With such an audience, rather than making a one-sentence exclamation I would probably offer a full-fledged natural narrative, starting out with something like "The funniest thing happened today. I have this friend Bill, you know, and he hates banks with a passion. . . ." In short, display texts have a high degree of detachability both from prior discourse and from the immediate personal concerns of the participants. Consequently, in speech situations where the topic of conversation is not predefined, they have an enormous freedom of occurrence. In extreme cases, the tellable can take precedence over the current topic in almost any speech situation. The appearance of an escaped elephant would be grounds for an exclamatory interruption no matter who is talking or what the subject is. Even though the blatant beast may pose no physical threat to the interlocutors, he must be coped with verbally on the spot.

The second important feature of the tellable is that we love to elaborate on it. This is the point on which display texts differ most radically from informing texts. To return to the case of Bill at the bank, I suggested that if my interlocutors didn't know Bill, I would have to present my news as a natural narrative rather than an exclamation. But notice that even if my addressees already know all about Bill, the natural narrative would very likely occur anyway. The exchange might run as follows:

A: You're not going to believe this. *Bill* went to the *bank* today!
B: No!
C: You're joking!
A: I'm not kidding. I walk into the bank at about 11 o'clock, and there he is, standing at the teller's window with a sock full of change. I couldn't believe it! So I went up to him and I says, "Well, *Bill*, fancy meeting you here!" I says, "Whatcha up to, Bill? Opening an account?" And he got all red, and he kinda looks up at me and growls, "None o' your damn business."
B: Geez! He'll never live it down.
C: I can hardly wait to see him.
A: I thought I'd die laughing, him standing there with that crazy sock, looking up at me. Can you imagine![14]

The effectiveness of the exchange of information going on in such a dialogue has little to do with its efficiency. A's contributions are exceedingly redundant. Actually, there is no real way even of defining the efficiency of the exchange here, since there is no predefinition of what information is required by the situation. A can pile detail upon detail, and can even be blatantly repetitive, because he is understood to be enabling his audience to imagine and comprehend the state of affairs more fully and to savor it for a longer time. A is informing his audience, too, in this case. But his point is display, and the form of his utterance, like that of any utterance, can only be

---

14. Notice that a purely interpretive or descriptive display, rather than a narrative one, could also follow A's initial exclamation. That is, A's elaboration could run something like "Yep, I guess he must have run out of old socks, either that or he decided interest rates were high enough to make it worth the risk. . . ."

understood in terms of its point, as both Grice and Labov insist. In the end, tellability can take precedence over assertibility itself. As with exclamations, a natural narrator is not required to inform. With his Audience's permission, he can tell a story his interlocutors have already heard. The display context also allows text-internal repetition; that is, it allows me to reiterate what I just said and what all the participants therefore already know. Our tolerance, indeed propensity, for elaboration when dealing with the tellable suggests that, in Gricean terms, the standards of quantity, quality, and manner for display texts differ from those Grice suggests for declarative speech acts in his maxims. "Informativeness," "perspicuity," "brevity," and "clarity" are not the criteria by which we determine the effectiveness of a display text, though there are limits on how much elaboration and repetition we will find worth it. When those limits are reached in conversation, we simply move on to something else. Even the truthfulness requirement can be bent in the interests of effective elaboration. I have now no precise answer to the question of how Grice's maxims might be adjusted to accommodate these differences, but I think adjustments could be made without great violence to the theory as a whole. In particular, building the idea of tellability into the maxim of Relation would in no way threaten the validity of the Cooperative Principle. Furthermore, I think Grice would agree to the need for such an accommodation, a fact which some of his critics (notably R. Lakoff, 1974) apparently fail to recognize. Grice is aware that his maxims as formulated are incomplete. With regard to relevance in particular, Grice concludes that what he really wants the maxim of Relation to express is the hearer's right to "expect that an aspect of an utterance which it is within the power of the speaker to eliminate or vary, even if it is introduced unreflectively, will have a purpose connected with what is currently being communicated, unless, of course, its presence can be explained in some other way." (III, 15) This extended view of relevance clearly has space for the tellable, while the "exchange of information" approach does not. It is worth adding that allowing for the tellable in Grice's schema would help answer some of the questions about relevance that trouble him most, namely, what kinds of topical foci there are and how topics get established and changed in conversation.

As might be expected, these two features—contextual detachability and susceptibility to elaboration—are equally important characteristics of literary utterances, too. Literary works do not depend for their relevance on prior discourse, since there is none in the literary speech situation except in special cases like sequels, parodies, or rejoinders; nor do we expect literary works to relate to our immediate surroundings and specific personal concerns, though they certainly may. In fact, we assume the literary utterance is expressly designed to be as fully "detachable" as possible, since its success is in part gauged by the breadth of its Audience and since its legitimate addressee is ultimately anyone who can read or hear. We do not require literary works to be informative. Text-internally, the literary speech situation admits of enormous elaboration, accumulation of detail, and even pure repetition (as for example in the Faulkner and Kerouac passages quoted in chapter two). Indeed, one might say that what literary works chiefly do is elaborate on the states of affairs they posit. There is even a sense in which literary works, like natural narratives, can be viewed as elaborations on their abstracts, as the long chapter summaries of many early novels suggest. Finally, literary works can be repeated in their entirety. As with natural narratives, we can choose to hear the good ones again and again.

These facts about display texts cannot surprise us in the least, given the communicative purpose they are designed to serve, a purpose I have described as that of verbally representing states of affairs and experiences which are held to be unusual or problematic in such a way that the addressee will respond affectively in the intended way, adopt the intended evaluation and interpretation, take pleasure in doing so, and generally find the whole undertaking worth it.

The view that literary works are verbal displays designed to re-create, interpret, and evaluate experience is a familiar one to most literary scholars. The important point for the present argument is that this re-creative, interpretive activity is not unique to literature. At the very least, both literary and natural narrative are examples of it. This means that to a great extent these two utterance types exploit the same aspects of our linguistic competence. In Gricean terms, it means that the speech posture we adopt when we pick up a novel (and probably many other varieties of literature) is much the same as the one we adopt in conversation when an interlocutor says, "Wait till I tell you. . . ." To the extent that these claims are true, literature as a body need not and cannot be set apart as a use of the language different from all other uses; the many formal similarities between literary and natural narrative need not and cannot be viewed as accidental. The kind of relation that holds between reader and literary work need not and cannot be viewed as resulting from a suspension of or an immunity to the rules governing other discourse; rather it is a relationship that commonly characterizes discourse outside literature and that must be accounted for by the general rules for talk, rather than by special rules for literary discourse.

It is ironic that speech act philosophers and linguists have been so slow to recognize the extent to which assertions and representative discourse in general are used for purposes other than informing, reminding, or displaying knowledge at exams (these are the three classes of assertions recognized by Forman, 1974). In a sense, it means that they have made the same mistake about "ordinary language" that the poeticians made: they have assumed that spoken language is normally used only for immediate, utilitarian purposes such as informing or inducing action. The noninformative use of assertion, when recognized at all, is often treated as a nuisance. Gordon and Lakoff (1971:69), for example, observe that the Non-obviousness Condition does not seem to hold for "small talk," as if small talk, for all its smallness, could be treated as an uninteresting exception. R. Lakoff (1972:916) similarly views small talk as an exception to the Nonobviousness Condition. Grice, in his discussion of meaning in assertions proposes to "eliminate the amusement case" (V, 15) by postulating for it a different kind of meaning—as if it were thereby eliminated. This failure to recognize the full range of uses to which assertions are put very likely explains why literary speech acts have looked as if their "normal" illocutionary force were suspended. The plain fact is that we will never be able to describe conversation at all until we find a way to deal with the "amusement case" and "small talk." And we will never be able to describe the literary speech situation without stating its relation to such conversational types. Consider, for example, Grice's characterization of the "over-the-wall chat" as having a "second-order aim," namely, that "each party should for the time being identify himself with the transitory conversational interests of the other" (II, 11). Is this "second-order aim" not strangely reminiscent of the tie that binds the reader of a novel or lyric to its author?

Fortunately, some linguists are beginning to recognize the inadequacy of analyzing declarative speech acts as utterances primarily used to inform. Larkin and O'Malley (1973) use a barrage of conversational data to argue that the informing use of declarative speech acts is not the prime use at all and that noninforming assertions are at least as common and important as informing ones, if not more so. R. Lakoff (1973, 1974) pointedly observes that conversations governed uniquely by the maxims Grice formulates would be boring to the last degree and quite unlike our usual exchanges.[15] More generally, American linguists in the last four or five years have begun to attend to the emotive or expressive side of language, the side that

---

15. Lakoff also shows that Grice's maxims as formulated are normally sacrificed if they threaten to clash with the rules of politeness. On the basis of this

formal predicate calculus was designed to eliminate. This is a prospect which bodes well for the literary linguist.

---

observation, Lakoff argues that Grice's maxims are really a subset of the rules of politeness. I do not think this claim holds up. It is obviously not for the sake of politeness that Grice's maxims get compromised in display texts. The plausible generalization would seem to be that a cooperative speaker will usually compromise the maxims in the interests of his hearer's feelings, that is, in the interest of maintaining in the hearer the desired attitude to what the speaker is saying. This generalization could account for both the politeness case, the tellability case, and a number of the examples raised by Larkin and O'Malley. As this emotive argument suggests, a description of display texts, and indeed a basic typology of assertions may have to wait for a theory of perlocutions. Jerry Sadock's hypothesis (Sadock, 1974) that all speech acts are perlocutions and that illocutions are only one subset of perlocutions seems to suggest a possible way out for the display text. As long as answers to questions are seen as the norm for assertions, all kinds of declarative speech acts, including warning, dispute, advising, and confessing will be problematic.

Chapter Five

Literary Cooperation
and Implicature

> If a writer omits something
> because he does not know it then
> there is a hole in the story.
> ERNEST HEMINGWAY,
> Interview, *Paris Review*, 1958

So far I have discussed what are probably the three most obvious factors which an account of the literary speech situation would have to include: literary works belong to the class of utterances addressed to an Audience; within this class they belong to the subclass of utterances that presuppose a process of preparation and selection prior to the delivery of the utterance; and they belong to the subclass of utterances whose relevance is tellability and whose point is to display experience. In establishing these features, I have relied on both psychological evidence—people's attitudes toward what is said in a given context—and grammatical evidence—what actually does get said. I have suggested that these features represent information which is presupposed by participants in a literary speech situation, and I have tried to stress that they are features which also form part of the context of other utterance types. From the linguist's point of view, this latter observation means that there is independent motivation for including such features as these in a grammar of discourse; from the critic's point of view, it means that, at least so far, no motivation has been found for viewing literary discourse as generically distinct from our other linguistic activities or as exploiting any kind of communicative competence other than that which we rely on in nonliterary speech situations.

I propose now to explore further the view of utterance or text interpretation that Grice derives from his concept of the Cooperative Principle and to examine its applicability to literature. In keeping with my own general concerns, I will be looking in what follows at how the Cooperative Principle (hereafter referred to as CP) works in narrative utterances, what special cooperation is required for fictional utterances, and how we handle and interpret deviance in display texts. I am assuming, as I think we must, that the CP (formulated by Grice as "Make your contribution such as is required at the stage at which it occurs, by the accepted purpose or direction of the talk-exchange in which you are engaged") does hold for representative discourse whose purpose is not or not only informative, even though we do need to expand or alter Grice's maxims to accommodate such assertions. In the case of literature, the assumption that the writer is trying to communicate *something* is obviously a crucial one.

1. Text interpretation and implicature

Any description of text interpretation or decoding has to make use of some concept of construction, reconstruction, or "filling in." Ohmann's view of reading, for example, is typical in this respect: "The reader constructs (imagines) a speaker and a set of circumstances to accompany the quasi-speech-act," and so on. Fillmore (1974:IV, 4) offers the following description of the interpretive act:

> A text induces its interpreter to construct an image, or maybe a
> set of alternative images. The image the interpreter creates early

in the text guides his interpretation of successive portions of the text and these in turn induce him to enrich or modify that image. While the image-construction and image-revision is going on, the interpreter is also trying to figure out what the creator of the text is doing—what the nature of the communication situation is. And that, too, may have an influence on the image-creating process.

Let me stress that Fillmore's description is intended to apply to our interpretation of any discourse, not just literary works.

On the basis of his CP model of conversation, Grice derives an approach to text interpretation which allows us to be somewhat more specific about how this image-construction process comes about linguistically. The view Grice proposes is simply this: in a given speech situation, if the hearer knows that the speaker is observing the CP and its attendant maxims, the hearer, in decoding the speaker's utterance, will make all the deductions and inferences necessary to maintain the assumption that the speaker is observing the CP. Hence, to return to Grice's example, if A says to B "Bill is in Oxford or in London," then B, in order to maintain the assumption that A is observing the CP, will infer that A does not know exactly where Bill is. Grice adopts the general term *implicature* to refer to the various kinds of calculations by which we make sense of what we hear. The speaker who says "Bill is in Oxford or in London" is thus said to have *implicated* (as opposed to having *said*) that he does not know exactly where Bill is. Implicatures which are required to maintain the assumption that the CP is in force are called *conversational implicatures*. Conversational implicata, then, are "the assumptions required in order to maintain the supposition that the CP and maxims are being observed on a given occasion" (III, 1). What a speaker implicates on a given occasion is distinguishable from what he says, that is, from the literal and conventional meaning of the words he uses; what is said and what is implicated together form the meaning of the utterance in that context.

The coherence of any conversation, text, or extended utterance almost invariably depends a great deal on implicatures. Consider the simple exchange:

A: I have a headache
B: I have some aspirin in my purse.

B here implicates, among other things, that he/she is willing to make the aspirin available to A. A is entitled to assume B's willingness, since otherwise B's remark would be a violation of the maxim of relation. In the following more bizarre exchange:

A: I have a headache
B: What time is it?

B could be implicating that he believes the time of day has something to do with A's headache, or that he does not wish to discuss A's headache, or that it may be a suitable time for A to leave off doing whatever has given him the headache. Here, as in many cases of implicature, more than one explanation is possible, a fact which is exploited a great deal by writers of literature and also by politicians, press agents, advertisers, and other speakers interested in multiple meanings. Notice that B's odd response in this exchange could also be due to the fact that B has not heard A's remark or has not heard it correctly. In this case, B implicates nothing at all.

Causal and chronological sequence are frequently established by implicature. On Grice's account, in a sentence like "I wrote some letters, attended a meeting, and had lunch with a friend," an implicature is present to the effect that I did the actions in that order. If I do not wish to implicate this, I must explicitly cancel the implicature by adding a clause like "but not necessarily in that order." In a sentence like "Bill dropped the plate and it broke" both temporal and causal sequence are implicated. Where the temporal interpretation is absent, causation alone can be implicated as in "they were busy talking and missed the boat." Here, an implicature of temporal sequence is ruled out because the first clause is a progressive, denoting a state of affairs rather than an event. Again, the causal implicature may be canceled. I could say "they were busy talking and missed the boat, though they may have intended to miss it anyway."

The question of how causal and chronological links are established between clauses is one that has troubled linguists a great deal, and I will not enter into a detailed discussion of it here. Suffice it to say that any analysis of narrativity will ultimately have to give an account of our ability to implicate causality and time sequence. The rudiments of such an account may be found in the following algorithm proposed by C. Ruhl. Although Ruhl is addressing himself to sequences of clauses lexically joined by *and*, I think we can agree with Grice that "in many cases the idea of conjunction might be regarded as present even without an explicit conjunctive device" (IV, 3). Ruhl proposes:

> If a structure A-*and*-B can be analyzed as a temporal sequence, it will be. If it can further be analyzed that A is a precondition for B, it will be. And if A can be analyzed as a decisive condition—that is, a cause—of B, it will be. Only if the first stage—the temporal sequence—is not reached, will the co-ordinate structure be analyzed as symmetric. (quoted by Schmerling, 1975:214n)

(Symmetric conjunction means a logical conjunction that implicates no priority relations between the conjoined clauses, as in "Bill is in London and Jane is in Rio.") Ruhl's rule is not accurate in detail, as Schmerling (1975) points out, and it is obviously in need of elaboration.[1] I offer it only as an example of the kind of statement

---

1. If I am not mistaken, any rule of asymmetric conjunction needs to distinguish between narrative clauses as defined by Labov, that is, simple past tense clauses, and other kinds of clauses which less readily implicate temporal se-

we may eventually want to make about the pragmatics of narrative and of the kind of generalization the implicature analysis allows us to make.

Evaluated narrative of the type found in display texts relies on a far greater range of implicatures than those required to establish narrativity. According to Labov's analysis, a natural narrator is required to supply not only narrative sequence (Labov's complicating action and resolution) but also evaluative and orientative information, as well as abstract and coda. In Gricean terms, we would probably want to say that the CP and maxims as defined for narrative display texts require that the speaker know and reveal the whole story and that he enable us to understand the sequence of events and to adopt the desired attitude toward them. Given these obligations, for each expression he uses a storyteller must either say or implicate whether that expression is part of the narrative sequence, serves as background information required to understand the narrative sequence (orientation), or is evaluative information intended to influence our attitude to the sequence. Most of the time, narrators merely implicate what kind of relevance a given expression has. For example, in this sequence of nonnarrative orientation clauses from narrative (1) above,

1. I was gunnin' one night with that dog
2. we had to use live decoys in those days
3. a fellow named Jack Bumpus was with me

the relations among the clauses and their relationship to the narrative are not at all apparent; however, since the CP is in force, we

---

quence. The algorithm will vary, I think, according to whether the first conjunct does or does not denote an event. A number of Schmerling's counterexamples to analyses like Ruhl's and Grice's could be better understood if the difference between event and nonevent clauses were recognized, e.g., Schmerling's "be nice and kiss your granny" could not imply temporal sequence because the first clause is not an event.

calculate by implicature that the speaker believes this information will be useful later. If the live decoys, the dog, and Jack Bumpus played no role in what followed, to mention them would count as a violation of the maxims of Quantity and Relation and thus as a violation of the CP. Since we have no reason to think the speaker is trying to violate the CP and the maxims, we assume the information is preparatory to what follows. The narrator, furthermore, assumes we will calculate this implicature. Given the definition of a story and the assumption that the CP is in force, we calculate countless implicatures of this highly generalized and straightforward type in our dealings with narrators. On the basis of the maxim of Relation, we interpret information as narrative, orientative, or evaluative. Given the maxim of Quantity, we understand time gaps not as violations of sequence but as spaces where nothing important to the story happened; if we are not told how a character got from point A to point B, we assume he did so in some normal and untellable way.

2.   Rule-breaking and implicature

I have so far dealt only with rather routine cases of implicature, in which it is clear that the speaker is not knowingly violating any of the maxims or the CP. More detailed analysis would show, I believe, that such implicatures are the mainstay of conventional narrative, both natural and literary, and indeed form the basis of all routine decoding, as the Fillmore passage quoted earlier suggests. It ought to be clear that this reconstruction by implicature is not peculiar to fictive utterances or to literature, as many reader-oriented critics seem to think (see, for example, Ong 1975). Without implicature, it would take us a long time indeed to say anything at all. It is possible and very common, however, for speakers to fail to fulfill the conversational maxims. In conversation, unintentional failures occur all the time. Speakers get carried away on a subject and violate the maxim of Quantity, they make mistakes, become confused or incoherent, under- and overestimate what the hearer already knows, and so on. Errors of this type do not threaten the assumption that the CP is in force, that the speaker is at least trying to "make his contribution such as is required by the purposes of the exchange." They mean only that he isn't succeeding very well at the moment, whether for lack of verbal skill or for some other reason. On the whole, unintentional failures aren't very serious in conversation because the turn-taking system allows the hearer to correct the offending speaker, interrupt him, or break off the exchange. As might be expected, such unintended failures are much more serious in speaker/Audience situations where turn-taking is not in force and where the speaker is consequently indebted to the Audience and in a position of being judged. In these cases, unintentional failure can finally lead to a breakdown of the CP, usually attested to by illegitimate interruptions, indignant departures from the scene of the offense, or some other outbreak of hostility.

Cases in which a speaker *knowingly* fails to fulfill a maxim are much more interesting. Grice outlines four such cases:

1. He [a speaker] may quietly and unostentatiously *violate* a maxim; if so, in some cases he will be liable to mislead.

2. He may *opt out* from the operation both of the maxim and of the CP; he may say, indicate or allow it to become plain that he is unwilling to co-operate in the way in which the maxim requires. He may say, for example, "I cannot say more, my lips are sealed."

3. He may be faced by a *clash*; he may be unable, e.g., to fulfill the first maxim of Quantity ("Be as informative as is required") without violating the second maxim of quality ("Have adequate evidence for what you say").

4. He may *flout* a maxim; that is, he may *blatantly* fail to fulfill it. On the assumption that the speaker is able to fulfill the

> maxim and do so without violating another maxim (because
> of a clash), is not opting out, and is not, in view of the bla-
> tancy of his performance, trying to mislead, the hearer is
> faced with a minor problem: how can his saying what he did
> say be reconciled with the supposition that he is observing
> the overall CP? This situation is one which characteristically
> gives rise to a conversational implicature; and when a con-
> versational implicature is generated in this way, I shall say
> that a maxim is being *exploited*.
>
> (Grice, II, 12)

The first three cases, violation, opting out, and clashes, put the CP in jeopardy, and if serious enough they may cause it to break down. In the first two cases, it could be said that there is a lack of agreement about purposes of the exchange. In the third case there is agreement but inability to fulfill the purpose. Only in the fourth case, flouting, is the CP not ultimately in danger. This case is the most interesting to the present discussion, first because it is one of our favorite kinds of verbal play and second because it is the only kind of intentional nonfulfillment possible in the literary speech situation. In literary works, intentionally failing to observe a maxim always counts as flouting. I will elaborate on this claim shortly, but first, for purposes of clarity, I will offer a few nonliterary examples of how speakers exploit (or flout) maxims. The following are taken from or modeled on those Grice provides:

I. *Flouting the maxims of Quantity:*

a. A is writing a testimonial about a pupil who is a candidate for a philosophy job, and his letter reads as follows: "Dear Sir, Mr. X's command of English is excellent, and his attendance at tutorials has been regular, yours, etc."

Gloss: A can't be opting out, since if he wished to be uncooperative, why write at all? He can't be unable, through ignorance, to say more, since this man is his pupil, moreover, he knows that more information than this is wanted. He must, therefore, be wishing to impart information which he is reluctant to write down. This supposition is only tenable on the assumption that he thinks that Mr. X is no good at philosophy. This, then, is what he is implicating. (Grice, II, 16)

   b. A: Did John go to the party last night?
       B: He sure did, honey, and don't let anybody tell you any different!
Gloss: B has said more than is required. B has implicated there is some disagreement about whether John was at the party.

II. *Flouting the maxims of Quality:*

   a. (1) A: I hate to tell you this, but you flunked the test.
            B: Oh. That's just terrific.
Gloss: It is clear to both A and B that B has said something he does not believe; A knows that B knows that the violation is obvious to A. A calculates that B is implicating some proposition other than but related to the one he has actually said. The most obvious candidate is the reverse of what B said. Therefore B implicates that it is disastrous that he flunked the test.

       (2) Metaphor.

       (3) Meiosis. Of a man known to have broken up all the furniture, one says, "He was a little intoxicated." (Grice II, 18)

       (4) Hyperbole. "Bill hasn't been late in thirty years!"

   b. A says of B's wife, "She is probably deceiving him this evening."

Gloss: In a suitable context, or with a suitable gesture or tone of voice, it may be clear that I have no adequate reason for supposing this to be the case. My partner, to preserve the assumption that the conversational game is still being played, assumes that I am getting at some related proposition for the acceptance of which I *do* have a reasonable basis. The related proposition might well be that she is given to deceiving her husband, or possibly that she is the sort of person who wouldn't stop short of such conduct. (Grice, II, 18)

III. *Flouting the maxim of Relation:*

    a. A (unaware Bill is in the room): Bill makes me sick.
        B: Heard any good jokes lately?
Gloss: In failing to relate his remark to the preceding discourse, B is implicating either that Bill is in the room or at least that A's remark is inappropriate for discussion.

IV. *Flouting the maxims of Manner:*

    a. Obscurity:

        A: I saw you-know-who yesterday.
        B: You did?
        C: ?????
Gloss: A, by being deliberately obscure, implicates to B that he does not want C to know whom A is referring to.

    b. Failure to be brief or succinct:

Instead of saying "Miss X sang 'Home Sweet Home,' " a reviewer says "Miss X produced a series of sounds which corresponded closely with the score of 'Home Sweet Home.' "
Gloss: Why has he selected that rigmarole in place of the con-

cise and nearly synonymous "sang"? Presumably to indicate some striking difference between Miss X's performance and those to which the word "singing" is usually applied. The most obvious supposition is that Miss X's performance suffered from some hideous defect. The reviewer knows that this supposition is what is likely to spring to mind; so that is what he is implicating. (Grice, II, 21)

c. Deliberate ambiguity:

Blake's lines, "Never seek to tell thy love, Love that never told can be."

Gloss: Partly because of the sophistication of the poet and partly because of internal evidence (the ambiguity is kept up) there seems to be no alternative to supposing that the ambiguities are deliberate and that the poet is conveying both what he would be saying if one interpretation were intended rather than the other, and vice versa; though no doubt the poet is not explicitly *saying* any one of these things, but only conveying or suggesting them. (Grice, II, 20)

In all these cases of exploitation, "though some maxim is violated at the level of what is said, the hearer is entitled to assume that that maxim, or at least the overall CP, is observed at the level of what is implicated" (II, 16)[2] I suggested that exploitation is virtually the only kind of intentional nonfulfillment of maxims that the literary speech situation allows, that intentional failure to fulfill a maxim in literature always counts as flouting and is thus always intended to be resolved by implicature.

As an example, consider the third and fourth sentences of Sterne's *Life and Opinions of Tristram Shandy* (1760). Shandy, bemoaning

---

2. "Violate" is used here in the general sense of "fail to fulfill" as opposed to the special sense of "quiet and unostentatious violation" (or lying) which Grice gives it above (p. 159). Like Grice, I have also found it necessary upon occasion to use "violate" in these two senses, but I believe it is clear from the context which sense is intended in a given case.

the yet-to-be-revealed circumstances under which he was conceived, writes (emphasis mine):

> Believe me, *good folks*, this is not so inconsiderable a thing as many of you may think it;—you have all, I dare say, heard of the animal spirits, as how they are transfused from father to son, &c., &c.—and a great deal to that purpose:—Well, you may *take my word*, that nine parts in ten of a man's sense or his nonsense, his successes and miscarriages in this world depend on their motions and activity, and the different tracks and trains you put them into, so that when they are once set a-going, whether right or wrong, 'tis not a *halfpenny matter,—away they go* cluttering like *hey-go-mad*; and by making a road of it, as plain and as smooth as a garden-walk, which, when they are once used to, the Devil himself sometimes shall not be able to drive them off it.
>
> Pray, my dear, quoth my mother, have you not forgot to wind up the clock?

The reader of this passage (and remember he has just begun the book) already knows by the title that Sterne intends to treat the text as an autobiography or memoir. He knows, in other words, that Sterne intends him to bring to bear on the text his knowledge of, among other things, the rules for narration and the rules for written discourse. In so doing, the reader encounters numerous failures to fulfill the maxims of Manner, Quality, and Relation when he reads this passage. With regard to manner, the text is peppered with colloquialisms and other expressions reserved for spoken discourse (I have emphasized some of them). In addition, there are typographical abuses, notably the use of "&c." and the dashes, colons, and semicolons which allow a single sentence to run on for half a page. As for quantity, the passage is plagued with repetition. Nouns and adjectives come in redundant, legalistic doublets or quadruplets: "successes or miscarriages," "sense or nonsense," "motions and activity," "tracks and trains," "right or wrong," "plain and smooth." In addition, given that Shandy is assuming his readers "have all heard of the animal spirits" it is quite possible that his own reformulation of the doctrine is less relevant here than he thinks. This is the more true given the passage's role in the narrative. Quite clearly, Shandy intends here to give us orientative and evaluative commentary which will permit us to adopt the desired attitude to the circumstances of his conception. But he has not yet told us what the circumstances were, and we thus have no events to which to relate the lengthy evaluation. The first narrative clause in the book does not occur until the end of the chapter, with the sentence "Pray, quoth my mother . . . ," a sentence which itself lacks orientation and relevance. As the reader of *Tristram Shandy* quickly discovers, evaluation often precedes (and engulfs) the event in this book, and Shandy's failure to keep his orientations from blossoming into huge narrative digressions often pushes the event even farther into the offing.

In decoding this passage, the reader does not for a moment think that the failures to fulfill certain maxims that apply to Shandy's utterance are due to ignorance, carelessness, lack of skill, or uncooperativeness on Sterne's part. Rather, he interprets them as being ultimately in accord with the "accepted purpose of the [literary] exchange." In other words, Sterne is immediately understood to be *flouting* the rules for narrative and the rules for writing and to be observing the CP at the level of what is implicated. As in the Gricean examples in (4) above, we take it that Sterne here is indicating that the contrast between the manner we expected and the manner we get is related to his own display-producing intent. The violations themselves are amusing, and since amusement is an accepted purpose of display texts, Sterne at least implicates that his intent is to amuse us. He is also calling our attention to the difference between Shandy's way of ordering his experience and our own, to the lack of consensus between us and the fictional speaker. He may also be implicating, for example, a critique of contemporary stylistic norms or orientative information about Shandy's psychological makeup, which we will need to respond as desired to what follows. This opening passage leaves unanswered the question of whether we are to interpret the failures as intentional or unintentional on Tristram Shandy's part. Shandy, the fictional speaker, could be guilty of any or all the kinds of maxim nonfulfillment; Sterne, the real-world author, cannot.

As a second example, reconsider the opening sentence of *Pride and Prejudice* discussed earlier: "It is a truth universally acknowledged that a single man in possession of a fortune must be in want of a wife." At the point he encounters this sentence in the text, possibly the only knowledge the reader has about the "nature of the communication situation," as Fillmore would say, is the fact that he is reading a novel called *Pride and Prejudice* written by someone named Jane Austen. Let us assume that the label "novel" entitles the reader to assume he is confronting a narrative display text. (I will be supporting this claim a little later on.) Since the sentence in question immediately follows the narrative abstract (the title), contains no narrative clauses and no orientative information about setting and participants, the reader infers that the sentence is relevant either as a continuation of the abstract (the "brief summary of the point of the story") and/or as an evaluative statement about events to be narrated. On the basis of this information, the reader infers that the sentence is, as Ohmann says, "a tip-off to the fact that the narrator of the story is being ironic." I argued earlier that, contrary to Ohmann's claim, the fact that the text is fictional is neither necessary or sufficient grounds on which to justify this inference. Let me attempt a brief Gricean account.

In Grice's view, the words "true" and "truth" refer to properties of utterances, not states of affairs. On this account, then, if I say "it is true that Bill is a miser," I am making a comment not about Bill but about the assertion "Bill is a miser." If no such assertion has actually been made, I am implicating that someone might make such an assertion (Grice, III, 21ff). This is the case with Austen's sentence. The speaker of this sentence is making a claim about a hypothetical assertion regarding the interests of moneyed bachelors. Furthermore, the assertion about which the claim is made is one with which the reader is likely to disagree, that is, one he is likely to regard as failing to fulfill one or the other of the maxims of Quality. The speaker of Austen's sentence, however, says he believes this assertion does fulfill the maxims of Quality ("it is a truth") and also that he believes there is no disagreement about this fact (it is "universally acknowledged"). But there is disagreement—notably the reader's own. Consequently, from the reader's point of view, Austen's sentence itself fails to fulfill the first maxim of Quality, or at least the second.

There are a number of ways the reader could account for the failure. Where p is the assertion "a single man in possession of a fortune must be in want of a wife" and q is the assertion that p is a "truth universally acknowledged," he could infer:

1. The speaker actually does believe both p and q and is thus merely ignorant of the ways of bachelors and of what other people think about the ways of bachelors. In this case, the failure is *unintentional*.

2. The speaker believes p but not q. In this case, the speaker in saying q is *flouting* the second maxim of Quality, as in Grice's example 2(b) above, by saying something for which he lacks adequate evidence. He is implicating that many people besides himself believe p and that the reader should believe p too.

3. The speaker believes neither p nor q but is naively trying to get us to think he does. In this case, he is *violating* the maxims of Quality in order to mislead us either about the truth of p or about his own beliefs about q.

4. The speaker believes neither p nor q and is being *ironic*. In this case, the speaker is saying q is *flouting* the first maxim of Quality and is implicating that his attitude to p is something other than that expressed in q. As in Grice's example 2(a) above, the speaker

is most likely implicating that his attitude is the opposite of that expressed in q, i.e., he is implicating that he emphatically disbelieves that p and that q. But, as Grice points out, irony also involves the expression of an emotive attitude as well as a propositional one. Since the speaker of Austen's sentence is also implicating that p is an assertion which might be made, then in implicating that q is false, the speaker is also implicating an ironic (contemptuous, mocking) attitude to those who would make the assertion p.

The reader of Austen's sentence has no trouble deducing that Austen is saying what is said in (4) and that given the sentence's location in the text, she is further implicating that the ironic attitude to p is relevant to our correctly understanding and evaluating what is to follow. This is the "tip-off" Ohmann refers to. For some reason, we know unequivocally that the author is not trying to communicate (1), (2), or (3). Notice that it does remain possible at this point in the text that interpretations (1) through (3), as well as (4), could apply to the fictional speaker of Austen's novel. That is, the narrator could be someone other than Austen's fictional mouthpiece, someone stupid or naive enough to hold the beliefs and intentions necessary for the first three positions, though if this were the case, Austen would have to immediately and explicitly indicate it or risk a misunderstanding with the reader. Though this case would engender further implicatures, it would not alter the fact that what Austen is saying in the sentence is at least what is said in (4).

Just as it is possible to imagine a naive fictional narrator who, in uttering Austen's sentence, did not intend to be ironic (cf. Richardson's Pamela: "For what could he get by ruining such a poor young creature as me?" Letter III) so, as I suggested in chapter three (note 5), one can easily imagine real-life speech contexts in which Austen's sentence could be used in any of the ways outlined in (1) through (3), a letter to or from Ann Landers, for example. How do we know, then, that Austen is implicating disbelief in p and q? Similarly, how do we know right from the first dash that Sterne is flouting the rules rather than breaking them unintentionally or for some other reason? How do we know that we are smiling with Austen and Sterne and not at them?

Let us begin with the question of how we know the failures are not unintentional ones. In the case of the Sterne passage, one could argue simply that they are so numerous and extreme that no adult speaker of English could have produced them unintentionally. But actually, it is not difficult to imagine an utterance as babbling and incoherent as Tristram Shandy's occurring quite naturally in conversation. The fact that we see the failures in the passage as extreme, then, derives in part from the fact that we assume this utterance to have been composed in writing, subject to deliberation and revision. But even this is not enough. Within the realm of written composition, it is not difficult to imagine the occurrence of utterances as defective as this one. Run-on sentences, overuse of dashes and semicolons, confusion of formal and colloquial registers, failure to stick to the point—these are standard sins of student compositions and even of the drafts of more experienced writers, to say nothing of less monitored forms of written discourse like letters, diaries, suicide notes, or "writing behavior" in mental institutions. Clearly, it is not the intrinsic properties of the Sterne passage which tell us that in each case of an unfulfilled maxim, the nonfulfillment is intentional. It is the fact that the passage occurs in a work of literature. But what do we know about works of literature which tells us the failures are intentional? We know that had Sterne not intended his text to be this way, his publishers and editors would not have enabled it to appear this way. If the deviance in the passage were there because Sterne was ignorant of the basic rules for written discourse, literary narrative, and fictional autobiography or so unskilled as to be incapable of observing them, his text would never have evolved into a book (at least not in this form) any more than a high school essay with the same sins could appear in a scholarly journal. Similarly, suppose Jane Austen had not intended the opening sentence of her book to be ironic, in which case the sentence is a falsehood. Probably either Austen or her editor would have noticed it and changed it. And even if Austen had been a person whose knowledge of the social world was so limited that she sincerely believed the assertions *p* and *q* were true, it is mostly unlikely that her editor would not have anticipated the reader's disagreement and suggested some less polemical way of beginning the book. Indeed, if the entire text were as naive and prescriptive as the first sentence (taken literally), the editor would very likely have returned the manuscript; certainly we would not be reading the book as avidly as we do today.

In short, we know the violations in the Sterne and Austen passages are intentional because of what we know about the circumstances under which literary works are composed, edited, selected, published, and distributed. The literary pre-paration and pre-selection processes are designed to eliminate failures which result from carelessness or lack of skill. The more selection and revision processes we know a work has gone through, the less likely we will be to attribute apparent inconsistencies and inappropriatenesses to random and unintentional error. Recall Grice's expanded maxim of Relation: "An aspect of an utterance which it is within the power of the speaker to eliminate or vary, even if it is introduced unreflectively, will have a purpose connected with what is currently being communicated, unless, of course, its presence can be explained in some other way" (III, 15). The preparation and selection processes are designed to reduce the likelihood of there being any "other way" in works of literature. Textual criticism is built on this assumption. This is not to say, of course, that we do or should assume all literary works to be somehow perfect. It means only that in literary works, the range of deviations which will be construed as unintentional is smaller than in many other speech contexts. Put the other way around, in literary works the range of deviations which will be construed as intentional is much larger. All works of literature carry the message that there are at least some readers for whom unintentional failure in the text was not sufficient to bring about a breakdown of the CP, namely the readers who approved the text for publication.

It is one thing to know that the failures to fulfill relevant maxims in the Sterne and Austen passages are intentional; it is another to know that, of the four types of intentional nonfulfillment Grice discusses, we are dealing in these passages with cases of flouting, not opting out, clash, or violation. Why couldn't Austen be trying to mislead us (violation)? Why couldn't Sterne be trying to make his text boring and unreadable (opting out)? How do we know that these failures are of the kind that does not endanger the CP? In other words, how do we know that we are to assume the maxims and CP are being observed at the level of what is implicated, and that we are expected to resolve the violations by calculating implicatures? Again, it is our tacit knowledge of the literary speech situation that enables us to make the flouting interpretation, not the intrinsic features of the utterances themselves. The literary speech situation is such that it is virtually impossible for an author to be guilty of any of the other kinds of intentional nonfulfillment Grice mentions.

Consider Grice's cases of *opting out* and *clashes*. In both these cases, the speaker fails to "cooperate in the way in which the maxim requires," in the first case because he is unwilling to do so and in the second because he is unable to do so without violating another maxim. Neither of these cases can apply to the author in the literary speech situation because literary utterances, like all display texts, are never "required" at all. They are always volunteered. (Even works produced in response to desperate financial pressures are legitimately read as volunteered material.) It is impossible to imagine a speaker *volunteering* an utterance whose purpose he is unwilling to accomplish or whose purpose he knows in advance he is unable to accomplish. A speaker cannot volunteer the remark "I don't know what time it is" (except as an oblique way of asking for the time) for the same reason a speaker cannot volunteer the exclamation "It isn't incredible what big feet he has!" or start telling a story he does not believe to be tellable. As Grice's example 1(a) above suggests, volunteering an utterance is always opting in, and one cannot opt in and out at once. If a writer knows himself to be unwilling or unable to address his Audience satisfactorily, then he need not speak at all, and it will be contradictory in the first case and pointless in the second for him to do so. The speaker of a literary work may indeed opt out of the conventional rules for a given genre, as Sterne does, but because the writer is understood to be *seeking out* an Audience, this opting out cannot count as a genuine threat to the CP. It counts instead as flouting, and the writer implicates that breaking the rules was in accord with his communicative intent. He is exploiting the rules not to endanger the CP, but to fulfill it. Real opting out, on the other hand, does jeopardize the CP. The speaker who really opts out is genuinely refusing to "make his utterance adequate to the current purpose of the exchange." Similarly, it is possible to imagine a *clash* of sorts in the literary speech situation. A writer may want to write, say, about incest, but he knows he would clash with social, linguistic and literary taboos on the subject. If he goes ahead and talks about incest anyway, then willy-nilly he has *flouted* the taboos, for he never was required to talk about incest; and if he doesn't talk about it, the clash he confronted privately never becomes apparent to the reader.

The third type of intentional nonfulfillment Grice mentions is "quiet and unostentatious" *violation,* the case which produces lies or misrepresentations. This case is certainly possible in nonfictional display texts, though the literary selection process has an obligation to keep falsehoods of any consequence out of print. We have libel laws to cover this possibility. But in the case of fictional display texts, genuine lying is out of the question. Even if it were possible for an author (as opposed to a fictional narrator) to lie about his fictional world, or about his attitude to it, he could not thereby mislead. The reader would be unable to detect the lie unless he were given clues by the author, in which case the author has flouted rather than violated the maxim of Quality. This kind of flouting, as we shall see, does occur in novels.

In sum, the literary speech situation is such that at the level of author/reader interaction, all Grice's types of nonfulfillment except flouting either cannot arise or tend to be eliminated in the process of a text's becoming a work of literature. Given his knowledge of how literary works come into being, the reader is entitled to assume, among other things, that he and the writer are in agreement about the "purpose of the exchange"; that the writer was aware of the appropriateness conditions for the literary speech situation and for the genre he has selected; that he believes this version of the text successfully accomplishes his purpose and is "worth it" to us; and that at least some readers agree with him, notably the publishers, and perhaps the professor who assigned the book or the friend who recommended it. From the writer's point of view, these assumptions greatly increase the possibilities for exploiting maxims in his text. By the same token, it is these assumptions which entitle readers to treat an unusually wide range of deviations as floutings in literary works. In contexts where some or all of these assumptions are not in play, as with a teacher reading student term papers, for example, a reader may indeed be unable to decide whether a given deviation was unintentional, or the result of opting out (i.e., not trying), a clash, or flouting.

In distinguishing between the fictional speaker of a work of literature and its real-world speaker, the author, I have tacitly adopted the view that many literary works are, as Ohmann puts it, "imitation speech acts" (1974:54). Though I disagree with Ohmann on the consequences of that view, I think such an analysis is in itself correct and necessary if we are to describe the reader's role in the literary speech situation. Like Ohmann, I would apply this view only to the traditional category "imaginative literature"; however, as discussed in chapter three, I would not maintain that this category alone constitutes literature. In a great many cases, then, a literary work may be described as a display text that is composed and addressed to us by an author and in which one or more fictional speakers in a fictional speech situation form a discourse whose intended addressee may or may not include us, the readers of the work. Readers of such literary works are in theory attending to at least two utterances at once—the author's display text and the fictional speaker's discourse, whatever it is. (This duality is not always exploited by the author, as I shall discuss shortly.) At the level of the author's utterance, virtually all failures to fulfill the CP and maxims as they apply to display texts of the genre in question will be interpreted as flouting. Within the fictional speaker's utterance, however, all kinds of nonfulfillment are possible. For example, as I suggested earlier, the reader encountering the Sterne passage might quite legitimately hypothesize that the failure to fulfill the maxims of Relation and Manner are due to naiveté or ignorance on Shandy's part, but this hypothesis in no way alters the fact that Sterne is flouting those maxims. Authors, in others words, can mimetically represent all kinds of nonfulfillment, for what counts as a lie, a clash, an opting out, or an unintentional failure on the part of the fictional speaker (or writer) counts as a flouting on the part of the real-world author and involves an implicature that the nonfulfillment is in accord with the purpose of the exchange in which the reader and author are engaged.

Now there is an important connection to be made between the fact that an author can *mimetically* represent all kinds of nonfulfillment and the fact that he can *really* perform only one. Before making this connection, however, I shall offer a few novelistic examples of the ways in which the fictional speaker of a work of literature can fail to fulfill the CP and maxims as required. Obviously, in order to detect a violated maxim, we must have a predefined idea of how the CP and maxims are defined for the fictional utterance in the first place. For the sake of clarity, I have therefore chosen examples in which the fictional speech act has a definite real-world correlate—letters, memoir, biography, natural narrative, and so on —and will concern myself for the moment only with cases in which the fictional speaker fails to fulfill the CP and maxims as defined for the utterance type *he* is performing, as opposed to violations of purely novelistic norms to which the fictional speaker is not himself subject. In each case, the assumption is that, regardless of what the fictional speaker is doing, the author is producing a display text, and it is this assumption which determines the implicatures by which we resolve the fictional speaker's violations at the level of our dealings with the author.

Opting out

As it turns out, much of the deviance in *Tristram Shandy* actually results not from unintentional failure, but from opting out on Shandy's part. Opting out, you will recall, is the case in which the speaker "says, indicates or allows it to become plain that he is unwilling to cooperate in the way the maxim requires," and it is one of the cases that, I suggested, places the CP in jeopardy. Consider the following passage from chapter 6 of *Tristram Shandy*, in which Shandy addresses the reader:

> As you proceed further with me, the slight acquaintance which is now beginning betwixt us, will grow into familiarity; and that, unless one of us is in fault, will terminate in friendship.—*O diem praeclarum!*—then nothing which has touched me will be thought trifling in its nature or tedious in its telling. Therefore, my dear friend and companion, if you should think me somewhat sparing of my narrative on my first setting out,—bear with me,—and let me go on, and tell my story my own way:—or if I should seem now and then to trifle along the road,—or should sometimes put on a fool's cap with a bell to it, for a moment or two as we pass along,—don't fly off,—but rather courteously give me credit for a little more wisdom than appears upon my outside,—and as we jogg on, either laugh with me, or at me, or in short, do anything,— only keep your temper. (p. 11)

In this passage, Shandy opts out of several of the main obligations of the autobiographer, the obligations precisely *not* to "trifle along the way" (maxim of Relation), *not* to be "sparing of his narrative" (maxim of Quantity) and *not* to "put on a fool's cap with a bell to it" (maxim of Manner). The speaker of an autobiography is by definition engaged in an exchange requiring him to narrate the story of his life and adopt a serious evaluative attitude toward his narrative, or at least some attitude other than just humor. To the extent that the CP and maxims as defined for autobiographies include such requirements, Shandy's utterance, he warns us, will not be "such as is required for the purposes of the exchange." And indeed, it is not. The only maxim which Shandy does not fail to fulfill in his book is the maxim of Quality ("Do not say that which you know to be false").

Now this kind of opting out is serious indeed in a speaker/Audience situation, given the speaker's position of indebtedness. But in telling his Audience to "bear with him" and "keep his temper," Shandy opts out of even the indebtedness rule. He merely orders the Audience not to let his opting out jeopardize the CP. It is rather like answering an exam question with "I don't know, but don't hold it against me" or like withholding the punch line of a joke and expecting the Audience to laugh anyway. Though he knows he is engaged in a speaker/Audience situation, it turns out that for Shandy, what is "required for the purposes of the exchange" is no more than would be required if he and the reader were engaged in a casual conversation. Shandy's manner is colloquial and conversational, and, as critics have often noted, the rules of Relation and Quantity which Shandy observes are likewise those governing conversation, not autobiographies. Relevance in Shandy's text is not determined by whether a piece of information contributes to our understanding or evaluation of his life. Rather, tellability alone counts as sufficient relevance, just as it does in conversation. And as in conversation, only the most tenuous metaphorical, lexical, or semantic associations are required to motivate a change of subject. Or, if the information is tellable enough, no link to prior discourse is required at all:

> I will not finish that sentence till I have made an observation on the strange state of affairs between the reader and myself . . . for the very novelty of it alone, it must be worth your worships attending to. (p. 285)

To say that Shandy structures his utterance according to the rules of conversation is not to say that he is oblivious to his narrative obligations or to the fact that the point of the exchange has been pre-defined as autobiography. If he were, his violations would be unintentional. Shandy at least in part recognizes his autobiographical obligations, as the passages I have quoted suggest, and at least in part he fulfills them. But he does not consider himself uniquely bound by them. He reserves the right at any time to opt out of the marked speaker/Audience situation that autobiography presupposes and instead to treat his relation to the reader as a conversational one. Thus in the passage quoted earlier, he depicts himself and the reader as "companions" walking a road together; the purpose of the encounter is for them to become friends, for their "slight acquaintance" to "grow into familiarity." Any danger to the CP arising from this arrangement will be due not to Shandy's failure to fulfill the reader's Audience expectations (a personal failure), but to a deficiency in the friendship (an interpersonal failure). In sum, the speech situation Shandy recognizes in this passage is not a speaker/Audience one at all, but rather the one Grice described for the "over-the-wall-chat" in which the "common aim" is "a second order one, namely that each party should for the time being identify himself with the transitory conversational interests of the other" (II, 11). It is this speech situation—not a speaker/Audience one—in which "nothing which has touched me will be thought trifling in its nature, or tedious in its telling." Says Shandy himself, "Writing, when properly managed, (as you may be sure I think mine is) is but a different name for conversation" (109). Throughout his text, the rules for writing and the rules for autobiographical narrative are optional, and may be set aside at any time in favor of the rules for conversation. Obviously, much of the humor of *Tristram Shandy* results from this attempt to import the CP and maxims as defined for conversation into the autobiographical speech situation, a situation which is a priori marked with respect to conversation. The attempt is as hopeless as it is outrageous, since Shandy cannot incorporate into his text the one set of rules which most clearly distinguishes autobiography from conversation, namely the rules for turn-taking. The reader may indeed be walking a road with Tristram, but his mouth has been securely taped shut. As to why we should enjoy such a plight . . . I will not finish that sentence until chapter six. In the meantime, you must accept Tristram Shandy's explanation: "for the very novelty of it alone. . . ."

As I mentioned earlier, opting out is one kind of nonfulfillment which puts the CP in jeopardy. Shandy's opting out quite clearly does so. As an autobiography, his text is a disaster. (One need only imagine a historical researcher encountering it in the autobiography section of the library.) But at the highest level of analysis, the level at which the text is defined as a novel by Sterne, Shandy's opting out counts as Sterne's flouting, and rather than jeopardizing the CP, it is understood to be there as a contribution toward fulfilling Sterne's own communicative intent, the intent to produce a display text.[3] The difference between what Shandy says and what a speaker in his position might be expected to say is part of what Sterne is displaying.

Clashes

A clash occurs when a speaker is unable to fulfill one maxim in

---

3. It could be argued that Shandy is producing a display text, too, and intends to. This does not alter the fact that he has opted out of the rules for autobiography.

the way required because doing so would require him to violate another maxim. The fictional speaker of Tommaso Landolfi's short story "Gogol's Wife" (1963) is faced with several such clashes. He is writing a biography of Gogol, of which the given text purports to be one chapter. The "chapter" opens thus:

> At this point, confronted with the whole complicated affair of Nikolai Vassilevitch's wife, I am overcome by hesitation. Have I any right to disclose something which is unknown to the whole world, which my unforgettable friend himself kept hidden from the world (and he had his reasons), and which I am sure will give rise to all sorts of malicious and stupid misunderstandings? Something, moreover, which will very probably offend the sensibilities of all sorts of base, hypocritical people, and possibly of some honest people too, if there are any left? And finally, have I any right to disclose something before which my own spirit recoils, and even tends toward a more or less open disapproval?
>
> But the fact remains that, as a biographer, I have certain firm obligations. Believing as I do that every bit of information about so lofty a genius will turn out to be of value to us and to future generations, I cannot conceal something which in any case has no hope of being judged fairly and wisely until the end of time. (p. 298)

The speaker here is faced with a clash between the maxims of Quantity and Manner. As a biographer, he is required by the maxim of Quantity ("Make your contribution as informative as is required") to reveal information which would lead to an increased knowledge and understanding of the subject's life and character; at the same time the maxims of Manner (some subset of the "be polite" rules) require that he not knowingly cast his subject in a poor light or leave him open to unmerited criticism. Now it is clearly illegitimate to discuss such a clash in a biography. For to say that there is something to reveal and then fail to reveal it is to opt out of the maxim of Quantity and to put the CP in jeopardy. The kind of clash the speaker here faces is the kind writers have to resolve before publishing their texts. The speaker here resolves the clash in favor of Quantity, at the risk of endangering the CP by violating the maxims of Manner. He will, he decides, reveal to us the grim truth about Gogol's wife. Notice, too, that the grounds on which he resolves the clash are logically flawed. According to the last sentence quoted, the upcoming revelation will never be judged fairly but will nevertheless turn out to be of value. Since fair judgment is an important criterion of value in a biography, the speaker's beliefs ought to have led him to resolve his clash in the opposite way, in favor of Manner. The question remains whether this mistake is unintentional or intentional. (The horror to be revealed is that Gogol's wife was an inflatable rubber doll which the dying Gogol eventually exploded and burned along with some of his manuscripts. Gogol, in fact, was never married.) [4]

Pages later, a clash between the maxims of Quantity and Quality emerges:

> Finally, I should speak of her [Gogol's wife's] voice, which it was only once given me to hear. But I cannot do that without going more fully into the relationship between husband and wife, and in this I shall no longer be able to answer to the truth of everything with absolute certitude. On my conscience I could

---

4. Landolfi's parodic intent will perhaps be better understood in the light of the following passage from a real biography of Gogol. The reader will not fail to appreciate the similarities between this passage and those I have quoted from Landolfi's story, particularly as regards clashes:

It is striking that Gogol appears to have had no relationships with women, either in his free and easy St. Petersburg years or later. This circumstance has provided psychoanalysts with a great deal of material for strange hypotheses, but it would hardly pay to go into them. As always in such cases, a grain of truth is present, but the attempt to explain the whole body of Gogol's works, his religious upheaval, his illnesses on the basis of sexual inhibitions, is certainly farfetched. His sexual attitudes are usually explained by excessive onanism during his school days; and this is also said to have led to severe psychic depressions, since Gogol saw in it a grievous sin. Gogol himself emphatically denied this assertion at the end of his life. The alleged evidence for it lacks plausibility. It

not—so confused, both in itself and in my memory, is that which I now have to tell.

Here, then, as they occur to me, are some of my memories. (p. 302)

As the last line shows, the clash is again resolved in favor of Quantity, at the risk of violating the second maxim of Quality, "Do not say that for which you lack adequate evidence."

Finally, at the climax of the story, another clash between Quality and Quantity occurs:

> The true reason why I wished to see [what else Gogol had thrown in the fire besides his wife and his manuscripts] was because I had already glimpsed. But it was only a glimpse, and perhaps I should not allow myself to introduce even the slightest element of uncertainty into this true story. And yet, an eyewitness account is not complete without a mention of that which the witness knows with less than complete certainty. To cut a long story short, that something was a baby. (p. 309)

Again, the clash is resolved in favor of the maxim of Quantity at the expense of the maxim of Quality, and again, the grounds on which the clash is resolved ("an eyewitness account is not complete, etc. . . .") are logically flawed.

The speaker concludes his chapter by assessing the degree to which he has accomplished his communicative purpose:

> I hope I have thrown sufficient light on a most controversial question and that I have unveiled the mystery, if not of Gogol, then at least of his wife. In the course of this I have implicitly given the lie to the insensate accusation that he ill-treated or even beat

---

may be that there is something to these claims, but one should guard against exaggerations (Vsevolod Setchkarev, *Gogol: His Life and Works*, trans. Robert Kramer [New York: New York University Press, 1965], pp. 38–39).

> his wife, as well as other like absurdities. And what else can be
> the goal of a humble biographer such as the present writer but to
> serve the memory of that lofty genius who is the object of his
> study? (p. 309)

What Landolfi is implicating, of course, is that in resolving the
clashes the way he did, in favor of Quantity and at the expense of
Quality and Manner, the speaker quite undermines his communicative purpose and fails altogether to fulfill the CP and maxims as
required for biographies. He has given us a great deal of unreliable
information which casts more outrageous aspersions on Gogol's
character than the "absurdities" he intended to refute; furthermore,
the clashes are resolved on faulty logical grounds, which themselves
are enough to endanger the CP.

Unintentional failure

Unintentional failure on the part of a fictional speaker can result
from carelessness or ignorance or from some temporary or permanent perceptual limitation such as psychological trauma, obsession,
insanity, or delirium. Unintentional failure is often used in narrative
to produce what the Russian Formalists called "estrangement" or
"deautomatisation of perception." In all cases of unintentional failure on the part of the fictional speaker, the author implicates the
cause of the failure and calls our attention to the contrast between
what the speaker said and what we might have expected him to say.
One famous example is the opening passage of Faulkner's *The
Sound and the Fury* (1929) in which a mentally retarded man,
Benjy, describes a golf game:

> Through the fence, between the curling flower spaces, I could
> see them hitting. They were coming toward where the flag was
> and I went along the fence. Luster was hunting in the grass by
> the flower tree. Then they put the flag back and they went to the

table, and he hit and the other hit. Then they went on, and I went along the fence. Luster came away from the flower tree and we went along the fence and they stopped and we stopped and I looked through the fence while Luster was hunting in the grass.

"Here, caddie." He hit. They went away across the pasture. I held to the fence and watched them going away.

The passage, you will note, is a narrative, albeit a rudimentary one. It has an orientation (the first three sentences), a sequence of chronologically ordered narrative clauses, a resolution ("they went away") and even a coda of sorts ("I watched them going away"). It is certainly not a felicitous narrative, however. In Gricean terms, its infelicity arises mainly from violations of the maxims of Quantity and Manner. The orientation provides a good deal less information about participants and setting than the maxim of Quantity requires. Within the narrative sequence, causal relations are not indicated and information which has causal relevance is omitted. For example, in the putting sequence—"They took the flag out, and they were hitting. Then they put the flag back."—Benjy fails to state or implicate the causal connection among the three clauses. This discontinuity arises obviously from his failure to mention the ball, which he has either failed to see or failed to consider relevant. The maxims of Manner are violated in a way not unlike Grice's example 4(b) on page 162 (the reviewer who says "Miss X produced a series of sounds which closely resembled the score of 'Home Sweet Home'"). In both cases, the speaker uses paraphrase where briefer and more accurate terms are available. Benjy, for example, takes six clauses to say what could reduce to "they putted and then teed off at the next hole." The essential difference between the two examples, of course, is that Grice's reviewer has intentionally failed to use the word *sing*, whereas terms like *golf*, *putt*, *tee*, and *course* are unavailable to Benjy. By failing to use these terms, then, Benjy is implicating nothing at all, though, again, Faulkner is implicating a great deal. Perhaps the most striking fact about Benjy's narrative is that it is completely lacking in evaluation and in this respect fails in both Quantity and Manner.

With respect to Benjy, the violations in the passage are unintentional, but Faulkner, like Grice's reviewer, is flouting the maxims of Manner and Quantity. Both Faulkner and the reviewer are indicating that part of what they are trying to communicate is implicated by the contrast between what they have said and what they might have been expected to say. Given the context of the reviewer's remark (a review), the reader quickly relates the reviewer's flouting to his evaluative intent. Given the context of the Faulkner passage (the opening of a novel), the floutings are understood to be related to Faulkner's experience-displaying intent. Faulkner is implicating not that golf is a silly waste of time, but that among other things, the speaker of the story has some cognitive or perceptual impediment, that this fact is relevant to our understanding of what follows, and that he intends us to share, contemplate, and evaluate Benjy's view of the world and contrast it with our own.

Benjy's violations, especially his failure to orient, evaluate, and maintain causal sequence, produce a particularly modern form of estrangement to which we often apply terms like "alienation" or "the absurd." The narrative failures we observe in Benjy's passage are the same ones we commonly associate with the novelistic technique of such writers as Camus, Kafka, or Robbe-Grillet. It is probably not an accident that we should apply the term "alienation" ("making other") to the effect produced in us by disoriented, unevaluated, and causally incoherent narrative. According to Labov, it is exactly these features which, at a certain stage of our linguistic development, distinguish the way we render *vicarious* experience from the way we render *personal* experience. Labov's studies of child narrative showed that by the time children reach preadolescence (9-12 years), they are often able to produce competent and effective narratives of personal experience; however, they are quite unable to reproduce and evaluate vicarious experience. Here, for example, is a preadolescent account of an episode from the TV series *The Man from U.N.C.L.E.*:

(1) This kid—Napoleon got shot and he had to go on a mission. And so this kid, he went with Solo. So they went and this guy—they went through this window, and they caught him. And then he beat up them other people. And they went and then he said that this old lady was his mother and then he—and at the end he say that he was the guy's friend. (Labov, 1972:367)

Labov comments:

This is typical of many such narratives of vicarious experience that we collected. We begin in the middle of things without any orientation section; pronominal reference is many ways ambiguous and obscure throughout. But the meaningless and disoriented effect . . . has deeper roots. None of the remarkable events that occur is *evaluated*. (Labov, 1972:367)

The similarities between the *Man from U.N.C.L.E.* narrative and the Faulkner text are unmistakable. Labov contrasts the vicarious narrative with the following preadolescent narrative of *personal* experience:

(2) When I was in fourth grade—no, it was in third grade—this boy he stole my glove. He took my glove and said that his father found it downtown on the ground. (And you fight him?) I told him it was impossible for him to find downtown 'cause all those people were walking by and just his father was the only one that found it? So he got all (mad). Then I fought him. I knocked him all out in the street. So he say he give. And I kept on hitting him. Then he started crying and ran home to his father. And the father told him that he ain't find no glove.

One would need two drastically different grammars to describe narratives (1) and (2). Somewhere in the linguistic (and presumably the cognitive) competence of the ten-year-old, there is a radical distinction between vicarious and personal experience (and thus between first and third person narrative). Benjy, however, lacks this distinction. He uses only one grammar, the grammar of (1), to render all experiences, including personal ones. In fact, Faulkner actually obliterates the vicarious/personal distinction in the opening passage by interspersing the two kinds of experience and using the same language—the language of vicariousness—to render both. Benjy is both a spectator (of the golf game) and an agent in the passage, but his two roles are linguistically undistinguished in his speech. Benjy's speech may not be anything like that of a retarded adult, nor do we need to know anything about retarded speech to respond to Faulkner's style here. All we need to imagine Benjy's world is our own linguistic and cognitive past.

The narrator of Camus' *L'Etranger* (*The Stranger*, 1942) likewise uses the grammar of the various to render his own experience. (Due to the looseness of the standard English translation, this passage is given in French. The English version is given below.)

> Le concièrge a traversé la cour et m'a dit que le directeur me demandait. Je suis allé dans son bureau. Il m'a fait signer un certain nombre de pièces. J'ai vu qu'il était habillé de noir avec un pantalon rayé. Il a pris le téléphone en main et il m'a interpellé: "Les employés des pompes funèbres sont là depuis un moment. Je vais leur demander de venir fermer la bière. Voulez-vous auparavant voir votre mère une dernière fois?" J'ai dit non. Il a ordonné dans le téléphone en baissant la voix: "Figeac, dites aux hommes qu'ils peuvent aller." (pp. 30–31) [5]

---

5. "The keeper came across the yard and said the warden wished to see me. I went to his office and he got me to sign some document. I noticed that he was in black, with pin-stripe trousers. He picked up the telephone receiver and looked at me.

Though we have no reason to think Meursault does not understand the causal relations among the events narrated here, at no time does he assert those relations. As with Benjy's passage, the reader has to establish causality by implicature alone. And as with Benjy's passage, there are unexpected gaps in the sequence. In order to make sense of the passage, for example, we are required to infer that between the time the director picks up the phone and the time he asks Meursault the question, he has called a number and talked with someone else. We need to know this to understand the director's question, and Meursault might certainly have been expected to tell us the full sequence. Meursault's discourse is better oriented than Benjy's, in part because Meursault has an adult's vocabulary. The characters are identified, if only by profession, and the relevant objects are at least mentioned. Meursault knows what game is being played. But he does not provide us with any information about the "certain nombre" of papers he signs, information which both Meursault and his Audience could be expected to find relevant. He does describe the director's clothing, but the description lacks interest and relevance. In fact, it is scarcely a description at all. It is embedded on the narrative clause "*j'ai vu*" 'I noticed'; that is, it is presented as a mere observation with its orientative and evaluative function quite unclear. The only other even potentially evaluative expression, the phrase "*en baissant la voix*" 'lowering his voice', likewise lacks apparent relevance and thus comes across as a mere observation with no relation to Meursault himself. There is no attempt on Meursault's part to establish a personal evaluative stance with respect to the events. Finally, like Benjy and the narrator of (1)

"The undertaker's men arrived some moments ago, and they will be going to the mortuary to screw down the coffin. Shall I tell them to wait, for you to have a last glimpse of your mother?"
"No," I said.
He spoke into the receiver, lowering his voice.
"That's all right, Figeac. Tell the men to go there now."

above, Meursault uses, for the most part, the unmarked simple sentence with subject-verb-object word order. And he uses the *passé composé*, the tense of spoken, not written narrative.

These syntactic observations are important, for it is his syntax which most obviously invites us to link Meursault's speech with that of the child, and it is on this link that much of our sympathy for Meursault depends. Says Sartre, "The outsider he [Camus] wants to portray is precisely one of those terrible innocents who shock society by not accepting the rules of its game" (Sartre, 1955:28). Meursault's air of innocence, however, may well depend on the fact that he talks not like one who has not accepted the rules of the game but like one who has not yet learned them. Like Faulkner, Camus alienates (makes other) Meursault's personal experience by rendering it through and associating it with the child's grammar of vicarious experience. Readers of *L'Etranger* have, of course, long noted the impression of vicariousness Meursault's narrative gives. Sartre calls *L'Etranger* "a novel of discrepancy, divorce and disorientation" (p. 33). Camus himself described the "absurd" state of mind as one in which "the setting collapses." In the world of the absurd man, says Sartre, "one experience is as good as another. . . . Confronted with this 'quantitative ethic' all values collapse; thrown into this world, the absurd man, rebellious and irresponsible, has 'nothing to justify'. He is innocent" (Sartre, 1955:27). I believe Labov's data provide an insight into the linguistic basis of Meursault's "innocence" and the sense of "discrepancy, divorce and disorientation" his narrative gives us. Absence of setting, values, and justification are characteristics not (or not only) of the absurd man's world but also of the absurd man's language. They are the characteristics that cognitively and linguistically distinguish his world from our own adult one while at the same time associating his world with that of our own childhood, or rather with one of the subworlds of our childhood—the world of vicarious experience. This association plays a significant role in Camus's attempt to get us to

perceive Meursault as alienated without being alienated by him.[6]
The unintentional failures in the Faulkner and Camus passages
are mostly sins of omission. But it is also possible and on the whole
perhaps more common for fictional narrators to err not by failing to
evaluate, orient, and maintain causality but by failing to do so correctly. Consider, for example, Huckleberry Finn's description of
suppertime at the Widow Douglas's house:

> The widow rung a bell for supper, and you had to come to time.
> When you got to the table you couldn't go right to eating, but
> you had to wait for the widow to tuck down her head and grumble
> a little over the victuals, though there warn't really anything the
> matter with them. (p. 2)

Obviously, the widow is not grumbling but saying grace. In Montesquieu's *Lettres persanes* (*The Persian Letters*, 1721), the Persian
traveler Rica makes a similar mistake when he describes in a letter
his first trip to the Comédie Française (again, the English translation is below):

> Je vis hier une chose assez singulière, quoiqu'elle se passe tous
> les jours à Paris.
> Tout le peuple s'assemble sur la fin de l'après-midi et va jouer

---

6. Morally and critically speaking, Camus's attempt has been more successful
than we might wish it to be. Meursault's linguistic detachment and his rhetorical
innocence have helped foster the conventional view of Meursault as a victim of
social oppression and a man who "accepts death for the sake of truth," as
Camus himself put it. As Conor Cruise O'Brien (1970) points out, it is rather
startling that several generations of readers should have adopted this view of a
man who, besides committing a murder, collaborates in an acquaintance's sordid
plot to deceive and humiliate his mistress, stands by while the mistress gets
beaten up rather than calling the police, and lies in court to save the friend from
punishment for the beating. As O'Brien observes, the myth of Meursault's innocence and martyrdom is partly the result of the power of critics to overshadow
the book. But the kind of stylistic mechanisms I have been discussing contribute
as well. Meursault's detachment from his actions deadens their moral impact,
dehumanizes his victims, and helps the reader forget them, as everyone else in
the book does, when Meursault is brought to trial.

> une espèce de scène que j'ai entendu appeler comédie. Le grand
> mouvement est sur une estrade, qu'on nomme le théâtre. Aux
> deux côtés, on voit, dans de petits réduits, qu'on nomme loges,
> des hommes et des femmes qui jouent ensemble des scènes
> muettes, à peu près comme celles qui sont en usage en notre
> Perse. (p. 75)[7]

Rica has erroneously inferred that the audience members at the
Comédie are also actors in the play, and the remainder of his letter
continues based on this assumption.

In both these passages, the problem is not a failure to evaluate,
orient, or maintain causal sequence. Rather, the fictional speaker
maintains, evaluates, and orients the *wrong* causal sequence. In both
cases, the speaker says something that he believes to be true but that
the Audience knows to be false. It is not the case that the Widow
Douglas is "grumbling" and it is not (literally) the case that the
public has essembled at the Comédie to "jouer une espèce de scène"
'to *play* at a kind of dramatic performance.' Grice, you will recall,
does not concern himself with unintentional nonfulfillment at all,
and it is difficult to see how his model would handle this kind of
mistake. Clearly Twain and Montesquieu are flouting the first
maxim of Quality in these passages. They are saying what they know
to be false. The most we can say of Huck and Rica, however, is that
in using the verbs "grumble" and "*jouer*," 'play', they are unintentionally failing to fulfill the second maxim of Quality, "Do not say
that for which you lack adequate evidence," and those parts of their
subsequent discourse which presuppose the erroneous assertion
thereby fail to fulfill the maxim of Relation. This would be the case

---

7. Yesterday I saw a strange thing, though it happens every day in Paris.
All the people gather together after dinner, and play at a kind of dramatic
performance which I have heard called a comedy. The main action occurs on a
platform that is called the stage. On each side of it there are small recesses
called boxes, and here men and women play together at a dumb show, rather
like those to which we are accustomed in Persia.

with Huck's clause "though there warn't really anything the matter with them" and with much of the rest of Rica's letter on the Comédie. But perhaps such an analysis is not too far from the mark after all. Certainly the humor in both passages derives from the contrast between what the speaker says and what he might have been expected to say had he had adequate evidence. And certainly in both cases the author is calling our attention to the similarity (or even identity) between the evidence which the speaker observed and the kind of evidence on which the use of the words "grumble" and *"jouer"* is normally based. In both cases, as in the Faulkner passage, the evidence that the speaker is lacking is institutional, not sensory. It is evidence about what the characters observed believe themselves to be doing, evidence that the speaker could not know was lacking. Twain is implicating that the only difference between grumbling and grace is the subject's belief that he is saying grace; grace, then is as futile as grumbling. Montesquieu is implicating that the only difference between the behavior of the audience and of the actors at the Comédie is the audience's belief that it is not playacting; the audience, then, is as insincere as the players.

Violation

In a violation the speaker "quietly and unostentatiously violates a maxim" and is "in some cases . . . liable to mislead." Such cases are not very common in literature for the obvious reason that if the fictional speaker of a work of literature were to successfully violate a maxim in this manner, the reader would necessarily be unable to detect the violation on the basis of the fictional speaker's utterance alone. And if the violation is undetectable, it is, from the author's point of view, pointless. There appear to be two main ways in which authors can make violations on the part of the fictional speaker detectable to the reader, and I shall offer some examples of both, in order of increasing ambiguity.

First, the author can give the reader access to some speech act other than the one in which the violation occurred and can reveal the violation in this second utterance. This is the case, for example, in epistolary novels, where speaker A can write a letter to B in which he tells B a lie, then write to C and tell him the truth. Obviously, the reader needs a way of distinguishing which letter contains the lie. Usually, A will also tell C that he lied to B. Alternatively, the reader will infer from A's letters that A is more likely to lie to B than to C. B, for example, could be A's enemy or a woman A is trying to seduce under false pretenses. It is on the basis of such information that the reader of Laclos's *Dangerous Acquaintances* (1782), for example, distinguishes levels of sincerity between the letters Mme. de Mertueil and the Vicomte de Valmont write to each other and the letters they write to others. Eventually, this sincerity judgment gets ironically reversed when Valmont reveals that his love letters to the Présidente de Trouvel were in fact sincere, and he had actually been deceiving Mme. de Mertueil.

Alternatively, a violation may become apparent if the speech act in which it occurs is embedded inside the utterance of a second speaker. This is the case of one of Jorge Luís Borges's *ficciones* called "The Shape of the Sword" (1956). In this story the narrator, an Argentine traveler named Borges, stops overnight at the ranch of an enigmatic Irish immigrant who bears on his cheek a large curving scar, whose history he has never been willing to reveal. He agrees to tell Borges how he got the scar. His story runs thus: while fighting for Irish independence in the 1920s, he risks his life to rescue from the British a comrade named Moon who has become paralyzed by fear. Shortly after, he discovers the same comrade is really a spy and has betrayed him to the British. Just before his capture, he manages to seize the traitor and slash a curving cut in his cheek. The traitor flees to South America. Here the Irishman stops, and we read:

> I [Borges] waited in vain for the rest of the story. Finally I told him to go on.

Then a sob went through his body; and with a weak gentleness he pointed to the whitish curved scar.

"You don't believe me?" he stammered. "Don't you see that I carry written on my face the mark of my infamy? I have told you the story thus so that you would hear me to the end. I denounced the man who protected me; I am Vincent Moon. Now despise me." (p. 71)

Here the Irishman reveals that in telling his story he has deceived his listener by presenting himself as the betrayed hero instead of as the cowardly traitor Moon. For the duration of his narrative, in other words, the Irishman violates the first maxim of Quality ("Do not say that which you know to be false") with the intention, however, of ultimately revealing and correcting the violation. The case is complicated. At bottom the Irishman's problem is a clash. He believes that unless he violates the maxim of Quality he will be unable to fulfill the CP because his utterance will be intolerably distasteful to his listener. Paradoxically, then, to fulfill the CP, he feels he must place it in jeopardy by misleading the listener. The moment the violation is revealed by the Irishman, of course, it necessarily counts as a flouting on the part not only of the Irishman, but of Borges the narrator and Borges the author as well. Both the violation and the flouting are perceptible only because we have the contextual information that the Irishman has a scar, and we get this information only because we get the story secondhand. On its own, the Irishman's story is a perfectly felicitous narrative of personal experience and bears no sign of the lie.

Secondhandedness also plays an important role in my next example, Defoe's *Moll Flanders* (1722), a novel that, like *Tristram Shandy*, has the form of an autobiography. It is frequently, and I think correctly, argued that Defoe intends us to suspect Moll Flanders of misrepresenting herself and of trying to convince us she is less blameworthy and more penitent than she really is. Those who take this view find support for it in the book's preface, written by a fictional editor figure. Two remarks in particular cast doubt on Moll's penitent attitude. The editor reveals that Moll's original manuscript was "written in Language, more like one still in *Newgate* than one grown Penitent and Humble, as she afterwards pretends to be" (p. 1) and secondly that in her old age (when she apparently produced the manuscript) Moll "was not so extraordinary a Penitent, as she was at first" (p. 5). In order to maintain the assumption that in making these remarks the prefacer is fulfilling the maxim of Relation, the reader must infer that the prefacer is implicating that Moll's penitent attitude in the book is insincere and that we need to know this to properly interpret her text. Alternatively, one could infer that the prefacer's intentions are innocent and that the implicatures are Defoe's (the prefacer being Defoe's fictional creation). In any case, the evidence the two remarks provide is evidence that Moll's text itself does not supply. As in the Borges and the epistolary examples, we are given access to the evidence of violation through a speech act other than the one in which the putative violation occurs. Ironically, the prefacer's implicatures cast doubt on his sincerity, too. The communicative purpose he professes is "to recommend Virtue and generous Principles and to discourage and expose all sorts of Vice and Corruption of Manners" (p. 4). To a great extent, this aim can be achieved only if we believe in Moll's penitence. By suggesting the penitence is insincere, then, the prefacer undermines his own purpose.

I turn now to a second, less straightforward way in which an author can make a violation on the part of the fictional speaker apparent to the reader: the fictional speaker may unintentionally fail to make his violation "quiet and unostentatious" enough. He may, for example, be inconsistent or even contradict himself. Machado de Assis's novel *Dom Casmurro* (Brazil, 1900) provides an example interesting for its complexity. *Dom Casmurro* is a fictional memoir written by a middle-aged Rio de Janeiran nicknamed Dom Casmurro (the name means something like "Sir Misanthrope"). The central event in Dom Casmurro's story is the collapse of his marriage caused by his conviction that his wife Capitú has been unfaithful to him. The evidence for this claim is what Dom Casmurro believes to be an exact physical resemblance between his son Ezequiel and his recently deceased friend Escobar, a resemblance which Dom Casmurro takes to be proof that the child is not his own but Escobar's. Now it is clear to the reader that in claiming the child is not his own, Dom Casmurro is failing to fulfill the second maxim of Quality requiring adequate evidence. The question is whether he is doing so knowingly, in which case the failure is a *violation*, or whether he is so blinded by jealousy that he sincerely believes the evidence is adequate, in which case the failure is *unintentional*. The following passage occurs just following the bitter scene in which Dom Casmurro confronts his wife with his suspicions and calls for a separation:

> In the meantime, I had recalled the words of the late Gurgel that time at his house when he showed me the portrait of his wife, which resembled Capitú. You must remember them; if not, re-read the chapter. I do not place the number of it here, because I no longer remember which it is, but it cannot be far back. They come down to this: there are these inexplicable resemblances. . . .
> (p. 265)

The sentence remains uncompleted. In the chapter whose number he has forgotten, Dom Casmurro recounts an incident in which Gurgel, the father of a friend, points out a coincidental resemblance between Capitú and a photograph of his own deceased wife. Gurgel's words were "Sometimes, in life, there are these strange resemblances." The Gurgel incident, in other words, forms an innocent precedent for the resemblance between Ezequiel and Escobar, who is now also dead. It is obvious that Machado de Assis is calling our attention to this precedent here, implicating that we should keep in mind the inadequacy of Dom Casmurro's evidence. It is equally clear that Dom Casmurro is himself thinking of the parallel between the two cases. But in the midst of referring to the Gurgel case, he opts out of the maxim of Quantity as it is defined for written discourse. He fails to put down the relevant reference, on the grounds he has forgotten it, and he fails to complete the sentence paraphrasing Gurgel's words. As always, the reader must treat the opting out as a flouting on Machado de Assis's part and must determine what Machado de Assis is trying to implicate by it. A number of solutions are possible, of which these three are perhaps the most likely:

1. Dom Casmurro really did forget the chapter number. In this case his reason for opting out is sincere, and Machado de Assis is flouting the maxim of Quantity for the sheer fun of it. (Machado was a great fan of Sterne's).

2. In view of the weakness of Dom Casmurro's excuse, Machado de Assis is implicating first that in pleading forgetfulness, Dom Casmurro is lying, and second that the real reason Dom Casmurro is opting out is that he does not want to call attention to evidence that would undermine his case against Capitú.

3. In view of the weakness of Dom Casmurro's excuse, Machado de Assis is implicating that Dom Casmurro is indirectly or even subconsciously trying to call attention to evidence against him in order to confess by implicature what he is too guilt-ridden to confess outright. In this case, in pleading forgetfullness, Dom Casmurro is flouting the maxim of Quality and implicating that he remembers Gurgel's words all too well and wants us to remember them too.

The same three possibilities are raised on another occasion a few pages earlier when, in the middle of a chapter, Dom Casmurro interrupts himself to say:

> Pardon me, but this chapter ought to have been preceded by another, in which I would have told an incident that occurred a few weeks before, two months after Sancha had gone away. I will write it. I could place it ahead of this one before sending the

book to the printer, but it is too great a nuisance to have to change the page numbers. Let it go right here; after that the narration will proceed as it should right to the end. Besides, it is short. (p. 251)

Again, Dom Casmurro opts out of the rules for written discourse, and again his excuse is a weak one: the reordered chapter is short and it's too much trouble to change the page numbers. In the "misplaced" chapter, Dom Casmurro relates an incident in which his wife calls his attention to the "strange expression in Ezequiel's eyes," an expression which she says she has seen only twice before, in the eyes of a friend of her father's and in the eyes of Escobar. Again, then, the passage which occasions the opting out contains evidence which undermines Dom Casmurro's case against Capitú: if she had reason to believe Escobar was the father of her son, why would she call her husband's attention to any resemblance between them? Again, the three interpretations outlined above are possible.

Depending on which of the three interpretations he adopts for these two cases of opting out, the reader will respond differently to the crucial final passage of the book:

Well, whatever may be the solution, one thing remains and it is the sum of sums, the rest of the residuum, to wit, that my first love [Capitú] and my greatest friend [Escobar], both so loving me, both so loved, were destined to join together and deceive me. . . . May the earth rest lightly on them! Let us proceed to the *History of the Suburbs* [the next book Dom Casmurro proposes to write]. (p. 277)

For all readers, the first sentence of this passage fails to fulfill the second maxim of Quality. Hence, for all readers, Machado de Assis is flouting the maxim of Quality here. The question is what Machado de Assis is implicating that Dom Casmurro is doing. For the reader who has adopted interpretation (1) above, the failure is *unintentional.* Machado de Assis is implicating that Dom Casmurro is laboring under a hideous delusion. For the reader adopting interpretation (2), Dom Casmurro here *violates* the maxim of Quality. He knows his evidence is inadequate but is trying to conceal this fact and to mislead the Audience into believing Capitú was guilty. For the reader with interpretation (3), Dom Casmurro here *flouts* the maxim of Quality, implicating that he knows he was unjust and that he feels so guilty he cannot talk about it directly. Machado de Assis may be and probably is implicating at least all three interpretations, as in Grice's example of the multiply ambiguous line from Blake.[8]

My purpose in offering these examples is to show that it is possible for the fictional speaker of a work of literature to fail to fulfill the CP and maxims in at least the following ways: opting out, clash, unintentional failure, violation, and flouting. I have also suggested that in all such cases, the fictional speaker's failures count as flouting on the part of the author. In order to cooperate as the literary speech situation requires, the reader confronting a violated maxim in a literary work must interpret the violation as being in accord with the "accepted purpose or direction of the exchange" in which he and

---

8. Historically speaking, there does exist a fourth option for the reader of *Dom Casmurro.* For several decades after the novel appeared, the possibilities of the narrator's unreliability and the wife's innocence were not recognized. Dom Casmurro was viewed as the unfortunate victim of betrayal he claims to be, and Capitú was viewed as the beautiful, calculating social climber he says she was. This view of the novel still has credence in some quarters today. If this view is adopted, neither Machado de Assis nor Dom Casmurro has failed to fulfill either of the maxims of Quality, and Dom Casmurro's habit of opting out must be explained in some other way not directly connected with the subject of his narrative. This interpretation must be rejected, however, because it lacks explanatory power and because it requires the reader to make an unsupported assumption, namely the assumption that there is adequate evidence of adultery. Nevertheless, the fact that disagreement over narrator reliability can arise both in the case of *Moll Flanders* and *Dom Casmurro* demonstrates that toying with the maxims of Quality is a risky business indeed within literature as well as outside it. Unless an author makes very clear who is lying and who is not, he is liable to create misunderstandings himself.

the author are engaged. The reader must assume that regardless of what the fictional speaker is doing, the author is observing the CP as defined for display texts; and he must calculate all the implicatures necessary to maintain this assumption. Consequently, when a fictional speaker fails to fulfill a maxim, it will usually be the case that the author is implicating things in addition to what the fictional speaker is saying or implicating.

In all the examples discussed, the fictional speaker's failures have the same basic effect. In all, it is not only the experiences reported which are unusual and problematic, but the report itself. The verbal version the speaker offers fails to elicit our understanding of events or our agreement with the speaker's interpretation of events. The fictional speaker thus produces a lack of consensus, and the author implicates that this lack of consensus is part of what he is displaying, part of what he wants us to experience, evaluate, and interpret. He may intend us to replace the speaker's version with a better one, question our own interpretive faculties, or simply delight in the imaginative exercise of calculating "what's really going on." He may be implicating an ironic or critical comment on literature itself. As I shall be discussing in chapter six, display texts of this type, in which the verbal representation itself is problematic, are also common in nonliterary discourse.

One of the main reasons I chose to focus in this chapter on Grice's account of deviance is the fact that the presence of intentional deviance in works of literature has been one of the arguments most often adduced to support the poetic language doctrine. The fact that literary works tolerate and even relish linguistic deviance is often felt to be the conclusive evidence that the function of language in literary works is indeed not primarily communicative (whereas its function elsewhere is). More often, of course, the explicit or implicit assumptions are somewhat more value-laden: ordinary language will do well enough for the ordinary verbal activities of ordinary people, but as a vehicle for aesthetic expression it is so inadequate that no one could blame the poet for escaping the confines of its rules. In its extreme form, the argument views the rules governing ordinary language as incompatible with aesthetic creation and makes deviance the essence of poetry (cf. Mukařovský: "the violation of the norm of the standard, its systematic violation, is what makes possible the poetic utilization of language" [1932:20]). As support for a linguistically autonomous literature, the argument depends of course on the assumption that intentional deviance does not occur outside literature or does not occur in the same way it does in literature. Grice's account of rule-breaking in conversation clearly shows that intentional deviance does occur routinely outside literature. And the fact that Grice's account seems perfectly able to handle deviance within literature as well shows that there are no clear grounds for distinguishing the way deviance occurs in the two supposedly opposed realms of discourse. In this regard, it is perhaps worth reiterating that fictivity cannot be viewed as a form of "poetic deviance" either. As I discussed earlier, fictive or "imitation" speech acts are readily found in almost any realm of discourse, and our ability to produce and interpret them must be viewed as part of our normal linguistic and cognitive competence, not as some special by-product of it.

Chapter Six

Extending the Analysis

> All communication takes place
> across barriers. . . . Provided
> that communication is going on,
> the interposition of further
> barriers has a tantalizing effect.
> It teases us to more vigorous
> attempts, sharper alertness,
> greater efforts at compassion
> or sympathy.
>
> WALTER J. ONG S.J.,
> "Voice as Summons
> for Belief"

1. Generic rules and generic deviance

In choosing and developing the examples in the previous chapter, I deliberately skirted an important question which I propose to address now, namely the distinction between the rules governing the author's utterance and the rules governing the fictional speaker's utterance.

In discussing deviance in *Tristram Shandy*, I assumed that the norms against which we detect deviance in that work were the CP and maxims as defined for autobiography, the utterance type that Tristram Shandy is writing. Similarly, in the case of the Landolfi story, I assumed that the norms the reader was intended to bring to bear were the norms for biography, the utterance type Landolfi's narrator was producing. In *Dom Casmurro*, I specified deviance with respect to the CP and maxims as defined for memoirs, and I treated the Faulkner passage and Borges's Irishman's story as natural narratives. In all these examples, in short, I took it that the rules in force were the CP and maxims as defined for the utterance type which the fictional speaker claimed or appeared to be performing, and I assumed it was on the basis of these rules that we decoded the speaker's utterance, detected deviance, and calculated implicatures. Now this approach is correct as far as it goes, but it does not go quite far enough; for although this one set of appropriateness conditions (that is, the appropriateness conditions for the utterance type the fictional speaker is producing) are all we need to understand what the fictional speaker is saying and implicating in a fictional utterance, it is not enough for us to understand the full range of what the author or real world speaker is implicating. Landolfi's speaker has written a biography, Tristram Shandy an autobiography, and Dom Casmurro a memoir; but Landolfi has written a short story and Sterne and Machado de Assis have written novels. In order to cooperate fully with these authors, we need to bring to bear not only the appropriateness conditions governing biography, autobiography, or memoirs but also the appropriateness conditions governing novels and short stories.

For example, I claimed that much of the deviance in *Tristram Shandy* resulted from Shandy's opting out of the rules governing manner, relevance, and quantity in autobiographies, and that with respect to Sterne, this opting out counted as flouting. But certainly Sterne is flouting the rules for novels as well as the rules for autobiographies. In order to understand the full range of Sterne's implicatures, the reader must attend to the contrast between the given text and our expectations of novels, too. As is often noted, Sterne calls our attention to this contrast in the very title of his book, "life and opinions" instead of the novelistically conventional "life and adventures." Likewise, Faulkner intends Benjy's discourse to contrast both with the way most people narrate and with the way most novelists write, and he implicates a comment on both. When Dom Casmurro claims his wife deceived him, he has violated and Machado de Assis has flouted the maxim of Quality, which surely applies to memoirs; but Machado de Assis has in addition flouted a novelistic rule: he has failed to give us enough information to resolve the plot. Dom Casmurro's violation thus gives rise to two floutings and two sets of implicatures on Machado de Assis's part. When Landolfi's fictional biographer suffers a clash, Landolfi is flouting not only the rules for biography, which entitle us to expect discretion and reliability from the speaker, but also the rules for short stories, which entitle us to expect the speaker will have a definite story to tell. By means of the same clashes, then, Landolfi implicates both a parody of literary biographers (especially Gogol's) and a comment on our own short story expectations. When Shandy and Huck Finn fail to fulfill the maxims of Manner by using conspicuously oral forms in their written compositions, Sterne and Twain are flouting the rules for writing both as they apply to autobiography and to novels. In effect, the rules for writing apply twice in a text like *Huckleberry Finn*, and given the dual context, this same set of rules could be exploited to give rise to two sets of implicatures. In sum, in order to account for the full range of implicatures for which the reader of a literary work is responsible, a description of literary speech acts will, at least in some cases, have to take into account both the CP and maxims as defined for the work's genre and the CP and maxims as defined for the fictional speaker's utterance. While only the latter are required to decode what the fictional speaker is saying and implicating as well as what the author is saying, both sets of appropriateness conditions are required to decode what the author is implicating. Readers of fictional literary works, of course, automatically distribute their expectations in this way.

It is possible for these two sets of appropriateness conditions to work independently of each other. With respect to its fictional speaker, Nabokov's novel *Pale Fire* (1962) is an annotated edition of a poem, complete with foreword, text, commentary, and index; with respect to its author, *Pale Fire* is a novel, as the title page asserts. Now regardless of how the fictional speaker behaves with respect to the norms governing annotated editions of poems (and of course he behaves very badly indeed), the very fact that his utterance has the form of a work of literary criticism obviously counts as a flouting by Nabokov of the generic rules which Nabokov himself has brought into play by calling his text a novel. The generic deviance, in other words, exists independently of what the fictional speaker actually says in his utterance. In his epistolary novel, *Pamela* (1740), Richardson clearly intends us to regard Pamela's style as conforming to the appropriateness conditions for the speech exchange in which she is engaged, the young lady's personal letter; but he also intends Pamela's style to contrast with the prevailing formal, public, literary norm, to appear more spontaneous and ingenuous. He intends, that is, to fulfill one set of appropriateness conditions and to flout or exploit the other. Generic deviance is perceptible whether or not the fictional speaker breaks any of the rules to which his utterance is subject.

To say that literary works presuppose generic norms in addition to and separate from the norms governing the fictional speaker's utterance is to say that the reader who picks up a work of literature of a given genre already has a predefined idea of "what the nature of the communication situation is." Although the fictional discourse in a work of literature may in theory take any form at all, readers have certain expectations about what form it will take, and *they can be expected to decode the work according to those assumptions unless they are overtly invited or required to do otherwise.* Our most basic assumption in the literary speech situation is that we are dealing with a display text. But in the case of the novel, at least, we are

entitled to assume even more, for although novels can take the form
of memoirs, dialogues, letters, biographies, psychiatric interviews,
even books of literary criticism, there is little question that the initial hypothesis of the novel reader is that the fictional speech act
will take the form of a narrative display text. We do not ask why
Balzac did not construct *Père Goriot* (1834) as a dialogue, but we
do ask why Diderot did so construct *Jacques le fataliste* (1796). We
do not ask why Jane Eyre is a reliable narrator, but we do ask why
Dom Casmurro is not. As novels are viewed today at least, Dom
Casmurro's unreliability is *marked* with respect to Jane Eyre's reliability, and the dialogue form of *Jacques le fataliste* is marked with
respect to the uninterrupted narrative of *Père Goriot*. More generally, the claim is that the *unmarked* case for the novel is the one
in which the fictional speech situation reproduces the speech situation obtaining in real world narrative display texts: a speaker addresses to an Audience a narrative utterance whose point is display
and whose relevance is tellability; the speaker observes the CP and
maxims as specified for such utterances; that is, he knows the story,
provides all the relevant information, evaluates adequately, and
succeeds in making our Audience-ship worth it. In the unmarked
case, the speaker in addition observes all the rules governing written
discourse at the time of the work's composition. By written discourse, I mean here discourse composed in writing and intended for
publication, that is, addressed to an Audience whose exact size and
membership are unspecified in advance. These would include rules
governing grammar, style, text presentation, subject matter, and so
on.[1] Again, we are struck by the fact that the mayor of Casterbridge
uses dialect words but not by the fact that Jane Eyre does not.

In saying that these rules define the unmarked case for the novel,

---

1. There may be special writing rules for novels, such as rules defining pro-
logues and epilogues. For the most part, however, it would seem that the writing
norms for novels are the same as the norms governing public written discourse of
all kinds at a given period.

I do not necessarily claim that this case is statistically the most common, though it probably is. What I do claim is that regardless of what form the fictional utterance actually takes in a novel, the fact that the text is a novel automatically entitles the reader to bring these rules to bear on the fictional speech act. I believe such an analysis corresponds to our intuitions about novels at this point in history. The evidence of formal correspondences between literary and natural narrative discussed in chapter two provides additional support for this hypothesis.

Given the rules for the unmarked case, the reader of a novel will begin by analyzing information as either narrative, orientative, or evaluative and will continue to do so as long as and whenever he can make sense of the text that way. Unless otherwise specified, he will assume that the purpose of the exchange is for him to understand and adopt the desired attitude to a sequence of events being presented for their tellability. And even when the fictional speaker's purpose is revealed to be something other than narration, as in *Pale Fire*, any information which can be analyzed according to the rules for narrative display texts will be so analyzed by the reader. Even the first-time reader of *Pale Fire* knows by the second page that there is a story coming up. According to the rules for writing, a novel reader will assume the text is itself definitive, accurate, complete, stylistically appropriate, free of gross accidental errors, and "worth it" unless he is invited to think otherwise. It is with respect to these rules for narrative and written discourse that we detect what I have called "generic deviance." More importantly, these are the rules we need in order to describe what does *not* count as deviance in a novel and to explain how we decode what is not deviant. It is these rules that tell us that the opening sentence of *Pride and Prejudice* is a narrative abstract and not a piece of advice as to how we should run our lives or that the long opening description in Hardy's *Mayor of Casterbridge* (1886) is an orientation introducing the setting and main characters of an upcoming story and not merely a reflection on a scene "that might have been matched at almost any spot in any county in England at this time of year" (p. 12).

The claim that there is an unmarked speech situation for the novel answers another important question. To say that a novel is an imitation speech act (as opposed to an imitation of reality), one must be able to say what speech act a given novel is imitating. This is easy to do for works like *Pale Fire, Dom Casmurro, Tristram Shandy,* "Gogol's Wife," or *Pamela,* where the real-world speech act being imitated is explicitly identified. But very often, novelists do not explicitly identify who the fictional speaker is or what real-world speech act is being imitated. This is the case, for example, in *Pride and Prejudice* and *The Mayor of Casterbridge,* and in neither novel do we feel the author has flouted an appropriateness condition by failing to specify what the fictional discourse is imitating. Does this mean that *Pride and Prejudice* and *The Mayor of Casterbridge* are not actually imitation speech acts at all, that there is no real-world correlate for what the fictional speaker is doing? I think not. For to say that the nature of the fictional speech situation is not *stated* in third-person novels like these is not to say it is unspecified; rather, it is simply presupposed to be the unmarked case. We do not confront *Père Goriot* and *The Mayor of Casterbridge* in a vacuum nor are we intended to. We are intended to treat these novels as (imitation) written narrative display texts and to decode them according to the generic norms alone. The fact that these norms *can* be presupposed, the fact that third person novels are possible and readily decipherable even though the nature of the fictional speech situation is not stated is strong evidence that this unmarked case for the novel exists. We execute *In Cold Blood* the same way we execute a novel, because we execute novels in the same way we execute *In Cold Blood*—as if they were real-world narrative display texts.

As long as the fictional speaker of a novel does fulfill all the rules for narrative display texts and written discourse, the reader will execute the text as he would a real-world narrative display text. He will make all and only the implicatures necessary to maintain the assumption that the speaker is fulfilling the CP and maxims as defined for the unmarked case I have described, and he will assume that the author intends him to calculate exclusively these implicatures. This last point is important. It means that as long as the rules for the unmarked case are fulfilled, the implicatures we need to make sense of the author's utterance are all and only those we need to make sense of the fictional speaker's utterance as well as all and only those we would make if the text were a real-world narrative display text. None of the "additional implicatures" I discussed in the examples of flouting are required. This is the case in novels like *Jane Eyre, The Mayor of Casterbridge, Pride and Prejudice,* and *Père Goriot.* Put the other way around, unless the fictional speaker's text in some way does not fulfill the CP and maxims as defined for narrative display texts and published written composition (the generic norms), the author implicates nothing in addition to what the fictional speaker implicates. In the unmarked case, the duality of the reader's role is without consequence; the reader's position with respect to the speaker is the same as his position with respect to the author except that in the speaker's world the utterance is true and in the author's world it is not. There appear to be three main ways in which this unmarked case can be realized in a novel:

1.   The fictional speaker may be merely the fictional counterpart (*persona*) of the author. Unless we are overtly invited or instructed to think otherwise, we automatically take him to be such in any work of literature. This is the case traditionally called epic or third-person narrative.

2.   The author of a literary work may identify the fictional speaker as someone other than himself, usually by giving him a proper name. This is the configuration we normally call first-person narration. *Jane Eyre* is a good example of a first person novel in which the unmarked case is realized.

3.   While (1) above reproduces the real-life speech situation in

which a speaker tells a story which happened to someone else and
(2) reproduces the situation obtaining in real-life narrative of personal experience, the third possibility reproduces the situation in
which a speaker reproduces a story that someone else told him. In
this case, the fictional speech situation contains another; the fictional speaker embeds someone else's narrative utterance inside his
own discourse.

The third situation has a great many variants. The fictional
speaker may be retelling the other's utterance for the sake of its own
tellability, as in James's *The Turn of the Screw,* or he may be making
the other's utterance the subject of his own narrative, as in Borges's
"The Shape of the Sword." The former case also holds in Faulkner's
novel *The Reivers* (1962), which begins with the words "Grandfather said." With this phrase, the fictional speaker implicates that
he is the fictional counterpart of the author and also that he is recounting to us an oral narrative that his grandfather told him. In
this case, then, the speech situation in (2) above is embedded in
the speech situation in (1), and the reader is at least in theory attending to three utterances: Faulkner's novel, the grandson's report,
and the grandfather's story. The fact that the embedded story is oral
does not in itself count as deviance from the unmarked case for
novels, provided the speaker does not use explicitly oral expressions.
Oftentimes, if the reported utterance is written rather than oral, the
author's fictional counterpart will present himself only as an editor
figure, as in Defoe's *Moll Flanders.* In Prévost's *Manon Lescaut*
(1731), the fictional *homme de qualité* is setting down in writing
the oral narrative of personal experience told him by Des Grieux.
Here both the inner (embedded) and outer fictional speech situations are as in (2).

Further levels of embedding are possible. In Emily Brontë's
Wuthering Heights (1847), the fictional speaker reports to us his
own story (2) in which are embedded Bessie's narratives of personal experience (2), which in turn contain Bessie's reproductions

of Catherine's narratives of personal experience (3). In general, both in real-life and literary narrative, the limits on embedding are pragmatic rather than logical, and as in real-life second- or third-hand narrative, the speaker, reporter, or editor may or may not vouch for the accuracy of what the embedded speaker(s) say, and he may or may not agree with an embedded speaker's evaluative stance. However, as in real-life narration, unless the fictional speaker specifically states or implicates his doubt, disbelief, or disagreement, he implicates on the basis of the maxim of Quality that he does believe the utterance he is reporting or reproducing and does agree with the reported speaker's evaluative stance.

2.   Verbal jeopardy: deviance as a social act

I suggested earlier that if the fictional speaker of a novel fulfills the CP and maxims for the unmarked case, if his utterance is felicitous as a written narrative display text, then the implicatures required to make sense of his text are all and only those we need to make sense of the author's text and all and only those we would need if the fictional speech act were not fictional. In other words, a felicitous written, fictional, narrative display text *is* a felicitous novel. Obviously, this is not to say that when the fictional speaker's utterance does not fulfill the unmarked rules, the author's utterance is infelicitous as a novel. Rather, the deviance counts as a message that, as Riffaterre (1971) puts it, "there is something to discover." When the fictional speaker fails to fulfill any of the rules for the unmarked case or any other rules to which his utterance might be subject, his utterance and that of the author cease to coincide, and a second, additional range of implicatures is required to make sense of the author's utterance, the novel. As the examples in chapter five indicate, in the literary speech situation display texts can be used to challenge our views of the world as well as to corroborate them, to threaten our interpretive faculties as well as to validate them, to frustrate our expectations as well as to fulfill them, to shake our faith in the representative power of language as well as to affirm it. In the literary speech situation, in other words, rule-breaking can be the point of the utterance; the same is true of many speech situations outside literature, as I shall discuss shortly.

Within literature, this kind of linguistic subversiveness is associated especially with the so-called "new" or "anti-novel," where we find radically decreasing conformity to the unmarked case for novels and a concomitant radical increase in the number and difficulty of implicatures required to make sense of the given text. For example, at the level of the fictional speaker's text, we find in many twentieth-century novels a tendency to increase the limitations on the fictional speaker's ability to fulfill his communicative purpose. Obsessive jealousy leads Dom Casmurro to misjudge or misinterpret his wife's behavior, but in the fictional speaker of Alain Robbe-Grillet's *Jealousy* (1957) it brings about complete narrative and evaluative paralysis. Similarly, the cognitive impediment of Faulkner's Benjy, mental retardation, has much more drastic linguistic consequences than Huck Finn's ignorance or Pamela's naiveté. Tristram Shandy is perhaps overwrought and disorganized, but Dr. Kinbote, fictional speaker of Nabokov's *Pale Fire*, is hopelessly insane; Landolfi's fictional biographer and the journal-writer of Michel Butor's *Passing Time* (1958) have an equally tenuous grip on their senses. Dom Casmurro gets his chapters in the wrong order and can't be bothered correcting them, but the fictional speaker of Robbe-Grillet's *In the Labyrinth* (1959) couldn't solve his sequencing problems even if he wanted to, for he doesn't know the order of things in the first place. At one point in the text, we read:

> It is probably here that the scene occurs of the silent crowd moving in all directions around him, leaving the soldier alone at last in the centre of a huge circle of white faces. . . . But that scene leads to nothing. Besides, the soldier is no longer in the middle of a crowd either silent or noisy; he has left the café and is walking along the street. (pp. 153–54)

And while there is some question whether Dom Casmurro has fulfilled his communicative purpose, it is unclear whether the fictional speaker of *In the Labyrinth* has a communicative purpose or what that purpose is, though the most plausible hypothesis is that he is trying to construct a fictional narrative. The narrator of Julio Cortázar's story "Blow-up" (1959) spends his first few pages wondering if he has anything at all to communicate and wishing the typewriter could be entrusted to produce the text without his intervention.

The new novel is perhaps better characterized by its tendency toward increased generic deviance, deviance from the unmarked norms that is motivated at the level of the author only and not the fictional speaker. Both *Pale Fire* (1962) and *Dom Casmurro* (1900) are built around fictional speech acts that are not strictly narrative display texts. But while the rules for memoir—Dom Casmurro's rules—overlap substantially with the unmarked generic rules for novels, the rules for annotated editions—Dr. Kinbote's rules—overlap with them scarcely at all. In fact, in *Pale Fire* the two sets of rules in operation nearly exclude each other. To the extent that Professor Kinbote narrates, he violates (and Nabokov flouts) the rules for annotated editions; to the extent that Kinbote accomplishes his editing purposes, his text violates (and Nabokov flouts) the unmarked rules for novels. *Pale Fire* puts the CP in a kind of double jeopardy that is absent in *Dom Casmurro*.

Both Laclos's *Dangerous Acquaintances* (1782) and Guillermo Cabrera Infante's *Three Trapped Tigers* (Cuba, 1967) are made up of a succession of speech acts produced by a variety of fictional speakers. But in *Dangerous Acquaintances*, the speech acts are all of the same type, namely letters. The succession of speech acts making up *Three Trapped Tigers* includes a nightclub emcee's welcome, one letter, one side of a phone call, eleven excerpts from an unidentified series of psychiatric interviews, a set of seven parodies of Cuban writers transcribed by one of the characters from tape recordings, two Spanish translations of a hypothetical short story by an American tourist accompanied by his wife's comments and corrections, a transcript of a madwoman's mutterings copied down by one of the characters, and finally a large number and variety of narratives of personal experience, some oral, some written, and some unspecified as to mode of composition. The letter form used in *Dangerous Acquaintances* requires the fictional speaker to identify himself, his addressee, the time and place of composition, and the motive for writing. In *Three Trapped Tigers*, the fictional speakers almost never identify either themselves or their addressees, mainly because most of the speech acts presuppose face-to-face situations. The letter writers of *Dangerous Acquaintances* observe the rules for written French; the speakers of *Three Trapped Tigers* much of the time use spoken Cuban, as far removed from literary Spanish as Cockney is from the Queen's English. In *Dangerous Acquaintances*, because the fictional speaker and his addressee are separated, the addressee is usually as much in the dark about events as the reader. All the speech acts in *Three Trapped Tigers* presuppose a great deal more knowledge on the part of the addressee than the reader has. The fictional speakers do refer to each other in their various speech acts and to shared acquaintances and experiences, so that the reader willing to work at it can calculate who the characters are and who is speaking where. He can even find a story line of sorts, but he can scarcely believe the sketchy and rudimentary plot is what he is primarily supposed to be appreciating in the book.

Perhaps most characteristic of all is the new novel's tendency toward patterning that with respect to the rules for narrative is gratuitous. Robbe-Grillet's narrators dwell at great length on intricate visual patterns and correspondences whose relation to the plot is purely metaphorical; the fictional journal writer of *Passing Time* substitutes the usual schedule for journals (whereby each entry discusses what happened since the previous entry) with an intricate arithmetical progression whereby up to five chronologically separate periods are under discussion at the same time. Mario Vargas

Llosa in *The Green House* (Peru, 1966) intertwines several unrelated or tenuously related story lines. Julio Cortázar in his novel *Hopscotch* (1963) put his narrative in one half of the book and his external evaluation or metacommentary in the other, then invites us to read the chapters not sequentially but in a numerical order listed at the outset of the book. In all these cases, the deviance can be explained only as a flouting of the generic norms automatically brought into play by novels. All tend to trivialize the unmarked norms for narrative and for text construction by ruling out the possibility of decoding all but the smallest stretches of text according to those norms alone. In all, the reader's principal question becomes not *"then* what *happened?"* but *"now* what's he going to *say?"*

I have already suggested some ways in which we might use Grice's Cooperative Principle analysis to describe how readers detect and resolve such deviance as this in novels. The same model also suggests a sociolinguistic explanation of what the deviance is doing there in the first place. As Grice himself observes, the Cooperative Principle is not a purely grammatical construct but a social one as well, which can be used to describe many kinds of activities other than verbal ones. Linguistic cooperation, in other words, is one kind of social cooperation. By the same token, linguistic rule-breaking, far from being a purely grammatical act, is an act which carries social weight. It is a kind of noncooperation or, in some cases, uncooperativeness. I propose to conclude with a few remarks on what Grice's model can say about the social basis for and the display of linguistic rule-breaking. My remarks are intended to be anything but conclusive; I present them mainly by way of suggesting one direction in which the CP approach could be fruitfully developed.

I mentioned earlier that of the four kinds of nonfulfillment of maxims described by Grice, three (violation, opting out, and clash) jeopardize the CP and can cause it to break down. To these I added a third, gross unintentional failure, which is particularly dangerous to the CP in speaker/Audience situations, where correction or interruption are impossible. There are doubtless other kinds of dangerous noncooperation. The expression of hostility, for example, invariably both signals and provokes a breakdown of the CP, though it could be argued that verbal hostility is just the most extreme form of opting out. Of Grice's four kinds of nonfulfillment, only one, flouting, leaves the CP intact. I also argued that, owing to the conditions under which literary works are composed, published, and distributed, all the types of nonfulfillment except flouting either do not arise or tend to be eliminated in the process of a text's becoming a work of literature. Now to say that these "dangerous" kinds of nonfulfillment are ruled out for the author of a literary work is to say that in the literary speech situation, the CP is singularly secure and well-protected at the level of author/reader interaction. It is *hyperprotected.* This fact is crucial to our understanding of how deviance is used in literary works. For clearly it is *because* we know the CP to be hyperprotected in the literary speech situation that we can freely and joyfully jeopardize it or even cancel it there and expose ourselves to the chaotic consequences. Authors can mimetically represent all Grice's kinds of nonfulfillment including those kinds which threaten the CP *because* the literary speech situation is nearly immune to cases in which the CP is genuinely in danger. Our knowledge that the CP is hyperprotected in works of literature acts as a guarantee that, should the fictional speaker of the work break the rules and thereby jeopardize the CP, the jeopardy is almost certainly only mimetic. Ultimately, the CP can be restored by implicature. Given such a guarantee, the Audience is free to confront, explore, and interpret the communicative breakdown and to enjoy the display of the forbidden. It is this freedom that the "deviant" novels I have been discussing exploit. The game they play is not, or not only, the tellability game of natural narrative but also this other game, which I will call *verbal jeopardy.*

The game of verbal jeopardy is by no means unique to the literary speech situation. In fact, in any context where the CP is particularly secure, we invariably play at putting it in jeopardy or at canceling it altogether. It is common, for example, for terms of abuse to serve as terms of endearment or as compliments precisely because among intimates it would be almost impossible for the genuinely abusive use of the word to occur. Among good friends, invitations may take the form of near threats ("Look, Jake, you're staying for dinner and that's all there is to it. Now sit down and stop complaining.") and welcomes can sound like reprimands ("I figured that was you. Get in here and pour yourself some coffee.") In playful remarks such as these, the speaker flouts the maxim of Manner in such a way that his utterance, if taken literally, would very likely signal or provoke a breakdown of the CP. Since it is most unlikely for the speaker in such a context to have the attitude to his hearer that his utterance expresses, he implicates, by a kind of reversibility principle basic to all irony, that his attitude is the opposite of what his utterance expresses. The speaker gets his message across and in the process both he and his addressee take pleasure in *mimetically* jeopardizing the CP. Obviously, the felicity of such utterances depends entirely on the hearer's recognizing that the hostile interpretation is not intended, a fact which the speaker usually makes evident through gesture, intonation, and facial expression. (Anyone who has tried teasing in a language or culture not his own knows by bitter experience the importance of these cues.) Misunderstandings are possible however, and when they occur, the speaker must immediately take steps to restore the CP by reassuring the hearer he was "only kidding," and so on. Because it depends so crucially on the assumption that no real danger to the CP is intended, feigned hostility or uncooperativeness of this sort is safe and appropriate only among friends, where an accumulation of trust makes the CP virtually unassailable, as it is for entirely different reasons in the literary speech situation. Thus, teasing remarks cannot be addressed to just anyone. In fact, people very easily take offense at being teased by someone they do not know or like very well. In other words, even though a speaker's gestures and intonation make it perfectly clear that the hostile interpretation *is not* intended, a mimetically hostile remark will be safe and appropriate only if the context makes it entirely unlikely that the hostile interpretation *could* be intended. As long as we are assured that the flouting interpretation will prevail, jeopardizing the CP has the effect of reinforcing intimacy.

In many if not all societies, the game of verbal jeopardy has the status of a full-fledged ritual. According to Jean-Pierre Hallet,[2] married couples among the Ituri forest pygmies from time to time stage mock domestic quarrels in which everyone in the village participates as spectator and judge. In our own society we stage formal debates in much the same manner. Anthropologists have observed such verbal dueling rituals in a great many cultures, from Turkey to Guatemala to Harlem. The "point of the exchange" in verbal dueling is not cooperation, as defined in Grice's CP and maxims, but opposition. The participants are engaged in speaking not to produce some mutually desirable consequence but to determine a winner and a loser, a consequence desirable to one party and undesirable to the other. Yet given that noncooperation is understood to be the point of the exchange in rituals such as these, noncooperation counts as cooperation for the duration of the ritual. Hence, in failing to observe the CP within the fictional speech situation, the duelists are observing the CP as it is defined for the ritual, since their role in the ritual is precisely to feign uncooperativeness of a certain type. Within the fictional speech situation, the maxims and the CP itself are violated in a wide variety of ways; outside the fictional speech situation, they have only been flouted.

The CP is thus ultimately *unassailed* in the fictional speech situation, but it is the ritual context itself which independently guarantees that the CP is *unassailable* for the duration of the ritual, in the

---

2. I have taken this reference from Hallet's film, *Pygmies*. See also Jean-Pierre Hallet and Alex Pelle, *Pygmy Kitabu*, New York: Random House (1973).

same way that friendship guarantees it in teasing. The ritual context hyperprotects the CP. Hence, for a competitor in a verbal duel to express *genuine* hostility to his opponent, he must break the rules governing the ritual itself. He must fail to cooperate in a way in which the ritual prohibits. Here is an example, taken from Labov's study of the black adolescent verbal dueling ritual called "sounding" or "playing the dozens." Sounding is a verbal competition in which ritual insults or "sounds" of the following type are exchanged;

> Your mother so old she got spider webs under her arms.
>
> Your mother so skinny, about that skinny, she can get in a Cheerioat and say, "Hula hoop! Hula hoop!"
>
> You get your shoes from Buster Brown—brown on the top and all busted on the bottom.
>
> You got your suit from Woolworth! All wool but it ain't worth shit.
>
> I went to your house and ask your mother, could I go to the bathroom. She said, "The submarine jus' lef.'"
>
> I went to his house—I wanted to go to the bathroom,—and his mother gave me a pitchfork and a flashlight.
>
> Labov, 1972:297–353)

Like the feigned domestic quarrels of the pygmies, sounds reproduce in form an utterance type that in conversation invariably brings about or signals a breakdown of the CP. All the participants in sounding, including the Audience, understand, however, that the threat to the CP is only mimetic. The speakers are not really claiming to have the attitudes and beliefs their utterances express; they are flouting the CP. In order to maintain this supposition, however, the rules for sounding require that the sounders flout the maxim of Quality. Only insults which are obviously false are allowed. In other words, it must be impossible for the hearer to interpret the ritual insult as if it were a real one, *even though* he already knows it is not intended to be a real one. In sounding, this rule requiring blatant implausibility hyperprotects the CP:

> Sounds are directed at targets very close to the opponent (or at himself) but by social convention it is accepted that they do not denote attributes which persons actually possess. In Goffman's formulation, symbolic distance maintained serves to insulate this exchange from further consequence. The rules given above for sounding, and the development of sounds in bizarre and whimsical direction, all have the effect of preserving this ritual status. (Labov, 1972:352)

When a sounder does accidentally or intentionally fail to flout the maxim of Quality, then the hearer is entitled to interpret the breakdown of the CP as a reality rather than a pretense. He may take the insult personally. Labov examines several cases in which arguments, fights, and even death resulted from sounds which rang too true. He comments:

> As we examine these examples of sounding, the fundamental opposition between ritual insults and personal insults emerges. The appropriate responses are quite different. Ritual insults are answered by other ritual insults, while a personal insult is answered by denial, excuse or mitigation. . . . Sounds are not denied. (p. 335)

> There is no need to compile a great many such incidents to demonstrate the danger of a ritual sounding which is not obviously untrue. In dealing with strangers, it is considerably harder to say what is a safe sound, and there are any number of taboos which can be broken with serious results. (p. 341)

In similar fashion, the conventions governing formal debate permit the "honorable opponents" to ritually insult each other in ways they would not tolerate in normal conversation, but there are also conventional restrictions on what kinds of insults a debater may use. A formal debater can sound on his opponent's lack of experience or intelligence but not on the length of his nose or the conduct of his sister.

The speech situation in which these extraliterary forms of verbal jeopardy are played bears a close resemblance to the speech situation I have been postulating for fictional literary works. Like the literary speech situation, it is made up of:

1. a fictional speech situation.

2. an Audience (all verbal dueling rituals require an Audience; in friendly teasing, the addressee alone will do).

3. a hyperprotected CP. This hyperprotection may be based on mutual trust (as among friends), on convention (as in formal debate), or on both (as in sounding, and the pygmy domestic quarrels).

4. an understanding on the part of all participants that the first three elements are present and that the object of the exercise is display.

For verbal dueling rituals, the fictional speech situation is predefined as one within which the CP and maxims are in jeopardy or have broken down, and the rituals have additional conditions specifying and possibly restricting the kinds of noncooperation that can occur in the fictional speech situation. Given these factors and those in (2)–(4) above, all failures to fulfill the CP and maxims in the fictional speech situation count as flouting.

Unlike the verbal dueling rituals, works of literature do not *have* to be built around fictional speech situations in which the rules for language use are broken; but this is one of the possibilities the literary speech situation admits. As Peter Foulkes says, "The important conclusion, I believe, is not that some literary texts are characterized by deviant grammaticality, but that our reception of all literary texts is determined by a tentative willingness to enter into an esthetic relationship with deviant grammaticality" (Foulkes 1975:61). Not all works of literature use the fictional speech situation to play verbal jeopardy any more than do all rituals. In fact, as I argued earlier, the unmarked case for novels at least is the one in which the rules for written discourse and narrative display texts are *not* broken by the fictional speaker. The important fact, however, is not whether a given novelist chooses to exploit the hyperprotection of the CP in a given text but the fact that in the literary speech situation, the hyperprotection is there to be exploited. This fact, I would argue, explains why we are willing, as Foulkes says, to "enter into an aesthetic relationship with deviant grammaticality" in literary works. Failing to observe the CP is an act of social violence that we cannot normally take lightly. In literature, however, noncooperativeness can be taken lightly because it is, in Labov's terms, "insulated from further consequences." And again, this insulation comes from the context, the circumstances under which literary works are composed, selected, and so on. It is these circumstances that in the literary speech situation form the guarantee in (3) above, performing the same function as the sounders' rule requiring blatant implausibility. The guarantee enables us to display and explore what is surely one of the most problematic and threatening experiences of all, the collapse of communication itself.

The extraliterary varieties of verbal jeopardy I have mentioned offer a useful corrective to two of poetics' traditional assumptions about deviance in literature: the assumption that literature is the only context in which we "enter into an aesthetic relationship with grammatical deviance" and the assumption that deviance occurs in literature because ordinary language is impoverished and inadequate. Deviance occurs in literature primarily because the literary context is one that has the necessary guarantees we need in order to let deviance happen.

To say that the hostility expressed in the game of verbal jeopardy is without consequences is not to say it is nonexistent. As students of play have known for a long time, where there is mimetic hostility, there is also real hostility. The insulated contexts like games, rituals, and literary works in which we act out verbal and nonverbal violence are commonly believed to serve the social function of defusing and redirecting real hostility, or of allowing people to express real hostility in a nondestructive way. Hallet claims there were no real domestic quarrels among the pygmies he lived with. By the same token, it is no accident that Black English sounds revolve around those aspects of ghetto life that blacks and whites alike have always been taught to despise: poverty, dirt, old age, skin color, and so on. Similarly, it is no accident that verbal jeopardy has become the novelist's favorite game in the last thirty or forty years. The drastic deviance which we encounter in the new novel amounts to a declaration of war on the unmarked narrative and literary norms the novel presupposes and on the interpretation of experience which those norms have been used to affirm in our culture. This is a point Roland Barthes made twenty years ago in his essay "Literal Literature":

> In our present social circumstances . . . literature can exist only as the figure of its own problem, self-pursuing, self-scourging. Otherwise, whatever the generosity or the exactitude of its content, literature always ends by succumbing under the weight of a traditional form which compromises it insofar as it serves as an alibi for the alienated society which produces, consumes and justifies it. Robbe-Grillet's *The Voyeur* cannot be separated from what is today the constitutively reactionary status of literature, but by trying to asepticize the very form of narrative, it is perhaps preparing without achieving, a deconditioning of the reader in relation to the essentialist art of the bourgeois novel (Barthes, 1955:57–58)

Probably the one thing the new novelists share is a conviction that the unmarked speech situation for the novel is incompatible with their own view of contemporary experience. Their specific objections to the "bourgeois novel" vary a great deal. Robbe-Grillet objects to the unspoken ideological assumptions behind the evaluative stance of traditional novelists, and he tries to eliminate evaluation from his own texts. Many Third World writers object to the traditional downgrading of spoken language and to the enormous gap between the spoken language of their own largely illiterate nations and their still Europeanized (i.e., colonized) literary language. It is this message which Cabrera Infante's use of Cuban dialect carries. For other new novelists, the derived, institutionalized nature of literary discourse itself excludes the possibility of authentically representing experience in the literary speech situation, hence a proliferation of works in which fictional speakers devote large amounts of attention to works of art executed in media other than writing. Just as ghetto sounders use the language to protest the circumstances under which they live, so the new novelists "sound on" the circumstances under which they write and are read. It is a protest we will not fully understand until we have understood those circumstances themselves, until, that is, we have understood literature in its context and in its relation to our other linguistic activities. If we are to have a "science of literature," as called for by the Russian Formalists, we should understand from the outset that that science will be a social, not a mathematical one.

List of Works Cited

I. *Literary Texts*

Borges, Jorge Luis (1956). "The Shape of the Sword." Translated from the Spanish by Donald A. Yates in *Labyrinths,* eds. Donald A. Yates and James E. Irby. New York: New Directions, 1964.

Brontë, Charlotte (1847). *Jane Eyre.* New York: New American Library, 1960.

Camus, Albert (1942). *L'Etranger.* Paris: Gallimard, 1955. Translated as *The Stranger* by Stuart Gilbert. New York: Alfred Knopf, 1953.

———— (1956). *The Fall.* Translated from the French by Justin O'Brien. New York: Vintage, 1956.

Defoe, Daniel (1722). *Moll Flanders.* London: Oxford University Press, 1971.

Eliot, George [pseud.] (1861). *Silas Marner.* London: Oxford University Press, 1964.

Faulkner, William (1929). *The Sound and the Fury.* New York: Random House, 1956.

———— (1934). "Wash." In *The Collected Stories of William Faulkner.* New York: Random House, 1950.

Fitzgerald, F. Scott (1925). *The Great Gatsby.* New York: C. Scribner, 1953.

Kerouac, Jack (1962). *Big Sur.* New York: Bantam, 1963.

Landolfi, Tommaso (1963). "Gogol's Wife." Translated from the Italian by Wayland Young. Reprinted in *The Single Voice,* ed. Jerome Charyn. New York: Macmillan, 1969.

Machado de Assis, Joaquim Maria (1900). *Dom Casmurro.* Translated from the Portuguese by Helen Caldwell. New York: Noonday, 1953.

Melville, Herman (1853). "Bartleby the Scrivener." In *The Complete*

Short Stories of Herman Melville. New York: Random House, 1949.

Miller, Henry (1963). *Plexus*. New York: Grove Press, 1965.

Montesquieu, Baron de la Brède et de (1721). *Les Lettres persanes*. Paris: Garnier, 1963. Translated as *The Persian Letters* by George R. Healy. New York: Bobbs Merrill, 1964.

Robbe-Grillet, Alain (1959). *In the Labyrinth*. Translated from the French by Christine Brooke-Rose. London: Calder and Boyars, 1967.

Sterne, Laurence (1760-67). *Tristram Shandy*. New York: Odyssey, 1940.

Twain, Mark [pseud.] (1884). *Huckleberry Finn*. London: Chatto and Windus, 1938.

II. *Linguistics, Stylistics, Criticism*

Austin, J. L. *How to Do Things With Words*. New York: Oxford University Press, 1962.

Bailey, Richard W. (1972). "Toward the Integrity of Stylistics: Symbiosis vs. Parasitism." In Kachru and Stahlke, eds., *Current Trends in Stylistics*, 1972, pp. 97–102.

Barthes, Roland (1955). "Literal Literature." In *Critical Essays*. Translated by Richard Howard. Evanston: Northwestern University Press, 1972, pp. 51–58.

———— (1973). *The Pleasure of the Text*. Translated by Richard Miller. New York: Hill and Wang, 1975.

Brik, Osip M. (1927). "Contributions to the Study of Verse Language." Translated by C. H. Severens. In Matejka and Pomorska, eds., *Readings in Russian Poetics: Formalist and Structuralist Views*, 1971, pp. 117–125. (French translation in Todorov, *Théorie de la littérature: Textes des formalistes russes*, 1965).

Cercle Linguistique de Prague (see Prague Linguistic Circle).

Chatman, Seymour, ed. *Literary Style: A Symposium*. London: Oxford University Press, 1971.

————, and Levin, Samuel, eds. *Essays on the Language of Literature*. Boston: Houghton Mifflin, 1967.

Chlovski, V. (see Šklovskij).

Cole, Peter and Morgan, Jerry L., eds. *Syntax and Semantics, Vol. III: Speech Acts*. New York: Academic Press, 1975.

Davie, Donald and Wyka, Kasimierz, eds. *Poetics: Papers Read at the*

First International Conference of Work-in-Progress Devoted to the Problems of Poetics, Warsaw, August, 1960. The Hague: Mouton, 1961.

Delas, Daniel and Filliolet, Jacques. *Linguistique et poétique*. Paris: Larousse, 1973.

Duncan, Hugh. *Language and Literature in Society*. Chicago: University of Chicago Press, 1953.

Ehrmann, Jacques, ed. *Structuralism*. New York: Doubleday, 1970.

Eichenbaum, B. (see Èjxenbaum).

Èjxenbaum, Boris M. (1926). "The Theory of the Formal Method." Translated by I. R. Titunik. In Matejka and Pomorska, *Readings in Russian Poetics: Formalist and Structuralist Views*, 1971, pp. 3–37. (English translation also in Lemon and Reis, *Russian Formalist Criticism: Four Essays*, 1965; French translation in Todorov, *Théorie de la littérature: Textes des formalistes russes*, 1965.)

Elliott, Dale E. (1975). "Toward a Grammar of Exclamations." *Foundations of Language* 11 (1975):231–246.

Enkvist, Nils Erik; Spencer, John; and Gregory, Michael J. *Linguistics and Style*. Oxford: Oxford University Press, 1964.

Erlich, Victor. *Russian Formalism: History, Doctrine*. The Hague: Mouton, 1965.

Fillmore, Charles J. (1971). "Verbs of Judging: An Exercise in Semantic Description." In Fillmore and Langendoen, *Studies in Linguistic Semantics*, 1971, pp. 273–289.

———— (1974). "The Future of Semantics." In Fillmore, Lakoff, and Lakoff, *Berkeley Studies in Syntax and Semantics*, 1974, IV, 1–38.

———— (1974). "Pragmatics and the Description of Discourse." In Fillmore, Lakoff, and Lakoff, *Berkeley Studies in Syntax and Semantics*, 1974, V, 1–21.

————; Lakoff, George; and Lakoff, Robin, eds. *Berkeley Studies in Syntax and Semantics*, vol. 1. Berkeley: Institute of Human Learning and Department of Linguistics, University of California at Berkeley, 1974.

————, and Langendoen, D. T., eds. *Studies in Linguistic Semantics*. New York: Holt, 1971.

Forman, Donald (1974). "Uses of Declarative Sentences." In Fillmore, Lakoff, and Lakoff, *Berkeley Studies in Syntax and Semantics*, 1974, VI, 1–53.

Foulkes, A. P. *The Search for Literary Meaning.* Berne: Herbert Lang, 1975.

Fowler, Roger. *The Languages of Literature: Some Linguistic Contributions to Criticism.* New York: Barnes, Noble, 1971.

Freeman, Donald, ed. *Linguistics and Literary Style.* New York: Holt, 1970.

Garvin, Paul L., ed. and translator. *A Prague School Reader on Esthetics, Literary Structure, and Style.* Washington, D.C.: Washington Linguistics Club, 1955.

Goodman, Paul. *Speaking and Language: Defense of Poetry.* New York: Random House, 1971.

Gordon, David and Lakoff, George. "Conversational Postulates." *Papers from the Seventh Regional Meeting, Chicago Linguistic Society,* April, 1971. Chicago: Chicago Linguistic Society, 1971, pp. 63-85.

Grice, H. Paul. *Logic and Conversation.* 1967 William James Lectures, Harvard University. Unpublished manuscript, 1967. Excerpt in Cole and Morgan, *Syntax and Semantics, Vol. III: Speech Acts,* 1975.

Halliday, Michael A. K. "The Linguistic Study of Literary Texts." *Proceedings of the Ninth International Congress of Linguistics.* The Hague: Mouton, 1964. Revised reprint in Chatman and Levin, *Essays on the Language of Literature,* 1967, pp. 217-223.

——— (1971). "Linguistic Function and Literary Style: An Inquiry into the Language of William Golding's *The Inheritors.*" In Chatman, *Literary Style: A Symposium,* 1971, pp. 330-368.

Hamburger, Käte (1954). *The Logic of Literature.* Translated by Marilynn Rose. Bloomington: Indiana University Press, 1973.

Hartmann, Geoffrey (1966). "Structuralism: The Anglo-American Adventure." In Ehrmann, *Structuralism,* 1970, pp. 137-157.

Havránek, Bohuslav (1932). "The Functional Differentiation of the Standard Language." In Garvin, *A Prague School Reader on Esthetics, Literary Structure, and Style,* 1955, pp. 1-18.

———; Horálek, K.; Skalička, V.; and Trost, P. (1958). "Thèses collectives: réponses aux questions linguistiques." Quatrième Congrès Internationale de Slavistes, Moscow, 1958. Quoted in Vachek, *Dictionnaire de linguistique de l'Ecole de Prague,* 1964.

Hendricks, William O. "Three Models for the Description of Poetry." *Journal of Linguistics* 5 (1969):1-22.

Jakobson, Roman (1921). "On Realism in Art." Translated by Karol

Magassy. In Matejka and Pomorska, *Readings in Russian Poetics: Formalist and Structuralist Views*, 1971, pp. 38–46.

———— (1935). "The Dominant." Translated by Herbert Eagle. In Matejka and Pomorska, *Readings in Russian Poetics: Formalist and Structuralist Views*, 1971, pp. 82–87.

———— (1960). "Closing Statement: Linguistics and Poetics." In Sebeok, *Style in Language*, 1960, pp. 350–377.

————, and Bogatyrev, Petr (1929). "On the Boundary between Studies of Folklore and Literature." Translated by Herbert Eagle. In Matejka and Pomorska, *Readings in Russian Poetics: Formalist and Structuralist Views*, 1971, pp. 91–93.

Kachru, Braj B. and Stahlke, Herbert F. W., eds. *Current Trends in Stylistics*. Champaign: Linguistic Research, Inc., 1972.

Labov, William. *The Social Stratification of English in New York City*. Washington, D.C.: Center for Applied Linguistics, 1966.

————. *Language in the Inner City*. University Park: University of Pennsylvania Press, 1972.

————, and Waletzky, Joshua. "Narrative Analysis: Oral Versions of Personal Experience." *Essays on the Verbal and Visual Arts: Proceedings of the 1966 Annual Spring Meeting of the American Ethnological Society*. Seattle: University of Washington Press, 1967, pp. 12–45.

Lakoff, George. "Linguistics and Natural Logic." *Synthèse* 22 (1971): 151–171.

Lakoff, Robin. "Language in Context." *Language* 48 (1972):907–927.

————. "The Logic of Politeness; or Minding Your p's and q's." *Papers from the Ninth Regional Meeting, Chicago Linguistic Society*, April, 1973. Chicago: Chicago Linguistic Society, 1973, pp. 292–305.

Lakoff, Robin (1974a). "Why Women are Ladies." In Fillmore, Lakoff, and Lakoff, *Berkeley Studies in Syntax and Semantics*, 1974, XV, 1–45.

———— (1974b). "What You Can Do With Words." In Fillmore, Lakoff and Lakoff, *Berkeley Studies in Syntax and Semantics*, 1974, XVI, 1–55.

Larkin, Donald and O'Malley, Michael. "Declarative Sentences and the Rule-of-Conversation Hypothesis." *Papers from the Ninth Regional Meeting, Chicago Linguistic Society*, April, 1973. Chicago: Chicago Linguistic Society, 1973, pp. 301–320.

Lemon, Lee T. and Reis, Marion J., eds. and translators. *Russian Formalist Criticism: Four Essays*. Lincoln: University of Nebraska Press, 1965.

Levin, Samuel R. *Linguistic Structures in Poetry*. The Hague: Mouton, 1962.

Lodge, David. *The Language of Fiction: Essays in Criticism and Verbal Analysis of the English Novel*. London: Routledge and Kegan Paul, 1966.

Lyons, John. *Introduction to Theoretical Linguistics*. London: Cambridge University Press, 1968.

Mallarmé, Stéphane (1886–95). "Crisis in Poetry." In *Selected Prose Poems, Essays, and Letters*. Translated by Bradford Cook. Baltimore: Johns Hopkins University Press, 1956, pp. 34–43.

Matejka, Ladislav and Pomorska, Krystyna, eds. *Readings in Russian Poetics: Formalist and Structuralist Views*. Cambridge: MIT Press, 1971.

McCawley, James D. "Le téléscopage." *Communications* 20 (1973): 3–18.

Mukařovský, Jan (1932). "Standard Language and Poetic Language." In Garvin, *A Prague School Reader on Esthetics, Literary Structure, and Style*, 1955, pp. 19–35.

Nowottny, Winifred. *The Language Poets Use*. London: Athlone Press, 1962.

O'Brien, Conor Cruise. *Albert Camus of Europe and Africa*. New York: Viking, 1970.

Ohmann, Richard. "Speech Acts and the Definition of Literature." *Philosophy and Rhetoric* 4 (1971):1–19.

―――――. "Speech, Literature and the Space Between." *New Literary History* 5 (1974):37–63.

Ong, Walter J., S.J. *The Barbarian Within and Other Fugitive Essays and Studies*. New York: Macmillan, 1962.

―――――. "The Writer's Audience is Always a Fiction." *PMLA* 90 (1974):9–21.

Prague Linguistic Circle. "Thèses." *Travaux du Cercle Linguistique de Prague* 1 (1929):7–29.

Riffaterre, Michael. "Criteria for Style Analysis." *Word* 15 (1959): 156–175. Reprinted in Chatman and Levin, *Essays on the Language of Literature*, 1967.

————. "Stylistic Context." *Word* 16 (1960):207–18. Reprinted in Chatman and Levin, *Essays on the Language of Literature*, 1967.

————. "Le formalisme français." In *Essais de stylistique structurale*, ed. and translated by Daniel Delas. Paris: Flammarion, 1971.

Rilke, Rainer Maria (1922). Letter to Countess Margo Sizzo-Crouz. Translated by Eva Rennie. In *Selected Letters*. New York: Doubleday, 1960.

Sacks, Harvey; Schegloff, Emanuel A.; and Jefferson, Gail (n.d.). "A Simplest Systematics for the Organization of Turn-taking for Conversation." Mimeographed.

Sadock, Jerrold M. *Toward a Linguistic Theory of Speech Acts*. New York: Academic Press, 1974.

Sartre, Jean Paul (1943). "Camus' *The Outsider*." In *Literary and Philosophical Essays*. Translated by Annette Michelson. New York: Criterion Books, 1955.

Saussure, Ferdinand de (1915). *Course in General Linguistics*. Translated by Wade Baskin. New York: Philosophical Library, 1959.

Schegloff, Emanuel A. "Recycled Turn Beginnings: A Precise Repair Mechanism in Conversation's Turn-taking Organization." Public Lecture in the series Language in the Context of Space, Time, and Society, Summer Institute of Linguistics, University of Michigan, July, 1973. Mimeographed.

Schmerling, Susan F. "Asymmetric Conjunction and Rules of Conversation." In Cole and Morgan, *Syntax and Semantics, Vol. III: Speech Acts*, 1975, pp. 211–232.

Shklovsky, V. (see Šklovskij).

Searle, John R. *Speech Acts: An Essay in the Philosophy of Language*. Cambridge: Cambridge University Press, 1969.

———— (1973). "A Classification of Illocutionary Acts." *Language in Society* 5 (1976):1–23.

Sebeok, Thomas A., ed. *Style in Language*. Cambridge: MIT Press, 1960.

Šklovskij, Viktor (1917). "Art as Technique." Translated in Lemon and Reis, *Russian Formalist Criticism: Four Essays*, 1965, pp. 3–24. (French translation in Todorov, *Théorie de la littérature: Textes des formalistes russes*, 1965.)

Spitzer, Leo. *Linguistics and Literary History: Essays in Stylistics*. Princeton: University Press, 1948.

Stankiewicz, Edward (1961). "Poetic and Non-Poetic Language in their Interrelation." In Davie et al., *Poetics: Papers Read at the First International Conference of Work-in-Progress Devoted to the Problems of Poetics*, 1961, pp. 11–23.

Todorov, Tsvetan, ed. and translator. *Théorie de la littérature: Textes des formalistes russes*. Paris: Seuil, 1965.

————. *Introduction à la littérature fantastique*. Paris: Seuil, 1970.

Tomasevskij, Boris (1928). "La nouvelle école d'histoire littéraire en Russie." *Revue des Etudes Slaves* 8 (1928): 226–240.

Traugott, Elizabeth. "Generative Semantics and the Concept of Literary Discourse." *Journal of Literary Semantics* 2 (1973): 5–22.

Tynjanov, Jurij and Jakobson, Roman (1929). "Problems in the Study of Literature and Language. Translated by Herbert Eagle. In Matejka and Pomorska, *Readings in Russian Poetics: Formalist and Structuralist Views*, 1971, pp. 79–81.

Uitti, Karl D. *Linguistics and Literary Theory*. Englewood Cliffs: Prentice Hall, 1969.

————."Philology: Factualness and History." In Chatman, *Literary Style: A Symposium*, 1971, pp. 111–132.

Vachek, Josef, ed. *A Prague School Reader in Linguistics*. Bloomington: Indiana University Press, 1964.

————. *The Linguistic School of Prague: An Introduction to Its Theory and Practice*. Bloomington: Indiana University Press, 1966.

————. *Dictionnaire de linguistique de l'Ecole de Prague*. Utrecht: Spectrum, 1966.

Valéry, Paul (1938). "Poetry and Abstract Thought." In *The Art of Poetry*. Translated by Denise Folliot, *Collected Works of Paul Valéry*, Vol. 7, ed. Jackson Matthews. New York: Pantheon Books, Bollingen Series, 1958, pp. 52–81.

Wellek, René. "The Theory of Literary History." *Travaux du Cercle Linguistique de Prague* 4 (1936): 173–191.

Index